James Renwick, Jared Sparks

Memoir of Sir Benjamin Thompson, Count Rumford, with notices of his daughter

James Renwick, Jared Sparks

Memoir of Sir Benjamin Thompson, Count Rumford, with notices of his daughter

ISBN/EAN: 9783741178719

Manufactured in Europe, USA, Canada, Australia, Japa

Cover: Foto ©Andreas Hilbeck / pixelio.de

Manufactured and distributed by brebook publishing software (www.brebook.com)

James Renwick, Jared Sparks

Memoir of Sir Benjamin Thompson, Count Rumford, with notices of his daughter

THE LIBRARY
OF
AMERICAN BIOGRAPHY
CONDUCTED BY
Jared Sparks.

COUNT RUMFORD.

BOSTON.
CHARLES C. LITTLE AND JAMES BROWN.
MDCCCXLV.

THE

LIBRARY

OF

AMERICAN BIOGRAPHY.

CONDUCTED
BY JARED SPARKS.

SECOND SERIES.

VOL. V.

BOSTON:
CHARLES C. LITTLE AND JAMES BROWN.
1848.

LIVES

OF

COUNT RUMFORD,

ZEBULON MONTGOMERY PIKE,

AND

SAMUEL GORTON.

BOSTON:
CHARLES C. LITTLE AND JAMES BROWN.
1848.

CONTENTS.

LIFE OF COUNT RUMFORD.
BY JAMES RENWICK, LL. D.

Preface 3

CHAPTER I.

Introduction. — His Birth and Parentage. — Education. — Mercantile Pursuits. — Employment as a Teacher. — Settlement at Concord. — First Marriage. 5

CHAPTER II.

He receives the Commission of Major. — Jealousy of the Officers. — He is suspected of Disaffection. — Threatened by a Mob. — Flies to Woburn, and thence to Boston. — His Reception there. — He returns to Woburn. — Is again threatened. — His Trial and Acquittal. — His Efforts to obtain a Commission in the Continental Army. 23

CHAPTER III.

He leaves America. — His Arrival and Reception in London. — First scientific Papers. — Mission to America. — Return to England. . . 41

CHAPTER IV.

He visits Germany. — *Forms the Acquaintance of Prince Maximilian of Deux-Ponts.* — *Is introduced to the Elector of Bavaria.* — *Returns to England.* — *Is knighted by the King.* — *Enters the Service of the Elector.* — *His Reforms in the Bavarian Army.* — *Military Workhouse at Manheim.* 61

CHAPTER V.

Measures for suppressing Mendicancy in Bavaria. — *Establishment of the Military Workhouse at Munich.* 80

CHAPTER VI.

Principles and Details of Establishments for the Relief of the Poor. 93

CHAPTER VII.

Opposition he experienced in Bavaria. — *Military School at Munich.* — *Projects for improving the Breed of Horses and horned Cattle; and for diminishing the Evil of Usury.* — *Landscape Garden at Munich.* — *Monument erected in it.* — *He returns to London.* — *His Improvements in Fireplaces.* — *Remedy for the Smoking of Chimneys.* 117

CHAPTER VIII.

His Visit to Dublin. — *Further Improvements in heating Boilers.* — *Heating by Steam.* — *Dis-*

cussion in Relation to the Heating of Dwellings.
—Ventilation of Apartments.—Warm Bathing.
—Renewal and Continuance of his Communications with the United States. 137

CHAPTER IX.

He revisits Bavaria.—Is appointed Chief of the Council of Regency.—His Success in maintaining the Neutrality of Munich.—Appointed Minister of Bavaria at the Court of St. James, which refuses to receive him in that Capacity.—Invited to return to the United States.—Establishment of the Royal Institution.—Death of the Elector Charles Theodore.—Influence of that Event on his future Plans.—Bids Adieu to Bavaria, and visits Paris.—Marries Madame Lavoisier, and fixes his Residence at Auteuil. 152

CHAPTER X.

Loss of his Papers.—Further Experiments on the Force of Gunpowder.—Experiments on the Gases; on the Absorption of Moisture; on the Light yielded by Combustion; and on colored Shadows.—His Discoveries in Relation to accidental Colors.—His Experiments on the chemical Effects of Light. 169

CHAPTER XI.

He proves that Heat is not influenced by Gravitation.—Demonstrates that Liquids are very imperfect Conductors, and Gases absolute Non-Conductors of Heat. — Explains the Manner in which Heat is propagated by Fluids. — Explanation of many natural Phenomena. — Experiments on the Radiation of Heat. — On the Heat developed by Friction. — His Thermoscope and Calorimeter. — Prizes instituted by him. — Views of his Character. — His Death. 184

APPENDIX.

No. I. — *Count Rumford's Donations to the American Academy of Arts and Sciences, and to Harvard University.* 202
No. II. — *Reasons assigned by Count Rumford for leaving his Country.* 210

LIFE OF ZEBULON MONTGOMERY PIKE.

BY HENRY WHITING.

CHAPTER I.

His Birth and early Education. — Obtains a Commission in the Army. — His Promotion. — Appointed to command an Expedition up the Mississippi. — Departs from St. Louis. — Demoyne Rapids. — Speech to the Indians. — Remarks on the Indian Trade. 219

CHAPTER II.

Arrives at Prairie du Chien. — Council with the Indians. — Falls of St. Anthony. — Hunting Excursion. — Reaches Red Cedar Lake and the Sources of the Mississippi. — British Trading Establishments. — Returns to the Falls of St. Anthony, and thence to St. Louis. . . . 239

CHAPTER III.

Expedition to the Sources of the Red River. — Leaves St. Louis and ascends the Missouri in Boats. — Osage Indians. — Pawnees — He reaches the Head-Waters of the Arkansas River. — Hunting Buffaloes. — Disasters and Sufferings of his Party among the Mountains. — He builds a Fort. — Taken by the Spaniards, and conducted to Santa Fe. 259

CHAPTER IV.

Sent to the Interior of New Mexico. — Deprived of his Papers. — Returns to the United States through Texas. — Commendation of his Services by the Secretary at War. — Burr's Conspiracy. — Pike prepares a Narrative of his Expeditions. 276

CHAPTER V.

War of 1812. — Pike promoted to the Command of a Regiment. — Stationed on Lake Champlain. — Plan of Operations for the Campaign

CONTENTS.

of 1813 on Lake Ontario. — Pike promoted to the Rank of Brigadier-General. — Remarks on the Military Operations. 285

CHAPTER VI.

Commodore Chauncy's Fleet embarks on Lake Ontario with Troops under the Command of General Pike. — Arrives at York. — The Troops land at that Place. — Major Forsyth and the Riflemen. — Attack upon York. — Death of General Pike. — Surrender of the Town to the Americans. — Remarks. 297

LIFE OF SAMUEL GORTON.

BY JOHN M. MACKIE.

CHAPTER I.

Introduction. 317

CHAPTER II.

Gorton's Birth. — Ancestors. — Early Education. — Arrival in Boston. — Removal to Plymouth. — Difficulties with Ralph Smith. — Banishment from Plymouth. 320

CHAPTER III.

Gorton goes to Aquetneck. — Hardships of his Journey. — The Settlement at Aquetneck. —

Gorton's Difficulties with the Authorities. — His Punishment. 331

CHAPTER IV.

Removes to Providence, and settles in Pawtuxet. — Controversies then prevailing in this Settlement. — Part taken in them by Gorton. — Unlawful Interference of the Massachusetts Authorities. — Gorton refuses to submit to their Jurisdiction. — Removes from Pawtuxet. . . 336

CHAPTER V.

Founds Shawomet. — His Disputes with the Indian Chiefs Pomham and Sochonocho. — Massachusetts takes Part with the latter. — Armed Commission sent by Massachusetts to Shawomet. — It is opposed by Force. — Truce between the Parties. — Gorton and his Company consent to go to Massachusetts. — Are treated as Prisoners of War. — Are imprisoned in Boston. 346

CHAPTER VI.

Gorton and his Fellow-Prisoners accused of Heresy in Court. — The Trial. — The Accused found guilty. — Their Sentence. — Gorton confined in Charlestown. — Prisoners released. 350

CHAPTER VII.

Gorton and his Friends kindly treated in Boston. — Expelled by the Governor. — They go to

Aquetneck. — Are kindly received by the Narragansett Indians. — Subjection of the latter to the English Crown. — Gorton, with two of his Friends, goes to England. — They complain of the Massachusetts Government to the English Commissioners. — Their Complaint favorably received, and an Order issued to Massachusetts. — Gorton preaches in England with great Success. — Is accused before a Committee of Parliament of preaching without License. — Is acquitted. 367

CHAPTER VIII.

Returns to America, and disembarks at Boston. — Warrant issued against him by the Governor of Massachusetts. — He proceeds to Shawomet, then called Warwick. — Massachusetts relinquishes her Claims to Warwick. — Gorton's public Services after his Return from England. — His Mode of Life. — Death. — Family. 374

CHAPTER IX.

Gorton's Character. — His Relations with the Indians. — His Opinions. 382

APPENDIX.

Account of Samuel Gorton's Writings. . . . 411

LIFE

OF

BENJAMIN THOMPSON,

COUNT OF RUMFORD;

BY

JAMES RENWICK, LL.D.

PREFACE.

With the exception of his own works, the materials for a biography of Count Rumford are scanty. The only accessible printed documents that have been found are, the "*Eloge*" of Cuvier, the "Inaugural Address" of Professor Bigelow, and a memoir in the "Literary Miscellany," published at Cambridge, in the years 1805 and 1806. In addition to these materials, the author has been furnished with manuscript "Outlines of the Family, Infancy, and Childhood of Benjamin Thompson, Count of Rumford," by his half-brother, Josiah Pierce, late of Baldwin, Maine; with copies of a part of his correspondence with Colonel Loammi Baldwin; and with several letters written by himself, together with a few memoranda and accounts relating to his earlier years. For these papers he has been indebted to the kindness of Mr. James F. Baldwin, of Boston, and Mr. Josiah Pierce, of Gorham, Maine. They relate chiefly to the events which occurred before Rumford left America. In regard to subse-

PREFACE.

quent events, ittle more could be done than to arrange, in a condensed form, facts and inferences which must have been hitherto sought in many separate volumes.

COLUMBIA COLLEGE, *January 1st*, 1845.

COUNT RUMFORD.

CHAPTER I.

Introduction. — His Birth and Parentage. — Education. — Mercantile Pursuits. — Employment as a Teacher. — Settlement at Concord. — First Marriage.

THE state of Massachusetts may be justly proud of having given birth to him, whom posterity will know under the name of Rumford. Next to Franklin's, his name is the proudest among those of Americans, who have gained distinction in the fields of science; and, like him, he was as remarkable for the practical character of his investigations, as for the depth of his philosophical research. Unlike Franklin, however, who died surrounded by countrymen grateful to him for having been among the foremost in the struggle, by which their independence of foreign rule was achieved, the best years of Rumford's life were spent in the service of foreign countries; his rewards were the tribute of foreign nations; and his last hours were spent among a people alien to him in race and language. He was, in truth, lost to the land of his birth before it had taken a place among nations; and she rejected, as a son, one who might have rendered worthy service both in the field and cabinet. More fortunate, however, than exiles usually are, he reaped, in foreign climes, rank, honors, and fortune; and he who was scornfully refused admission into the yet undisciplined ranks of his own countrymen, and even thought unworthy to live in quiet in the humble village of his nativity, reached the command of armies, prompted the deliberations of cabinets, graced the circles of the most polished courts, and was admitted to fellowship by the most learned institutions of Europe.

BENJAMIN THOMPSON, afterwards COUNT OF RUMFORD, was born at Woburn, in the colony of Massachusetts, on the 26th March, 1753. His ancestors appear to have been among the first settlers of that town; and the name, as well as the circumstances under which that part of the continent was settled, shows that they were of English blood. By papers yet in existence, it appears that his progenitors had, for three generations, held landed property in Woburn, which they cultivated, and upon the produce of which they had been able to maintain themselves in comfort, and bring up families, among whom the paternal property was at each descent divided, until the share of each descendant finally became small.

The grandfather of Count Rumford held a commission in the militia of the province, at a time when it was a post of danger as well as of honor. His appointment as ensign, signed by Governor Belcher, bears date the 12th of August, 1738; and it is believed that he rose to the rank of Captain, by which title he was known. At a time when military rank was granted only on grounds that might at the present day be styled aristocratic, the possession of this rank affords evidence of the estimation in which Captain Ebenezer Thompson was held by his neighbors, as well as by the rulers of the colony.

Benjamin Thompson, the father of Count Rumford, died at an early age, and little is in consequence known of him but his name. Rumford's mother was named Ruth Simonds, the daughter of a neighboring farmer; and the young couple continued to reside, until the death of the husband, in the house of his father. Rumford was but eight months old when his father died, and, with his mother, continued to dwell with his grandfather for about two years more. In the month of March, 1756, however, Mrs. Thompson again married. The name of her second husband was Josiah Pierce, also a resident of

Woburn; and when he took home his bride, she was accompanied by her son.

Previous to this time, the grandfather had also died; for there is still extant an agreement among such of his heirs as were of age, and the guardians of a son and the grandson, which bears date, October 16th, 1755. We shall quote a portion of this, as an interesting memorial of the simplicity of the age, and of the humble patrimony to which Benjamin Thompson, the future Count of the Holy Roman Empire, was born the heir. Among other things, it is agreed that Ruth Thompson, his mother, shall have liberty "to improve one half of the garden, at the west end of the mansion," with a further "privilege of land to raise beans for sauce," and that the guardian of her brother-in-law shall "give the said widow eighty weight of beef, eight bushels of rye, two bushels of malt, and two barrels of cider for the present year," and further that she shall "have liberty of gathering apples to bake, and three bushels of apples for winter, yearly and every year."

However moderate this paper would seem to indicate the inheritance of Rumford, it was sufficient to provide for his maintenance and education. He did not go to the house of his stepfather as a burden, but the latter carefully stipulated for the allowance of two shillings and five pence currency per week, from the guardian of his step-son, until his ward should attain the age of seven years. According to his own statement to Cuvier, however, it would appear that Benjamin Thompson did not receive a fair proportion of the estate of his grandfather, who left by far the largest share of his estate to his youngest son.

The wise foresight of the first settlers of Massachusetts had provided for their posterity the means of a sound elementary, and even of a liberal education; and while the system carefully guarded against the appearance of its being eleemosynary, it was yet open to all. To the public school of his native town, young Thompson was, according to the custom of the day, sent as soon as he was able to repair thither. Here he was speedily taught reading, writing, and the elements of arithmetic; and, in compliance with the sound old method, he acquired a grammatical knowledge of his own language through the study of the Latin tongue. His instructor was John Fowle, who is stated to have been "a gentleman of liberal education, and an excellent teacher."

Even at an early age, young Thompson was distinguished among his fellows for quickness of apprehension and energy of character. No recollection is, indeed, preserved of his having exhibited any striking proofs of his possessing a genius superior to those around him. It is, however, stated that he was not satisfied with the ordinary routine of a schoolboy's plays, but was continually in search of new and curious plans of amusement. These plans were rapidly conceived, and afforded evidence both of ingenuity in the invention and self-possession in the execution. They were also pursued with untiring perseverance, and marked that sense of confidence in his own powers, which was in after life so distinctive a feature of his character.

However skilful might be the teacher at Woburn, it does not appear that the school afforded facilities for education of an elevated character; and it would seem that, by the age of eleven years, young Thompson had acquired all that was there taught. He now joined the school of a Mr. Hill, at Medford, under whose tuition he made a further and rapid progress. Among other studies, he pursued that of mathematics with success, and attained a knowledge of the principles of astronomy, the union of which was exhibited in the calculation of eclipses of the sun and moon.

In the course of his studies, he devoted his whole soul to the pursuit in which he was engaged; and it is said that he never abandoned any task until he had completed it, and never left any undertaking incomplete.

With such dispositions, he was, at the early age of thirteen, considered qualified to enter upon the preparation for the profession or occupation to which he was to owe his future livelihood. By one account, he was first placed under the charge of Dr. Hay, a physician in Woburn, for the purpose of qualifying himself for the practice of medicine. Here it would seem that he paid more attention to the mechanical matters connected with that study, than to the healing art itself, and amused himself with attempting to manufacture surgical instruments. The age of sixteen, at which his residence with Dr. Hay is said to have occurred, contradicts a more authentic account of his early years, which states that he was no more than thirteen when he was bound apprentice to Mr. John Appleton, a respectable merchant of the town of Salem.

There is no reason to doubt that young Thompson fulfilled the duties of his station as clerk with faithfulness; and his abandoning commercial pursuits is to be ascribed to the circumstances of the times, and not to any failure on his part in industry or assiduity. The routine of a counting-room, however extensive or arduous in its details, was not sufficient to engross the mind, or occupy the whole thoughts, of the future philosopher. We therefore learn that, while in the service of Mr. Appleton, he did not neglect the studies in which he had previously delighted; but, with better opportunities for procuring books, he extended his acquaintance with mathematical and physical science.

Nor were his hands idle while his mind was occupied; but, encouraged by his success in engraving, with the rudest tools, the initials of his companions' names upon the handles of their penknives, he ventured upon the more ambitious essay of cutting a plate from whence a label for marking his books might be struck. The execution is said to have been such, as would have been creditable to an artist; and, when we consider that there is no positive record of any work of this description having been successfully executed at that time in the colonies, Rumford may perhaps be ranked as the earliest of American engravers. The whole design is about four inches by three. The centre is occupied by an oval medallion, within which is an escutcheon blazoned with a coat of arms surmounted by a helmet, with its lambrequin. By a mistake almost amounting to prophecy, the helmet is of that character, facing full to the front, with beaver open, and bars, which marks, in heraldic symbols, the rank of nobility, instead of the less

ambitious basnet of the simple gentleman or
esquire. The medallion is represented as suspended from the truncated branch of a tree;
from another broken limb hang a compass and
square, and at the root of the tree lie books,
another compass, and a sword. The tree grows
upon the shore of the sea, on whose waves are
seen the bow and foremast of a ship under full
sail. In the upper angle of the plate, to the
right, is the eye of Providence, surrounded by
rays of light. Such a design marks a poetic
fancy, and the drawing exhibits no mean skill
in perspective and design. With the exception
of the helmet, the heraldry is correct, and displays an acquaintance with a subject little known
beyond the narrow circle of those who study it,
in aristocratic countries, as a profession.

Among other matters to which he applied his
leisure hours, while at Salem, was the oft-exploded and oft-renewed search for the perpetual
motion, a project so frequently entertained by
those whose inventive genius is not regulated by
a sound knowledge of mechanical laws. In this
direction he entertained such hopes of success,
that, quitting Salem at nightfall, he travelled to
Woburn to communicate his supposed discovery
to his old school-fellow and friend, Loammi Baldwin, and returned in time to resume his station
at the counter in the morning. The more ma-

ture judgment and deeper mechanical knowledge of Baldwin had satisfied him, that such projects were impossible, and Thompson had the good sense to abandon his fruitless attempt.

While he remained in the employ of Mr. Appleton, an event occurred which was widely celebrated in the colonies. The stamp tax, imposed by the law of a legislature in which they were not represented, and which had in consequence excited so much complaint, was removed, and the act of Parliament repealed. As is well known, this event, which was, in fact, a victory over an attempted oppression, caused the most lively joy throughout the colonies; but the mercantile interest, on which the tax fell with the greatest weight, was the loudest in its expressions of joy.

To give the public excitement vent, it was proposed, at Salem, to celebrate the occasion by a display of fireworks; and, in the absence of any professional pyrotechnist, Thompson, whose studies had taught him the composition of the necessary articles, volunteered to prepare them. He was not, however, aware of all the danger of the undertaking, nor acquainted with the precautions required to guard against explosion. The shop of a neighboring apothecary was used as a laboratory, and the apparatus for preparing the explosive compound was his pestle and mortar. It will not surprise the reader to learn, that, in the midst of the preparations, a violent explosion occurred, and that the operator was much injured. In addition to the mere shock, his clothes took fire, and, before assistance reached him, he was severely burnt. So serious was the injury, that his life was despaired of; and, after being removed to his mother's residence at Woburn, he lay in great danger and suffering for several weeks. His sight was for a time lost, and the skin of his face and breast came off. No sooner had he recovered his strength, than he returned to Salem, to resume his duties in Mr. Appleton's establishment. Here he continued until the renewed attempts of the mother country to levy taxes upon the colonies led to the adoption of the famous non-importation agreement. By this, nearly the whole external commerce of the colonies, confined by the navigation acts chiefly to British ports, was at once brought to a close. Mr. Appleton had, in consequence, no longer need of a clerk, and was, no doubt, happy to free himself from the obligation of supporting one. We therefore hear no more of the indentures of apprenticeship, and Thompson returned to his mother's residence at Woburn.

The non-importation agreement was entered into with the most pure and patriotic motives. The parties to it gave up, in all cases, the hopes of increasing their fortunes, and in many instances the means of livelihood. Yet it may be questioned whether any act was ever more impolitic, or injurious, with the exception of those, which, in imitation of it, were adopted previous to the war of 1812. The repeal of the Stamp Act had been forced upon the British ministry by the instances of the merchants and manufacturers engaged in the commerce with America. This agreement converted those warm and influential friends into bitter enemies; and the war which followed, instead of being looked upon as one that tore the entrails of a common country, was sustained by the people of England as if it were against a foreign foe. The capital engaged in trade in the colonies ceased to give returns, and the merchants, instead of living upon the income, were compelled to consume the principal, and thus became unable to furnish loans or pay contributions; the country, dependent at the time upon England for many of the articles of prime necessity, was found, when hostilities commenced, without a sufficient supply of arms, ammunition, clothing, or camp equipage, all of which the intuitive sagacity of merchants would have provided in abundance, had a free importation continued.

If Thompson were in reality disaffected to the cause of his country's independence, it might be ascribed to his sufferings on this occasion, when, prepared to enter into active life, his occupation was suddenly taken away. We shall, however, see that there is good reason to believe that no such feeling existed in his mind.

Thus deprived of the opportunity of supporting himself in trade, Thompson sought to gain a support by teaching the elements of that knowledge in which he was already a proficient. During the winter of 1769, therefore, he taught a school at Wilmington, and spent the summer of that year at Woburn, in the study of anatomy and physiology. It is to this period we must refer his residence with Dr. Hay, of which mention has already been made.

The ensuing winter, he resumed his commercial pursuits, and was engaged as a clerk in a dry-goods store in Boston, kept by Hopestill Capen. In this capacity he was in Boston during the occurrence of what is usually known as the "Boston Massacre." On this occasion, while many, terrified at the report that the English soldiers were engaged in the slaughter of the inhabitants of Boston, retired from the streets, and shut themselves in their houses, Thompson was among those who prepared themselves for resistance. Arming himself, he rushed in haste towards the scene of action; but ere he reached it, the tumult had subsided.

When no fresh importations take place, stocks of foreign goods are speedily exhausted; and the business of Mr. Capen came soon to a close. Thompson therefore again returned to Woburn, and resumed his favorite studies. While he was thus without any positive employment, the annual course of lectures on experimental philosophy was about to be delivered, in the halls of Harvard College, by Professor Winthrop. This seemed to offer an opportunity for acquiring knowledge for which he had long sighed in vain. His friend Baldwin, although not a matriculated student, had obtained permission to attend those lectures, and Thompson's instances soon obtained him the same privilege.

The two friends daily proceeded on foot to attend the lectures, and returned in the same manner. In defiance of fatigue, they had no sooner reached their homes than they set to work to construct a rude apparatus, by which they repeated the experiments they had witnessed, or contrived new ones to illustrate the principles that had been expounded to them. Undeterred by his former mishap, but wiser in avoiding danger than before, Thompson planned new methods for examining the manner in which gunpowder acts; and the experiments he then instituted became the germ of those, which he afterwards so successfully performed, and which are still cited among the highest existing authorities.

His zeal and success in acquiring knowledge had now probably begun to attract attention; for, in the autumn of the same year, 1770, Colonel Timothy Walker, of the town then called Rumford, in New Hampshire, sought him out, and requested him to take charge of an academy at that place. This thriving village, after bearing for a time the name of Rumford, is now known as Concord, the seat of government of the state of New Hampshire. It would appear, however, that, previous to his acceptance of this invitation, he had, for a short time, taught a school at Bradford, Massachusetts. The invitation of Colonel Walker was accepted; and, as the people of that place were wise enough to know, that, to elevate the teacher in the eyes of his pupils is among the best means of insuring the literary improvement of their children, Thompson found himself caressed and welcomed by a society not wanting in refinement or pretensions to fashion. His grace and personal advantages, which afterwards gained him access to the proudest circles of Europe, were already developed. His stature, of nearly six feet, his erect figure, his finely formed limbs, his bright blue eyes, his features chiselled in the Roman mould, and his dark auburn hair, rendered him a model of manly beauty. He had acquired an address in the highest degree prepossessing; and, at the counter of the Boston retailer, had learnt, from its fashionable customers, that polish of manner and dialect which obliterates all peculiarities that are provincial, and many of those which are national. He possessed solid acquirements far beyond the standard of the day, and had attained already the last and highest requisite for society, that of conversing with ease, and in a pure language, upon all the subjects with a knowledge of which his mind was stored. In addition, he possessed the most fascinating of all accomplishments, for he had a fine voice, and, although far from a proficient in music as a science, sang with much taste, and performed on several musical instruments.

With such personal and mental advantages, it is not surprising that he should have turned the heads, or affected the hearts, of the belles of a country village. Among the rest, Mrs. Rolfe, the widow of a Colonel, and possessed in her own right of an estate considered large in those days, made him the object of a tender preference; and in spite of the disparity of their years, she retained enough of her youthful attractions to render it probable, that a feeling more creditable than one arising from interested motives led him to seek her hand. The *dénouement* of the courtship, however, can hardly be contemplated with-

out a smile. On the closing of his school for
the season, in the year 1772, he being then
nineteen years of age, the widow gave him a
seat in her carriage, and they proceeded together
to Boston. Here his first step was to fit himself
out in the extreme of the fashion of the day.
From a settlement of an account with Mr. Cyrus
Baldwin, of Boston, it would appear that the
favorite color of his dress was scarlet, which had
not yet gone out of vogue in consequence of
ideas of the English attachment, that were afterwards associated with it; and we may therefore
infer, that he did not refuse to deck his splendid
figure in that brilliant hue on this important occasion.

When the tailor and haberdasher had performed their duties, Thompson again entered the
carriage with Mrs. Rolfe, and proceeded to visit
his mother. The apparition of him, who had
been so long known in Woburn as the studious
boy, the retired student, or the humble teacher
of the village school, in a splendid equipage, accompanied by a gorgeous dame, and decked out
in the picturesque and fanciful garments of the
day, whose brilliant dyes we still admire in contemporary pictures of Copley, produced no little
sensation in the quiet world of Woburn. His
mother's astonishment and dismay, at the apparent
extravagance of her son, left her no language for

greeting, but the exclamation, "Why, Ben, my child! how could you spend your whole winter's wages in this way?"

Her maternal solicitude seems wholly to have overcome the feminine tact, by which love affairs are usually so soon discovered, and in the presence of Mrs. Rolfe explanation was not easy. He therefore sought his old preceptor in physiology, Dr. Hay, and committed to him the task of announcing his intended nuptials to his mother. She was taken so much by surprise with the intelligence, that she could give no reply; and it was not until the following morning that she gave her assent. The sanction of his only surviving parent being obtained, the fair widow and her youthful lover drove back to Rumford, and were soon after married.

We have thus reached the first step of young Thompson towards fortune and distinction. We have seen him left in infancy an orphan, not destitute, but with slender means; acquiring, with industry and perseverance, the elements of a sound education; laboring, with faithfulness and industry, to prepare himself for the mercantile profession, yet not neglecting the new means thrown in his way for improving himself in science and useful knowledge. We have then seen him thrown out of employ by one of the convulsions to which business is liable, supporting his reverse with fortitude, and laboring in the often ungrateful and always irksome task of teaching a school, until, by his personal merits and accomplishments, he was thought worthy to receive the hand of a lady holding an acknowledged rank in the aristocracy of the colonies, and possessed of an ample fortune. With the latter event a new era in his history commences.

CHAPTER II.

He receives the Commission of Major. — Jealousy of the Officers. — He is suspected of Disaffection. — Threatened by a Mob. — Flies to Woburn, and thence to Boston. — His Reception there. — He returns to Woburn. — Is again threatened. — His Trial and Acquittal. — His Efforts to obtain a Commission in the Continental Army.

The marriage of young Thompson to Mrs. Rolfe took place in the year 1772, when he was in the twentieth year of his age. This connection, in which his bride had committed to him her fortune as unreservedly as her hand, gave him at once a station in a society, in which the distinctions of rank were at that time preserved with even more punctilio, than in countries where they are guarded by titles and patents of nobility.

The elements of which that society was made up were, however, in a state of commotion. The strong attachment borne by the preceding generation to the mother country, an attachment manifested by the free outpouring of blood, and the contribution of all the treasure that a community far from rich could afford, had begun to give way under her repeated encroachments on the privileges the colonists claimed to have inherited from their Saxon ancestors. The colonies did not complain, that they were excluded from all direct communication with the rest of the world, except Europe south of Cape Finisterre. That the lucrative offices in the gift of the crown were conferred almost wholly upon those born in Great Britain, was felt to be a wrong by a few influential families, but caused no discontent in the body of the people; and that the duties on all imports from abroad should go into the coffers of the crown, was admitted as the result of colonial dependence. But when the Parliament of the United Kingdom undertook to pass acts for levying taxes within the colonies themselves, the inhabitants claimed that it was the birthright of Englishmen that they should be taxed only with their own assent, or by a body in which they were fairly represented; and for the rights of Englishmen they finally risked their lives and fortunes.

The question was one of ancient date in the colonies. They held, from the first, that they were the subjects of the crown, not of the King and Parliament of England; and, in the colony of New York, an indictment and conviction for treason had been the consequence of a petition to the Parliament for redress of injuries alleged to have been committed by governors appointed by the King. The colonists now sought, by petitions addressed to the King, protection against the oppressive acts of Parliament; and while, in fact, tending rapidly to a rupture with him, as the executive of the British empire, in theory they were his most loyal subjects.

The question, as debated by the intelligent, was among the nicest that could occur in constitutional law; but the people solved its difficulties in a summary manner. They felt themselves oppressed, and finally rushed almost spontaneously to arms to redress their wrongs. Thompson seems to have taken little interest in the subjects which agitated the public mind. Elevated, at an early age, to a fortune and station beyond his hopes, he gave himself up to the pleasures and festivities of the society to which his newly acquired rank and wealth entitled him. With his bride he was to be seen at all places of public resort, and on all occasions where the fashion and intelligence of the colony were assembled. Among other excursions was one to Portsmouth, then the seat of the government of New Hampshire, where they attended at a military review. Here he was presented to his Excellency John Wentworth, the Governor of the colony.

The Governor was not slow to perceive the merit of Thompson. In the stormy political atmosphere in which he was enveloped, it was probably a relief to meet with a person who had not irretrievably engaged himself on one side or the other, and whose mind was left free to direct his conversation to subjects of literature and science. He must have been a bad judge of mankind, had he not been able to perceive that Thompson possessed qualities that might fit him to be influential with his countrymen; and he may have thought it important to attach a young man of so much promise, and already so highly favored by fortune, to himself, and, through himself, to the cause he so warmly espoused.

Whatever motives may have influenced Governor Wentworth, their effect was speedily seen in a very decided act, the consequences of which were felt throughout the whole of Rumford's future life. A vacancy having occurred in a regiment of the militia of New Hampshire, the Governor immediately conferred the commission of Major upon Benjamin Thompson, thus raising him at once directly over the heads of all the captains and subalterns of the corps, and indirectly giving him precedence over all the officers of those ranks in the militia of the province.

If Governor Wentworth hoped, by this act, to enlist Thompson in an open declaration of adherence to the cause of the mother country, he certainly failed; but, on the other hand, the receiver of so signal a mark of favor and esteem could not in decency take a position hostile to the wishes and cherished cause of his patron. Major Thompson, therefore, in the continued agitation which followed, with increasing violence, his appointment to this office, took no active part.

The wounded pride of the officers, over whose heads he had been elevated, was not long in exhibiting itself in open acts. Had Thompson possessed greater knowledge of the world, he would probably have declined the honor tendered him by the Governor; for no feeling is so easily wounded as that of military rank, and no resentment is more unforgiving than that which arises from the loss of expected promotion. That promotion shall be accorded on no other ground than seniority, is strenuously asserted by the great body of officers in all armies and navies, for the obvious reason that they form no exception to the great body of the human race, in which high talent and elevated genius are so far from being general, that they usually bear the epithet of extraordinary. In consequence, whatever may be the merit that causes the rise of an officer out of the regular course, he becomes an object of jealousy to those above him, of hatred to those over whose heads he has passed, and of envy to those who had from the first stood beneath him. The officers of the New Hampshire militia, for such reasons, were not unwilling to seek out, and believe they had detected, delinquencies in Thompson; and these, whether real or fancied, were loudly proclaimed to the people.

The open partisans of the mother country were few in number, compared with the avowed opponents to her oppressive acts. In the early part of the struggle, when the pen and the press were the instruments of warfare, the number of the former was limited to the holders of government offices; and there are some curious instances on record of those, who had been the most violent Whigs, in the days of opposition to the Stamp Act, becoming active apologists for the tax on tea, because they had in the mean time been appointed to office. In fact, the crisis to which affairs were hurrying was not foreseen; and with the higher classes the contest seemed to have none but the old aspect of a struggle between the *outs* and the in. The heat of the popular commotion lay hidden beneath a comparatively cool, although heaving surface, as the molten lava continues its current of liquid fire beneath its indurated crust.

When, however, the signs of the times indicated an approach to a decision by arms, there were many on both sides of the question who had hostages in the hands of fortune, in the form of wives, families, and invested property. To these any war, and particularly a civil one, was of course an object of terror; and thus, while the noise of the contest grew louder and louder on both sides, fewer were to be seen taking an active part in it. Among those who were so placed that they might lose all, and could probably gain little, by the organization of an armed resistance, was Major Thompson. He appeared to have attained the highest objects to which he could aspire, fortune, military rank, an affectionate wife; and his felicity was crowned by the birth of a daughter.

The more active of the patriots, however, were not willing that any should refrain from expressing their opinions. The various reasons for abstaining from agitation, belief in the supreme authority of the Parliament of England, hesitation to break old and familiar ties, doubts of the ability of the colonies to enter into a successful contest, or the mere desire for the maintenance of peace, were all ascribed to the one cause of disaffection to the liberties of their country.

From the first settlement of the New England colonies, the administration of their internal police had rested on no other support than public opinion. The warrant of the justice of the peace was obeyed as implicitly as the absolute monarch's *lettre de cachet;* its execution required no more force than the single constable, and no weapon but his staff of office; a quiet and order unknown in any preceding form of society had hitherto reigned throughout the land. But as the crisis approached, these orderly habits were suspended; the civic authorities lost their power of repressing tumult, or winked at what, in other times, they would have thought it their duty to suppress. Mobs collected, threatening and finally committing violence upon those obnoxious to them. To tar and feather the open advocates of the cause of the mother country became the cruel pastime of the mob; and when these had been thus driven to take refuge under the protection of the British soldiery, the quiet citizens, who, for one reason or another, eschewed resistance, were pointed out as the next victims, unless they should declare themselves openly on the popular side.

It is the boast of our revolution, that it was

stained by no blood shed upon the scaffold for political reasons. Would that we could say, that it was sullied by no acts which an impartial posterity may designate as crimes, or which sound policy will condemn as mistakes more injurious to the cause than positive crimes! The violence of mobs drove many a one, who would otherwise have lived as a quiet citizen, and faithfully obeyed a republican government, to take arms on the royal side. When war actually broke out, attainders and confiscations were the lot of many of those against whom no crime could be alleged, but that popular violence had driven them from their homes, or that they had yielded to the overwhelming force, which occupied the districts in which they resided. Nor had these confiscations the miserable excuse of expediency; for there is hardly any instance in which they brought funds to the support of the war.

Not only had Thompson refrained from taking an active part in the agitations of the day, but the jealousy and envy of the superseded officers pointed him out as disaffected; and the favor in which he was held by the royal governor was alleged as ample proof of his delinquency. The result was, that he was marked as a proper subject to receive a visit from the mob, and undergo the infliction of a suit of tar and feathers. The design was not kept so secret that information of it did not reach him, and he saw no resource or escape from the indignity except to retire from Concord. This he did in great haste, in the month of November, 1774, leaving his wife, and his infant daughter, whom, after an interval of many years, he called to share his European honors.

His steps were first directed to his native town, where he repaired to his father-in-law's house. Here he for a time endeavored to lose the sense of his misfortune in his favorite amusements of reading and performing philosophical experiments. The report of his supposed disaffection to the cause of liberty had, however, preceded him; and even Woburn, the place of his birth, was not a safe residence for him, and he had reason to fear that he might be torn violently from his mother's hearth, and subjected to personal indignity, if not to actual assault. He, in consequence, took lodgings in Charlestown, where he remained for some months, after which he removed to Boston, which was at the time garrisoned by the British army under the command of General Gage. At this time, the ministry of England, although determined to persist in their obnoxious measures, did not consider the submission of the colonies as hopeless. While they chose to exhibit an imposing force, they hardly dreamed that it would be resisted in arms, and seem to have been at least willing to gild the chains with which they proposed to fetter the colonies.

General Gage had married a lady of American birth, and was himself a landholder in one of the colonies. Such, indeed, was the nature of his connections, and his attachment to the soil, if not to the body of the people, that it would not have been an extraordinary event, had he held a lower rank and been on the half-pay list instead of active service, if he had been found, like Gates and Montgomery, serving in the armies of Congress.

Whether from inclination or in virtue of his instructions, he left no blandishment untried to soothe the surly temper of the people of Boston. Few, indeed, were willing to accept of hospitalities in which they could not but see baits by which they were to be allured from their principles. Many, too, had the natural feeling that a public foe can hardly be treated as a private friend. Thompson, however, had no such repugnance to social intercourse with the officers of the British army. It is well known, that between the officers of hostile civilized nations a feeling of mutual esteem often grows up, which, in times of truce, or even in actual battle, leads to the exchange of chivalrous courtesies; and Thompson's mind was of that elevated cast, which would have made it possible that he should be on terms of intimacy with those, whom he might expect, after no long interval, to oppose in the field. Whatever may have been the cause, he was speedily admitted to the circles of the General, and became intimate with many of the officers of the army.

Thompson could not have been insensible to the charms of a society new to him in its forms, and probably marked by a refinement he had not before witnessed. It has been often questioned, whether the camp or the court is the best school for polished manners; and the organization of the messes of the British army is such, as to produce between their members a high standard of good breeding. Towards those, whom they do not consider as entitled to admission within their circle, the officers often assume an air of exclusiveness that renders them intolerable; but where, from a desire to conciliate, or from feelings of respect, they open their arms to strangers, none but those who have experienced the charm of their society can be aware of its fascination.

Driven from his home, on the one hand, by an angry populace, pursued to the house of his mother by the same excited feelings, and, on the other, received with distinction by the officers of England, it might have been expected that he could not have withstood the temptations held out to him. Many others, under less provocation, were seduced from their duty to their country, and even drawn into a course in opposition to their original principles. Major Thompson did resist, and, while he did not refuse the courtesies of General Gage and his officers, kept up his intercourse with his friends at Woburn, several of whom were in the habit of visiting him in Boston. Through these he anxiously inquired whether he might safely return to the place of his nativity; and at last, upon what he considered sufficient evidence that he ran no risk of further molestation, he left Boston for his mother's house. Here he had the pleasure of meeting his wife and daughter.

His friends, however, were not aware of the hatred with which he was regarded. He had hardly taken up his residence at his father-in-law's, when he was again threatened with violence. On a stormy morning in March, 1775, the house was surrounded by a body of men armed with muskets and bludgeons. The leader, after being informed, in answer to his inquiry, that Major Thompson was there, insisted that he should immediately leave his bed and come down to them. Fortunately, his friend Loammi Baldwin was at hand, and heard what was going forward before Thompson had time to dress himself. He immediately hastened to the spot, and, as

he had made himself conspicuous by his zeal for
the colonial cause, was listened to. His representations and assurances were received as sufficient, and the design of inflicting summary punishment on Thompson was abandoned.

Thompson must now have felt his position insecure. The hated name of Tory seemed to have been fixed upon him so indelibly, that it could not be removed, and no security seemed to be left to him, except within the lines of the royal army. He, however, continued to brave the danger, until the commencement of hostilities, in which he took an active part on the side of his countrymen, gave birth to a new state of things. The well-organized plans for resisting the forces of the crown had hitherto wanted the sanction of legal authority. The prosecution and punishment of the disaffected had been undertaken by self-constituted authorities, and was thus always summary, often unjust. No sooner had the first engagement taken place, than the Provincial Congress stepped into the place of the government, which an appeal to arms had abrogated. Committees of Safety, deriving their authority from the government *de facto*, took the place of voluntary associations. Before the committee of correspondence, organized in Woburn, Major Thompson demanded a trial, and the affair became the more pressing and important, in consequence of the arrival in the camp before Boston of the New Hampshire militia, which included the very persons with whom the charges against him had originated.

He was therefore placed in arrest, and public advertisement was made in the newspapers, summoning all persons, who knew any thing impeaching Major Thompson's character as a patriot, to appear and give their evidence.

The publicity thus given to the affair drew crowds to Woburn, and the meeting-house, in which the trial was held, could hardly contain the assemblage. No one deed or expression hostile to the American cause, of a date prior to his flight from Concord, was alleged against him; but the main feature of the charges lay in a subsequent act of benevolence, which he had performed in Boston. It appears, that, during the summer of 1774, two British grenadiers had deserted from Boston, and taken refuge at Concord. Here they had been hired as laborers upon his farm, an occupation of which they soon became weary, and he learned that nothing but a fear of punishment prevented them from rejoining their company. When he became a resident of Boston, and made the acquaintance of General Gage, he mentioned the circumstance to him, and received from him the assurance that, should they return to their colors, no notice would be taken of their offence. They, in consequence, soon after repaired to Boston, where they were well received.

Considering the extreme penalty with which desertion is visited by the military code, Major Thompson no doubt felt that he was performing a deed of benevolence; and unless in a state of actual war, he knew that his act was not forbidden either by law or usage. Such, however, was the excited and jealous state of feeling, that his interference in favor of these men was considered by the public as a proof of disaffection. By a voluntary association he would probably have been declared guilty; but the body before which he now appeared felt it their duty to proceed no further than strict law would warrant, and were convinced by the defence, which he ably conducted, that he had committed no act that could be possibly construed as a criminal offence. The court therefore declared, that it could not condemn him, and directed him to be released from arrest, but refused him a full acquittal. This course he denounced upon the spot as illegal and ungenerous, and the parties separated with feelings likely to widen the breach. He petitioned the Committee of Safety of the colony for an investigation by that board. The petition was referred to the Provincial Congress, but was not granted.

As, in the days of the French revolution, the camp afforded the only secure asylum from the terrors of the revolutionary tribunal, so Major Thompson now sought a refuge from civic persecution among his armed countrymen, who had by this time formed the siege of Boston. His friend Baldwin, who held a commission from the General Congress, was stationed at Chelsea, with a detachment of the army. Thither Thompson repaired; and, under his auspices and those of other friends, convinced, like Baldwin, of his loyalty to the cause of the revolution, a loyalty manifested by actual service in the battle of Lexington, he sought to be employed in the service of his country.

In the hopes of obtaining a commission, he paid great attention to tactics, and assisted at the drills of the yet undisciplined forces. He also took up the study of fortification, which he pursued with his usual ardor. In the pursuit of the object of his wishes, he from time to time visited the head-quarters at Cambridge, where he had an opportunity of repaying, in some degree, the obligations he had received from Harvard College. The buildings of that institution were required as barracks for the army, and the library and philosophical apparatus were consequently in danger of being dispersed or injured. Major Thompson was one of those, who assisted in packing and removing the books and instruments, and thus preserving them for use in more auspicious times.

Almost despairing of obtaining a commission, he next sought to be employed in some other manner; and, among other plans for this purpose, proposals were offered by him, which are still extant, for supplying the non-commissioned officers of the army with the epaulets that were made, by regulation, a part of their uniform.

For many years, no person who espoused the royal cause in the revolutionary struggle was an object of more obloquy than Major Thompson. When candidly considered, it will, we think, appear that, however indifferent he may have been to the question in dispute so long as it was conducted by mere argument, he did all in his power, when recourse was had to the sword, to obtain an opportunity to fight on the side of his country. Not only can no overt act of disloyalty be proved against him, but he must be acquitted of all treasonable intentions.

CHAPTER III.

He leaves America. — His Arrival and Reception in London. — First scientific Papers. — Mission to America. — Return to England.

TOWARDS the close of the summer of 1775, the position of Major Thompson had become irksome, and even dangerous. Suspicions, which it seemed impossible to allay, had shut against him all access to military rank in the Continental army; and the fact that his request had been denied reacted, to make what was before suspicion moral certainty. He now could not go from place to place within the lines of the army, without being pointed at as the famous Tory Thompson; and although military discipline sheltered him from actual violence, he was exposed to insults that a man of spirit could not brook, and which his position prevented him from resenting. If thus treated while countenanced by officers of rank and established character for patriotism, he might infer what awaited him when he should emerge from the outposts of the camp. All hope of return to his wife and child, or to the enjoyment of his fortune, was denied him; and he could not remain with the army after his offered service had been refused, without exciting suspicions more likely to be fatal to him than any to which he had been previously exposed

In this forlorn condition, the offers and promises to which he had before been deaf may have occurred to his mind. He knew that he had secured warm personal friends among the officers of the British army, and the inducements that had captivated many others had also been held out to him. It is, however, certain that he did not at first contemplate the decided step he finally took; for there is in existence a letter from him to a clerical friend in Boston, which puts it beyond doubt, that he had no expectation of visiting that place while it continued to be occupied by the British army. To his friends in the American army he stated, that, wearied with a hopeless pursuit, and fearful of his safety, he meant to proceed to one of the southern colonies, there to seek the means of support. His preparations for departure were conducted openly and methodically. He converted into money all the property he could dispose of, even to his share of the pew in the meeting-house at Woburn, paid off all his debts, and collected as much as he could of what was due him.

His arrangements were completed about the 10th October, 1775, and he at once left Cambridge. His half-brother, Josiah Pierce, accompanied him, at his request, to the nearest post town, when he took leave of him; and from that hour until the close of the revolutionary struggle, his friends and relatives were without any positive tidings of his fate.

It is now known that he reached Newport on the following day, in the neighborhood of which town he found a boat, belonging to the British frigate *Scarborough,* on board of which he was received. In the *Scarborough* he remained for some days; and from her he was landed at Boston, which was still in possession of General Gage and his army. So carefully were his plans of secrecy carried out, that, on the occupation of Boston by the American forces, no knowledge existed among the few remaining inhabitants of his having been at that place. A single report reached his friends, that he had been seen acting in the capacity of clerk to an officer holding the rank of major. This led to inquiry; and after the capture of New York, Colonel Baldwin writes from West Chester county, that he could not learn that he was with the enemy. Whatever may have been Thompson's original plan, his meeting with the boat of a man-of-war at Newport was evidently accidental; and it is even probable that he may have left Cambridge with no design of entering the service of England. To land at Boston could not have been a part of his original purpose, even if we had not the evidence that has already been quoted; for he might have proceeded thither from Chelsea by a much shorter, and probably equally safe road.

We have no intention of defending those, who enter in hostile guise the land of their birth; but, in a country where the doctrine that allegiance is not indefeasible is the very foundation, and still the daily practice, of the government, that the hatred entertained by their fathers against all the Tories of the revolution should have descended to a third generation seems a singular fact. Even the wounded majesty of kings, who are taught to hold that the obedience of their people is due to them by divine right, is more placable than our democratic sovereignty, which maintains that the subjects of foreign potentates may become its citizens at their own good pleasure. George the Third did not disdain the homage of an Erroll, although, within fifteen years, the head of that nobleman's father had fallen on the scaffold of his predecessor; and it would have been more honorable to our character as a nation, if the blood of a Delancey had been shed with his gallant cousins on the plain of Chippewa, instead of the field of Waterloo. For ourselves, when we read in history the American names of sailors, who bore the meteor flag of England through the terrors of the battle of the Nile, and of soldiers who led the charge of the British bayonets in many a well-fought field in the Peninsula, we cannot but think of the exclamation of George the Second, who, when victory was snatched from his grasp by the Irish brigade, in the service of France, cursed the laws which deprived him of the service of such subjects.

No palliation can be offered for those who deserted, or attempted to betray, a cause in which they had once enlisted; but the revolution was, to a certain extent, a cruel contest, and those who embraced the royal cause from pure motives before the declaration of independence, however much they erred in judgment, can hardly be said to have been traitors. The whole question of their demerit rests upon their subsequent conduct; and while those who joined in plundering and wasting their native fields are deservedly execrated, we cannot extend the same feeling to those, who merely refused to bear arms against the crown, to which, in their opinion, allegiance was due, nor even to those who made war in an open and honorable manner.

When the British commander was forced, by the occupation of the Heights of Dorchester, to evacuate Boston, he must have felt himself in a most painful position. The ministry of England had anticipated that his army would have been sufficient to prevent an outbreak, and when it did occur, had hoped that his force would have sufficed to rout what they considered to be an undisciplined rabble. The affair of Bunker's Hill, in which the English troops, although with immense loss, remained masters of the field, was claimed as an important victory, and no person in England was prepared for the news that the army had been driven to make its escape from Boston under circumstances resembling a flight. Had the English army gained a victory, it is probable that there would have been great competition for the honor of bearing the despatches. But when foiled and driven from its post, to find a messenger who would tell the disastrous news, was difficult. It is probable that no officer, of sufficient intelligence to explain the circumstances which led to the retreat of the royal troops, was willing to volunteer for the purpose; and had the commanding general made it a point of military duty, he might have committed his explanations to a lukewarm friend. In this emergency he thought of Major Thompson, to whom he committed his despatches, and who, reëmbarking in the ship that had brought him to Boston, proceeded directly to England, while the discomfited commander retired with his foiled army to Halifax.

The despatches were addressed to Lord George

Germain, Secretary of State for the department to which the affairs of the colonies were intrusted. The pride of Great Britain had spurned at the idea of considering the revolt of her colonies as a war, although by this time their armies had overrun Canada, and formed the siege of Quebec; and the State Department, and not that of War, was still the office through which the correspondence passed. Lord George Germain, who, under the name of Sackville, had narrowly escaped with his life for alleged cowardice at the battle of Minden, and had been dismissed from the army in disgrace, was now one of the most prominent members of the ministry; and it would seem, that, in the hope of retrieving his standing, he was the willing instrument of the King in his attempts on the liberties of the colonies. He was not, however, more fortunate in the cabinet than he had been in the field; and the administration, of which he formed a part, saw, under its rule, a greater number of disasters and disgraces than had ever before fallen to the lot of England.

These despatches brought Major Thompson into close communication with this powerful minister, who was so much struck by his merits, that he immediately tendered him an employment in the department over which he presided. Such an offer was far too flattering and advan-

tageous to be declined by a houseless and needy
exile, and he immediately entered upon the duties of his new office.

It is difficult to conceive what may have been
the plans and hopes of Major Thompson at the
time this unexpected good fortune presented itself. Bearing the despatches of an unfortunate
general, announcing the downfall of long-cherished expectations to a ministry already assailed
by a powerful opposition, to be graciously received was even more than he could well have
anticipated; and, this duty ended, it appeared
probable that he would be left to choose between seeking a precarious livelihood in a foreign country, and taking arms against that of
his birth. Other natives of Massachusetts, of no
mean repute, had preceded him, whose former
official stations might have been considered as
better qualifying them to advise the ministry, and
to whom such an appointment as he received
would have been a grateful boon. We may,
however, suspect that they had been found unsafe counsellors, and had given far too favorable
an account of the prospects of the royal cause.
Major Thompson was more recently from the
field of action, knew well the resolution of his
countrymen, had seen the forces they were embodying; and the very studies and observations

he had made to qualify himself for joining their ranks, enabled him to give information, which, however ungrateful, could not be gainsaid.

The great offices, the possession of which gave admission to the cabinet, were then, as they have been ever since the revolution of 1689, accessible only through a seat in Parliament, and could be held only so long as their incumbents were able to maintain a majority in the lower house. The direct influence of the crown could generally command a majority in the House of Peers, or even, in extreme cases, could obtain one by the creation of new peers; and although, by selecting ministers having parliamentary influence, their immediate adherents, united to those over whom the crown could exert an influence, might generally insure a favorable vote from the Commons, there was enough of independence left in a portion of the members to make a majority far from certain. In this state of things, it was all-important to the ministry that they should be night after night at their posts on the benches of the lower house, to explain and defend their measures. The duties of the great offices devolved, therefore, in many cases, on their subordinates, and they, in turn, if members of Parliament, and compelled to be in the house at the time of division, to swell the majorities of their party; or prevent its defeat, left the duty which had devolved upon them to their clerks.

In such a state of things, that whole drawers full of American despatches, written during the most critical period of the affairs of the colonies, should have been discovered unopened in the very office to which Major Thompson was now admitted, is not surprising; nor is it more so, that a young man of high talent, great industry and application, with an intellect sharpened and trained in a Yankee counting-house, should at once have rendered himself eminently useful. That he was so, we have undoubted evidence in the fact, that he speedily rose to the highest place in the department, having, in less than four years after his arrival in England, attained the post of under secretary of state.

While thus assiduous and successful in the performance of his duties, he was not wholly engrossed by them. His active mind found time for other pursuits, and he did not abandon those studies and inquiries into scientific subjects in which he had before taken so much delight. His military passion was not cooled; and the reflections, which he had indulged in the camp before Boston, now bore fruit in the proposal of an important change in the equipment of the horse-guards, which was at once adopted, and has not yet gone out of use.

Possessed, in virtue of his office, of an honorable station in society, and an adequate income to support its rank, he became entitled to admission into the highest circles both of fashion and science; and in the "Philosophical Transactions" of the Royal Society, to whose meetings he soon acquired access, he found a channel through which his philosophical researches might be published under the most favorable auspices.

As early as 1777, Major Thompson made some curious and interesting experiments on the strength of solid bodies. These were never published, and would probably have been superseded by more full investigations made by subsequent experiments. In 1778, he employed himself in experiments on the strength of gunpowder and the velocity of military projectiles; and these were followed up by a cruise of some months in the Channel fleet, where he proposed to repeat his investigations on a larger scale. In this expectation he appears to have been disappointed, and the pressure of his official duties prevented him from renewing the attempts.

These experiments were a continuation of the inquiries into which, as has been seen, he had entered before his removal to Concord, and as early as 1770. The apparatus which he employed was cheap and simple, as was necessary in the operations of an individual unaided by public funds. The experiments were undertaken without any knowledge of those in which Hutton had been engaged in 1775, but which were not published until 1778. Both had made free use of the previous labors of Robins; and Major Thompson, in repeating his calculations before publication, employed a formula of Hutton's, instead of one of Euler's, of which he had originally made use, because he found it simpler, while it gave identical results. In this respect only was he indebted to the previous labors of Hutton; and it is to be remarked, to his credit, that, while Hutton had not finished the task he had undertaken, but was employed, at various times, from the year 1783 to 1791, in making experiments by which to complete his theory, the paper of Major Thompson, published in 1781, contains some of his most important principles, established upon a sufficient basis of facts, as well as several others which did not fall within the limits of Hutton's inquiries. These facts and principles are now so familiar, and have, under the authority of Hutton, directed the practice of the artillerists of all countries, that we need merely refer to the circumstance, that, while the individual results obtained by Thompson are much fewer, the theory he founded on them is as accurate as that obtained by Hutton.

We have no positive account of the labors

and services of Major Thompson in the department over which Lord George Germain presided. It is certain, however, that they must have been valuable; for, as has already been stated, within four years from the time that he first arrived in London, he was appointed under secretary of state. This rapid promotion of a person unconnected with any aristocratic family, and entirely unsupported by parliamentary influence, is almost unexampled in the history of English statesmen. Parliament affords, in that country, almost the sole avenue to appointments of trust and honor, still more to those of emolument. The aristocracy, indeed, by a wise instinct, seeks to draw to its support all young men, however ignoble in birth, who, by their fame for scholarship and talent at either university, promise to be valuable friends, or threaten to become dangerous enemies. The rotten-borough system, however objectionable on many accounts, possessed at least one merit, that of giving opportunities for entering the national legislature to persons, who, had their advancement depended upon merely popular grounds, might have been lost to the service of their country.

Major Thompson, however, had never been in a position to attract the notice of those, who held the nomination to seats in Parliament as a part of their hereditary estate; and his labors at the desk, or in the philosophical discussions of the Royal Society, were not of the description that could make either the ministry or their opponents hope to find in him an adroit debater. Lord George Germain himself was the proprietor of boroughs; but it does not appear, that he thought of employing the talent of his *protégé* in that direction, and it is probable that he derived too much benefit from Thompson's devotion to his official duties, to desire to divert him from them, even had he thought him qualified to enter the lists with Charles Fox, Burke, and others, who were now united in opposition to the ministry of North, and the colonial policy of Germain.

The important post to which Major Thompson was advanced, in 1780, did not satisfy his ambition. According to his own statement to Cuvier, he was disgusted with the want of judgment displayed by his principal, for which he was now in a position to be held personally responsible. This much is certain, the war in America was daily assuming a more unsatisfactory character; one army had already surrendered; another had with difficulty made its escape from a similar fate; and all hopes of driving the revolted colonies to submission were at an end, for their existence as a nation had been acknowledged by one of the great powers of

Europe, and two of them were united in the war against the mother country.

England, so far from being able to send fresh levies of troops to supply those lost in battle or by disease, was compelled to look to her own defence against invasion; and her fleets had, in her own narrow seas, been compelled to retire without fighting before the superior forces of the allies of the United States. In this critical juncture of affairs, the parliamentary opposition was daily gaining in strength and boldness, and did not hesitate to talk in a tone of reproach and menace to the ministers, by whose alleged incapacity the national dishonor had been caused. It became evident that England must submit to a peace, in which the independence of her former colonies must form an essential article; and still more evident, that any peace must be preceded by the resignation of the ministry that had caused and conducted the war, or at least of the Secretary of State within whose department the direction of colonial affairs had fallen.

Finally, the news of the capitulation of Lord Cornwallis at Yorktown reached England. While this appeared to have no immediate effect in depriving the ministry of a majority in the House of Commons, or to lessen the confidence reposed in them by the crown, it was not long ere the existence of a division in the cabinet became apparent. Lord North, the premier, in a full house, abandoned Lord George Germain to the attacks of the opposition; and the latter, in consequence, tendered his resignation. His departure from office was, however, by the favor of the King, graced with honors certainly merited by his devotion to the royal will, but which were more suitable as awards for a successful minister, than as consolations for one yielding to the pressure of misfortune. A peerage, which gave him precedence over all barons, was granted him, on the representation, that, were he elevated only to that rank of nobility, his own lawyer, and the page of his father, would take precedence of him; and he sunk the name of Germain, which he had taken to entitle him to property left him under that condition, in his paternal epithet of Sackville.

The manner and circumstances of his retirement from office left him the power of rewarding his friends and adherents; among whom he did not forget Major Thompson, but obtained for him an appointment of all others the most gratifying.

We have seen that Thompson had, at an early age, attained the rank of a field-officer. By the title, which this commission conferred upon him, he was proud to be known; and in virtue of it, he had sought to be employed in the service of his native country, when it had recourse to arms. His military ambition had lain dormant in the office of the Secretary of State, but had not been extinguished; and although the usages of the British army seemed to shut him out from all access to a rank equal to that he held in the New Hampshire militia, a plan presented itself by which his desires could be gratified. Besides the regiments of the British regular army, and the subsidized battalions of the German princes, England had sought to enlist natives of America in her service; and this with such success, that it has been estimated, that, at one period or other during the seven years' continuance of the war of independence, at least twenty thousand persons born in her revolted colonies had received her pay and worn her uniform. To effect this, her agents had not been scrupulous in granting commissions to persons believed to possess influence, and in forming corps unknown upon the official army list.

The natural consequences were, that, while those who received commissions were of such stations in life as to become tied by feelings of honor to the royal cause, the common soldiers, cajoled, flattered, or threatened until they enlisted, took the earliest opportunity to desert their colors, and the proportion of officers became excessive. While some of these were men, whom mere desperation, in fortune and character, had led to espouse what they anticipated must be the gaining cause, in the hopes of becoming rich by the confiscations and attainders they saw impending over rebels, there were others whom a pure and holy, however mistaken, feeling of loyalty had animated. Dissolving all the local and disjointed corps, it was now proposed to unite those who had served as cavalry, and still remained with their standards, in a single regiment of dragoons, forming a part of the regular army of England. The advantages to be attained by such officers as might be thought worthy of admission into this regiment were great; among them was the attainment of a rank acknowledged throughout all the territories of the British empire, instead of one merely local; the right of receiving promotion by seniority or purchase, according to well-known and established rules, and, finally, the certainty of half pay to the close of life, even if not required to do duty.

Such was the value of the boon, that the organization of this regiment held out to a number of his unfortunate, and, as far as England was concerned, meritorious countrymen, that it may be suspected that the active benevolence of Rumford, which afterwards became so conspicuous, had no small share in the plan. From whatever source it may have originated, it is at least certain, that he was charged with the duty of organizing the regiment and selecting its officers. For this purpose, he at once received the commission of Major, which now, instead of bearing the signature of a colonial Governor, was graced by the royal sign-manual; and, in a short time, he was promoted to the rank of Lieutenant-Colonel, in which capacity the command of the regiment devolved upon him.

Colonel Thompson did not receive his commission until the capitulation of Lord Cornwallis, at Yorktown, had put an end to all chance of the subjugation of the states that had united in the declaration of independence. We need not, therefore, inquire whether he came out to America with the design of carrying a war of aggression against the country of his nativity. Whatever may have been his intentions, it was at least his good fortune that he never saw the blood of his compatriots shed in battle. According to traditions still handed down in New York, he was stationed on Long Island, where he was occupied in organizing his regiment out of the scattered and broken bands of loyalist rangers.

Whether it was the intention of the ministry to employ this regiment in America, in the event of the continuance of the war, or to call it to

Great Britain to aid in the defence of that country against a threatened invasion, cannot now be known This much is clear; the employment of the Tories had been found to have widened the breach between the mother country and her former colonies, and it would have been good policy to have withdrawn every person of American birth from the continent to serve in other parts of the empire. That it was, in all probability, intended that the regiment organized by Colonel Thompson was not to continue to serve in America is rendered probable by the fact, that he certainly returned to England, with some, at least, of his officers, if not with the whole corps, previous to the signature of the preliminaries of peace. Could this intention be shown to have existed, the only blot on Rumford's character, in the estimation of his countrymen, would be wiped away.

CHAPTER IV.

He visits Germany. — Forms the Acquaintance of Prince Maximilian of Deux-Ponts. — Is introduced to the Elector of Bavaria. — Returns to England. — Is knighted by the King. — Enters the Service of the Elector. — His Reforms in the Bavarian Army. — Military Workhouse at Manheim.

COLONEL THOMPSON, as we have seen, left America for England before the intelligence of the signature of the preliminaries of peace reached him. When he arrived in Europe, however, he found hostilities at an end; and although his regiment was not disbanded, and there is no reason to doubt that he might have, for a time at least, enjoyed his full pay, the dull routine of a soldier's life in time of peace had no charms for him. He therefore at once requested leave of absence, for the purpose of visiting the continent of Europe; and he is said to have entertained the idea of offering his services to Austria, which power was at the time engaged in a war with the Turks.

Taking France in his way, he had reached Strasburg, the last possession of that country on the side of Germany, when an incident occurred, that changed his plans, and opened to him a new and more extended career. A review being held of the garrison of that important place, he presented himself as a spectator, mounted on a superb English horse, and in the full uniform of his rank as colonel of dragoons. Several years had elapsed since it had been possible for a British officer to be seen in a French garrison town, in consequence of the war between the two nations; and we believe, that even when France was open to them, few Englishmen would have been found to have paid Frenchmen the compliment of putting on their uniforms to appear at a parade. The attendance of Colonel Thompson at the ceremony was received as an act of courtesy; and the French officers, of rank equal to his own, eagerly, and without introduction, sought his acquaintance. Among them was Prince Maximilian of Deux-Ponts, afterwards King of Bavaria, who commanded one of the regiments of the garrison. This Prince, like Colonel Thompson, had just returned from America, where he had served in the army of Rochambeau, and been present at the surrender of Cornwallis.*

This circumstance probably furnished subjects

---

* His portrait is to be seen in Trumbull's Picture of the Capitulation of Yorktown, in the rotunda of the Capitol.

of conversation in which both were interested; and the result of the interview was, to produce, in the Prince's mind, a most favorable impression of the character and talents of Colonel Thompson. Learning his design of seeking service in the Austrian army, and seeing that he was in fact without a country, the Prince recommended him to visit Munich, and inquire whether, in the employ of Bavaria, he might not find an opening better adapted to his views and more promising to his ambition. For this purpose, he tendered him an introduction to the Elector, of whom he was the nephew and presumptive heir.

Colonel Thompson, furnished with a recommendation from so high a source, immediately proceeded to Munich, and presented himself to the Elector of Bavaria, upon whom he made an impression as favorable as upon Prince Maximilian.

At the very first audience of his Serene Highness he received the offer of a situation, at the court, of dignity and importance; and when he declined respectfully any immediate decision, many flattering inducements were held out to him to remain, at least for a time, at Munich. He, however, remained firm to his purpose of visiting Vienna, preferring, as it would seem, a chance of seeing active service, in the war with the Turks, to the less exciting occupations that the peaceful relations of the Bavarian electorate could alone promise. During his residence at Vienna, he probably learned that the Turkish war was drawing to a close, and that the imperial service, in consequence, was little more likely to fulfil his desires of obtaining military renown than the Bavarian. Here, also, he was followed by letters from the Elector, who continued to correspond with him until he received his promise to come and reside at Munich, provided he could obtain the consent of the King of Great Britain to enter the service of a foreign potentate.

Having made this promise, Colonel Thompson quitted Vienna, and returned to London, where he immediately made application for permission to accept the employment offered to him by the Bavarian Elector.

His request was at once granted, and the permission was accompanied by tokens of favor that show, in the clearest light, how highly his previous services had been estimated by the government of England. While his resignation of the command of his regiment was accepted, he was permitted to retain the half-pay of his rank, which was continued to him until his death, and the honor of knighthood was conferred upon him.

It is probable, that, had Colonel Thompson continued to reside in England, he would neither have sought nor accepted the last-named distinction. His ambition would probably have taught him to wait for the Order of the Bath, the appropriate meed of military service, to which the rank he had already attained in the army might at no distant day have furnished an opening. But, leaving England, the rank of knight was valuable, not only as giving him an established degree of precedence, but as a clear and distinct evidence of the value of his services to the sovereign whose employ he was about to quit, and a passport to the confidence of him whose servant he was henceforth to become.

Thus graced by the King of Great Britain, Colonel Thompson forthwith repaired to Munich, which he reached before the close of the year 1784. Here he was immediately placed in a confidential station, near the person of the reigning prince, with the appointments of aid-de-camp and chamberlain.

Charles Theodore, who then ruled over Bavaria, was a highly enlightened prince. His views were directed to the advancement of the prosperity and happiness of his subjects, which, he wisely saw, was the surest mode of increasing his own consideration as a member of the German empire, as well as of rendering him more respected by the powers of Europe at large. In these views he met with no support from his own nobility; and, even had the strict etiquette of German courts permitted him to seek counsellors in persons of inferior rank, the low state of education would have prevented him from finding any qualified to aid him in his endeavors. As might have been expected from a German prince, his army claimed his earliest attention. This was, at the time when Sir Benjamin Thompson became a resident in Bavaria, little more than a shadow. The troops raised by a rigorous conscription had, even nominally, a scanty pay; but the system, then common to nearly the whole continent of Europe, of regiments, and even companies, being held as property by their commanders, had opened the door to abuses by which the condition of the soldier had been rendered miserable in the extreme, and the efficiency of the army destroyed. Thompson's first step was to relieve both the soldier and the state from the impositions of this class of officers; and thus, while he effected no inconsiderable saving in the expense of maintaining the army, he materially improved the condition of the men.

He next directed his attention to the arms and clothing, both of which were rendered more convenient and serviceable; and he simplified the exercise and manœuvres to such a degree, as to lessen the labor, which, under the old system, had pressed so severely upon both officers and privates. The time thus left at their disposal was not permitted to pass without an appropriate and useful occupation. Ground for a garden was allotted to each regiment, in which the men were encouraged to cultivate the vegetables, by which their scanty rations might be eked out, and their food rendered more wholesome and palatable.

The soldier, thus furnished with an occupation both interesting and advantageous, was assimilated more closely to the citizen, an approximation which was mutually advantageous; for, while the former had no occupation but the care of his arms and the performance of his military exercise, he looked down with contempt on the laboring class, from the midst of whom he had been taken; and at the same time, his evil habits, the natural consequence of idleness, furnished a pernicious example to the latter.

One of the greatest evils attendant on the former military system, was the growth of the numerous children of the soldiers in idleness and ignorance. For the instruction of these in the rudiments of letters, and in arts by which they might obtain an honest livelihood, schools were established in each regiment; and the system adopted in these was so well contrived, that they neither required funds from the treasures of the state, nor trenched upon the pay or comforts of the soldiers.

To the military, thus elevated in moral and physical condition, it became possible to hold out, as a reward for meritorious service, the prospect of receiving a commission, thus anticipating by several years that principle, which was found so efficient in exciting to the highest pitch of prowess the armies of revolutionary France. The artillery service, as being more closely connected with scientific research, became a special object of his attention. In order to rest its improvement upon sound principles, he made many experiments in extension of those he had formerly instituted.

The result of his exertions was, that the plans of gun-carriages and equipments, proposed and introduced by him, made the Bavarian artillery superior, at least in its material part, to any on the continent of Europe. To accomplish the improvement of the artillery, a new foundery for cannon was erected, under his direction, at Munich, in addition to that already existing at Manheim. This was furnished with machinery made under his directions, and very superior to any previously seen on the continent.

When we look upon the valuable services, which Sir Benjamin Thompson thus rendered the military establishment of Bavaria, which he may almost be said to have created, and which he placed upon a footing that required no change, even when her troops were brought into line with the choicest troops of Napoleon, we cannot but recall to our recollection the fact, that his tenders of service were scornfully rejected in his native country, and that she was compelled to intrust the formation of her code of tactics and discipline, in succession, to three persons of foreign birth. The brilliancy of Rumford's scientific discoveries has overpowered the lustre of his military performances; but the latter were such as have placed him high among that useful class, who organize the battalions by which others, with more good fortune, achieve victories. Whether he would have distinguished himself as much in the field, as he did in this less brilliant branch of military duty, we can only conjecture; for, as we shall see hereafter, he was not allowed any opportunities of commanding in the field, in the wars of which, before his death, Bavaria was often the seat, and almost always a party.

The labors of Sir Benjamin Thompson, in remodelling the military establishment of the Bavarian electorate, were not performed for an ungrateful master; nor, while he enjoyed the favor of the Prince, were the people insensible to his merits. He speedily received the appointments of a member of the Council of State, and of Major-General in the army; and, as the statutes of German knighthood prevented his receiving a Bavarian order, the Elector procured for him, from King Stanislaus, of Poland, the decorations of two of the chivalric orders of that country. The scientific men of the electorate, to testify their sense of his acquirements and talents, admitted him as a member of the two academies of Munich and Manheim.

In order that we may not have occasion to interrupt the narrative, by recording the further honors he attained in Germany, it may be here stated, that, on a visit to Prussia, in 1787, he was elected a member of the Academy of Sciences at Berlin; that, in Bavaria, he attained the military rank of Lieutenant-General, was commander-in-chief of the general staff, minister of war, and superintendent of the police of the electorate; that he was, for a short time, chief of the regency that exercised sovereignty during the absence of the Elector; and that, in the interval between the death of the Emperor Joseph and the coronation of his successor, Leopold, the Elector, becoming vicar of the empire, availed himself of the prerogatives of that office to make him a Count of the Holy Roman Empire. In receiving the last dignity, he chose a title in remembrance of the country of his nativity, and of the place endeared by recollections both of pleasure and pain, and was thenceforth known as Count of Rumford, from one of the names by which the residence of his wife had been distinguished.

Rumford's occupations in Bavaria are set forth by himself in one of his essays.

"I have been employed by his Eelctoral Highness in various public services, and particularly in arranging his military affairs, and introducing a new system of order, discipline, and economy, among his troops.

"In the execution of this commission, ever mindful of that great and important truth, that no political arrangement can be really good, except in so far as it contributes to the general good of society, I have endeavored, in all my operations, to unite the interest of the soldier with the interest of civil society, and to render the military forces, even in time of peace, subservient to the public good.

"To facilitate and promote these important objects, to establish a respectable standing force, which should do the least possible harm to the population, morals, manufactures, and agriculture of the country, it was necessary to make soldiers citizens, and citizens soldiers. To this end, the situation of the soldier was made as easy, comfortable, and eligible as possible; his pay was increased, he was comfortably and even elegantly clothed, and he was allowed every kind of liberty not inconsistent with good order and due subordination; his military exercises were simplified, his instruction rendered short and easy, and all obsolete and useless customs and usages were banished from the service. Great attention was paid to the neatness and cleanliness of the soldiers' barracks and quarters, and which extended even to the external appearance of the buildings; and nothing was left undone that could tend to make the men comfortable in their dwellings. Schools were established in all the regiments, for instructing the soldiers in reading, writing, and arithmetic; and into these schools not only the soldiers and their children, but also the children of the neighboring citizens and peasants, were admitted *gratis,* and even school books, paper, pens, and ink, were furnished for them at the expense of the sovereign.

"Besides these schools of instruction, others, called schools of industry, were established in the regiments, where the soldiers and their children were taught various kinds of work, and from whence they were supplied with raw materials, to work for their own emolument.

"As nothing is so fatal to morals, and particularly to the morals of the lower class of mankind, as habitual idleness, every possible measure was adopted, that could be devised, to introduce a spirit of industry among the troops. Every encouragement was given to the soldiers to employ their leisure time, when they were off duty, in working for their own emolument."

The ordinary occupations of agricultural industry created a sufficient demand for the labor of the soldiery at particular seasons of the year, but at others no means of occupation existed. These were now created for them by undertaking public works, which had before been neglected or performed by other hands. New highways were opened, and the old ones repaired; marshes were drained, and rivers embanked.

It might be supposed, that such modes of employing the military force would have entailed an additional burden upon the state; but Rumford was enabled, by this very system, to diminish the cost of the military peace establishments. The army was distributed, throughout the cities of the electorate, in permanent garrisons. The recruits of the several regiments, of which these garrisons were composed, were drawn from among the neighboring inhabitants. They thus did not, on becoming soldiers, wholly abandon their occupations as citizens, but gladly accepted the furloughs that were freely tendered them, to return to their paternal homes, and labor for their friends and relations. When thus on furlough, they were entitled to no pay, although they still received their rations, and were permitted, at their own option, to lodge in the barracks.

By this system, it finally came to pass, that no more of the army was in the actual receipt of pay, than was sufficient to perform guard and garrison duty, except for about six weeks in each year, when the whole was assembled for field exercise; and yet no soldier was out of hearing of the call of the trumpet, and the entire army could be collected at its alarm posts within a few hours. This state of things, however, was not attained without effort on the part of the government. The labors of agriculture and the public works did not suffice to furnish occupation for the multitude, which the necessity of keeping up a commensurate military establishment compelled the Elector to retain as soldiers. To provide further occupation, the gardens of which we have already spoken were laid out in the neighborhood of each garrison. These were allotted by regiments, battalions, and companies, until each private had his prescribed portion. No compulsion was used to induce the soldier to work in these gardens, and he might enjoy his pay in idleness, instead of giving it up for the privilege of cultivating his allotment, and indemnifying himself by the sale of its productions. But all allotments that remained uncultivated were forfeited. These measures were effectual in reducing the demands on the military chest, but still more in bringing back the soldier from the proverbially dissolute habits of the camp to the quiet and virtuous enjoyment of the domestic circle. Marriages, before almost unknown, became frequent, and with their growing families arose a new demand on the benevolence of Rumford.

To furnish them with the means of support, without becoming a charge upon the state, was his next attempt. The articles, which form the ornaments of a military dress, are made of materials of no great cost, and derive their principal value from the labor expended upon them. This labor, he saw, might be performed, after a little instruction, by the wives and children of the soldiers. All that was necessary was a stock of materials, a few simple implements, and a building that might be occupied as a workshop. The capital for the first two objects he found in the military chests of the several regiments, and the sums thus appropriated became no more than a payment in advance for the articles of which the army had need. At Manheim, on the Rhine, an appropriate building, the property of the government, was found; and here a military workhouse was established, which, after a short time, supplied not merely the ornamental parts of the soldiers' equipments, but the whole of the clothing worn by the garrison of that place, at a less cost to the government, than when the articles had been purchased from private manufacturers.

The establishment at Manheim did not take this development until its doors had been thrown open to all, who were willing and able to work. It thus furnished a sure source of honest livelihood to the poor of that town, and had a decided and marked effect in diminishing the numbers of those, who sought the alms of the charitable. It was, indeed, a test by which those, who merely wanted an opportunity of earning their means of support by industry, could be distinguished from those who preferred to live in idleness by the practice of beggary.

The military workhouse at Manheim was an experiment. Every step in its establishment was taken with the greatest caution. As an economic measure, it was successful, as far as the interest of the government was concerned; but it had attained the still more important object of introducing habits of industry among a class, which had before been a charge upon the labor of others. No enlightened person can fail to see, that by such means the general prosperity of the community would be promoted; and yet we do not doubt, that there were many persons in Manheim who would have preferred that those, who obtained employment in the military workhouse, should continue dependent upon alms, rather than engage in occupations that appeared to rival their own. Our more enlightened times, and our more favored country, have seen attacks made upon the charitable institutions of our cities, and the penal establishments of our states, because trades and arts were practised in them that were supposed to come in competition with the voluntary labor of the citizens; and we have even seen great political parties yielding to the clamor raised against the instruction of convicts in manufactures. Demagogues have seized upon this feeling to serve them as a passport to power and emolument; and we have seen bodies composed of large numbers of industrious handicraftsmen thrown into agitation by the idea, ingeniously pressed upon them, that the compulsory labor of two or three hundred convicts would have an effect in lowering the rates of their own wages.

Had Bavaria enjoyed a popular and representative government, it is possible, indeed more than probable, that objections would have been urged against Rumford's attempt to manufacture the clothing and equipments of the army in establishments, where a class before idle was converted into one of workers; and we can almost fancy, that we hear the eloquence with which the ruin of the mechanics and artisans of Manheim would have been predicted by popular orators.

There can be little doubt, that, even under the arbitrary rule of the Elector of Bávaria, persons were not wanting, who, jealous of the influence of the foreign favorite, ventured to predict to the Prince the injurious consequences that were to follow the innovations of Rumford. The Elector, however, placed implicit confidence in his prudence and foresight, and, in fact, identified himself with the plans for ameliorating the condition of his soldiery. The experiment at Manheim thus had a fair trial, and was completely successful. Large numbers of those, who had before relied upon charity for support, were rendered industrious; and, while no branch of industry, which had previously flourished, sustained the least injury, the burden of supporting paupers, which, if voluntarily assumed, was not the less onerous, was materially lessened.

The plan of quartering the army in time of peace in permanent garrisons, by which, without depriving it of the capability of rendering it immediately effective, the pay of the soldiery could be saved for a large portion of the year, was not original. It had been previously practised in Prussia, and was, in fact, the secret by which a poor and comparatively feeble state was enabled to bring into the field, at a short notice, forces which, at the beginning of every war, gave her, for a time at least, a superiority over her more powerful and wealthy neighbors. Rumford had also seen it practised, but without being formally announced, in England, where the stationary position of the household troops in London enabled the government, by a rate of pay very moderate when compared with the wages of laborers, to command the service of men picked for their strength, stature, and personal beauty. Nor is the method unfavorable either to discipline or martial spirit, as is readily seen by the character of the Prussian army, and the superiority which the English guards have always held in the field over the marching regiments.

If Rumford, however, was not the author of this system, it assumed in his hands a more perfect form than it had previously exhibited in any other country, and the military force of Bavaria was rendered formidable in a degree far beyond her limited revenues and narrow territory.

The experiment at Manheim had another and much more important bearing. In the attempt to lessen the expense of the military establishment, and improve the condition of the soldier, Rumford had ascertained that a pauper population might, with little difficulty, and at a small original outlay, be rendered capable of supporting itself. In this discovery lay the germ of plans of vast importance, and which have, in fact, ameliorated the condition of all the civilized nations of the earth. Planned in reference to the circumstances of Bavaria, they are capable of being adapted to every varying form of society, and have made their way, in spite of natural and artificial obstacles, into the charitable system of many nations. Before, however, we can appreciate the value of these plans, it is necessary that we should recur to the social state of the lower classes of the Bavarian electorate at the time that they were laid, and he began to put them in practice.

CHAPTER V.

Measures for suppressing Mendicancy in Bavaria. — Establishment of the Military Workhouse at Munich.

THE state of Bavaria, at the time that Rumford became a resident of that electorate, is thus depicted by Cuvier.

"Most of those, who are called to power by adventitious circumstances, are led astray by the opinion of the vulgar. They know that they will infallibly be called men of genius, and be celebrated in prose and verse, if they succeed in changing the forms of government, or in extending the territory of their sovereign but a few additional leagues. Is it, therefore, astonishing, that intestine revolutions and foreign wars should disturb the peace of mankind? Mankind have themselves to blame. Happily for Count Rumford, Bavaria, at this period, had no such temptations for her ministers. Her constitution was fixed by the laws of the empire, and her frontiers defined by the more powerful states who were her neighbors. She was, in short, reduced to that condition, which most states consider so hard a one, namely, to have her attention confined to the sole object of ameliorating the fortune of her people.

"It is true, that she had much to do in this direction. Her sovereigns, who had been aggrandized, in recompense for their zeal in behalf of the Catholic faith, during the times of the wars of which disputes in religion were the cause, had, from that time, exhibited a zeal beyond that demanded by enlightened Catholicism. They had fostered religious devotion, but had made no provision for the encouragement of industry. There were more convents than manufactories in their states; their army was almost a shadow, while ignorance and idleness were conspicuous in every class of society."

Beggary, in particular, had become an evil of the most enormous magnitude. It had, in fact, been rendered in some degree respectable by the example of persons in stations, that, in other countries, would have precluded their asking or receiving alms. Thus the students in the German and Latin schools, the sisters of the religious order of charity, the directors of public hospitals, not to mention the mendicant orders of friars, had been permitted to go about from house to house, at stated periods, to ask assistance for themselves and their establishments, until the contributions they levied had become a sort of tax, payment of which could not be denied. In addition to beggars of this description, where a tacit toleration had grown up into a prescriptive right, there was a class whose claims were sanctioned by immemorial usage possessing the force of positive law. It had been, and was still, the practice, in Germany, that those who had served apprenticeships to any mechanical trade, should, before they settled themselves in its practice in the place of their nativity, travel for three or four years, for the purpose of completing their education. Proceeding, with this view, from town to town, they engaged as journeymen in places where they could find employment; but in those where no opportunity for working at their trades could be found, they were considered as having the right to beg assistance of the inhabitants, and particularly of those of the same occupation as themselves, to enable them to proceed to the next town. To refuse this demand was thought a piece of injustice; and as most of the mechanics and handicraftsmen had, in their youth, performed a tour of the same description, they usually contributed cheerfully and liberally to such adventurers.

Whatever may have been the case in more ancient times, this custom had, towards the close of the last century, become fruitful of abuses. Sufficient skill, in many mechanic arts, to enable the possessor to pass for an apprentice, is easily acquired; and although certificates from their former employers were required from them, such documents were easily counterfeited, or purchased from those in whose favor they had been issued. Under the pretence of being travelling journeymen, numbers of idle mendicants were continually strolling from town to town, and returning, to begin a new circuit, as soon as time had been allowed for their faces and persons to be forgotten.

With such examples of authorized mendicity, beggary had become a trade, and was handed down as a profession from generation to generation. Numbers had, therefore, grown up, not only unacquainted with any description of work, but with the greatest aversion to regular labor. Crime had become rife among them, and they were callous to all sense of shame. The number of those who strolled about the country demanding rather than praying for alms, and who led a life of indolence and the grossest debauchery, was incredible. Even in the great towns, where a better police existed than in the country, beggars swarmed; and in the capital itself, their importunities were so bold, that passengers were actually forced to comply with their demands. The greater portion of these sturdy beggars were stout and healthy persons, who had embraced the vocation from choice, and who added insolence and threats to their importunity, thus extorting from fear what would have been denied by charity.

Their boldness had increased to such a degree in Munich, that they entered the dwellings of the inhabitants, stealing whatever they could lay their hands upon; the churches, which, as is usual in Catholic countries, were open daily, and at all hours, were their chosen resort; and those who repaired to them for devotion were prevented from saying their prayers until they had complied with their importunities. Even the celebration of mass did not put a stop to the nuisance, and the interruption of divine service became a positive scandal.

To excite compassion, many of the beggars had recourse to practices of the most inhuman and horrid description. Those who had children of their own would expose them naked in the streets, and keep them without food, in order that their unaffected cries of distress might excite sympathy; and as they became old enough to see that the distress of their parents was not real, they were unmercifully beaten when they did not succeed in bringing back a prescribed sum. Even the unaffected and simple narration of their being liable to such punishment often served as an incentive to charity. Those, who had no children of their own, did not hesitate to steal them from their parents, and, restrained by no natural affection, were in the habit of making them more likely to excite commiseration by depriving them of sight, or maiming their limbs.

The success and impunity of beggars by profession was such, as not only to attach them to their trade, but to induce others to join them; and thus a distinct class, or caste, existed, which seemed to assume the form of an organized community. Each beggar had his peculiar beat in the cities, within which no other ventured to ask for alms, and the beats became property, to be disposed of or inherited.

In such a state of things, it is not surprising, that the whole of the lower classes began to assimilate with the begging caste. In the great towns, the children of the poorer classes made a practice of begging; the herdsmen and shepherds stationed themselves on the road-side, to levy contributions from travellers; and their employers soon learnt to derive benefit from their booty by proportioning their wages to the value of their stand. The evil extended still further in the country villages; for there the children, even of the richest farmers, made a practice of begging from strangers, and it was rare to meet a woman walking on the road, who did not ask for charity.

From the foregoing statement, which is abridged from Rumford's own narrative, it would appear that mendicity had made such progress in Bavaria, as to threaten to subvert the foundations of society. A native of a country where, in his youth, beggary was wholly unknown, and long resident in England, where a strict system of poor laws had driven it to hide itself, the boldness and impunity with which it was practised in Bavaria must have been far more revolting to him, than to those who had witnessed it from their youth. It therefore must have attracted his attention at an early period, and he must have felt it as one of the duties he owed to his princely benefactor, to point out means for repressing the evil, or extinguishing it altogether.

Whatever may have been his designs, he, however, suppressed them, until the success of the establishment at Manheim gave him good grounds for believing, that he might, by vigorous yet gentle measures, relieve Bavaria of this scourge. He saw, that, with persons such as have been described, admonition, and even punishment, would be ineffectual, and that to endeavor to reform their habits, by making them virtuous in the first place, was impossible. He therefore proposed to reverse the order, and, by creating good habits, endeavor to bring them back to the practice of virtue; and, of the habits most likely to conduce to that end, he laid the greatest stress on cleanliness. "Virtue," says he, "never dwelt long with filth and nastiness; nor do I believe, that there ever was a person *scrupulously attentive to cleanliness*, who was a consummate villain." Such being the principles on which he proposed to proceed in his contemplated reform, and the hearty approbation of the Elector being obtained, he began to prepare for carrying his plans into effect.

The first requisite was a building of sufficient

extent to furnish work-rooms for all the beggars of Munich. One was found in a suburb, which had been built for a manufactory, but which had for many years been deserted, and was then falling to ruin. Preparations were made for repairing it, and a part was even rebuilt. It was of sufficient extent to furnish large halls for carrying on various branches of manufacture, as the spinning of hemp, flax, cotton, woollen, and worsted, and weaving, with all the processes necessary to finish the cloth, with store-rooms, offices, and dwelling-rooms for the officers. A kitchen, with a bakehouse and refectory, and workshops for carpenters and smiths, were added to the buildings; and when they were completed, they were furnished with machinery, tools, and a stock of raw materials.

While the building was undergoing repair, and receiving its furniture, preparations were quietly made for arresting, within the space of a few hours, all the beggars of the neighborhood of Munich, and for preventing their escape to prey upon other parts of the country. The infantry of the army, being stationed in fixed garrisons, were at his disposal in all the towns; and to occupy the country, and scour the roads, four regiments of cavalry were cantoned in the electorate, in such manner, that every town and village was occupied, and small parties so stationed that they might daily patrole between adjacent posts, without being compelled to call upon the inhabitants for food, forage, or quarters.

Although the experiment at Manheim had shown that it was sufficient, with those who were willing to work, to provide them with opportunities for so doing, and that they would thereafter support themselves, Rumford was aware, that with those unwilling and unaccustomed to work, and among whom were to be found many infirm with age, helpless from infancy, or suffering from bodily infirmity, large sums would be necessary to render them comfortable. For these he proposed to rely chiefly upon the voluntary contributions of the inhabitants. He trusted, that the pressure of the evil had been so burdensome to the people of Munich, that, could they be satisfied that the proposed measures were certain of success, they would gladly unite in defraying the expense. He was aware, however, that so many imperfect and ineffectual plans had been proposed, for some of which considerable amounts had been raised and wasted, that the inhabitants of Munich began to look upon all proposals of the sort as a job. He therefore determined to carry his project into execution in the first instance, and, after entirely removing the evil, call upon the public to support the establishment. His scheme for the organization of the workhouse was therefore prepared in secret, and measures were taken to carry his plan into sudden and immediate effect.

New year's day, of the year 1790, was chosen for the purpose. This day had been considered, by the pious, as peculiarly appropriate for almsgiving; and, in consequence, the beggars were sure, on that occasion, to be found on their beats. Early in the morning of that day, Rumford assembled, at his lodgings, the field-officers of the garrison and the magistrates of the city. He, at the same time, caused the subaltern and non-commissioned officers to be stationed in the streets, there to await further orders. Having explained his intentions to those whom he had invited to meet him, he proceeded into the street, accompanied by the chief magistrate, and followed by the officers, each with one of the inferior magistrates. The procession had hardly passed from the house, when Rumford was accosted by a beggar, whom he arrested upon the spot, and delivered to an orderly, to be conveyed to the town-hall. Calling then upon those who were with him to remark, that he had with his own hands arrested the first beggar, he requested them to disperse themselves through the different quarters of the town, and, by the aid of the military, whom they would find waiting for orders, take into custody all whom they should discover asking for alms.

Such was the extent of the evil, that means of no other description would probably have sufficed. The police officers of the city were known, and would have been avoided; private soldiers would not have been asked for alms; and it was necessary that persons, such as would naturally be objects of importunity, should condescend to the task of making arrests. To overcome the repugnance which would naturally be felt to such a task, Rumford, in his full uniform, and decorated with his orders, made the first capture; and, with such an example before them, his companions did not hesitate, but performed their duty so thoroughly, that in less than an hour not a single beggar was to be found in the streets.

Those who were arrested were conducted to the town-hall, when, after their names were inscribed, they were dismissed, with orders to repair the next day to the "Military Workhouse." Here, they were told, they would find well-heated rooms, a warm dinner, and work provided for such as were able to perform it. They were also told, that they must beg no more, but that persons were appointed, who would inquire into their circumstances, and grant them, in regular weekly sums, such amounts as they were in actual need of.

That compliance with the direction to repair daily to the workhouse might be strictly enforced, the military guards stationed throughout the town received orders to arrest all the beggars they should meet with, and seek for those, who, after being arrested, had failed to obey; and rewards were given for every person, of either description, arrested by them.

The ensuing day, the beneficial effects of the preparatory acts were visible; the beggars either repaired to the workhouse or carefully hid themselves. It was now a propitious time to lay the plan of the establishment before the inhabitants of Munich, and ask their aid in carrying it into effect. The details of the plan were prefaced by an address drawn up by Professor Babo, in which the fatal consequences of mendicity were pointed out; and this address was distributed to all the heads of families. In the distribution Rumford himself took a part, by calling with it upon the principal inhabitants, and personally requesting their aid.

CHAPTER VI.

Principles and Details of Establishments for the Relief of the Poor.

THE whole subject of the management of the poor, and the distribution of alms, was placed under the direction of a commission composed of the highest officers of state; the presidents of the several councils of war, regency, ecclesiastical affairs, and finance. Each of these was permitted to choose a member of the council, over which he presided, as his assistant; and it was made the duty of the person thus chosen to be present at every meeting of the commission. Thus, while the name and station of the most important members of the ministry gave weight to the directing board, it was provided, that the laborious part of the business should be performed by persons whose attention to it was rendered imperative.

No emolument whatever was granted to the members of the commission for their services; but they were allowed a secretary, clerk, and accountant, who received their pay from the treasury, and not from the funds collected for the support of the poor. That no suspicion might arise of the possibility of the misapplication of the funds raised by subscription, they were placed in the hands of a private banker, and accounts of the receipts and disbursements were directed to be made every three months.

To facilitate the inspection of the poor, the city was divided into sixteen districts, each of which was directed by a respectable inhabitant, elected for the purpose, and who had, as assistants, a priest, a physician, a surgeon, and an apothecary. These undertook their duties without reward, and the apothecary furnished his medicines without charging any profit.

The address and plan of management having been published, subscriptions were sought, and Rumford was not disappointed in his expectation of obtaining funds sufficient for the object. Arrangements were made by which subscriptions might be received and acknowledged from those, who did not choose to disclose their names, and boxes were placed in public situations, where those who thought proper might place their contributions; but no one was to be ever solicited to put anything into the boxes, nor were alms allowed to be asked on any occasion whatever.

Among other impositions which the growth of beggary had created, was one, which weighed heavily on the dealers in food of every description. The beggars had succeeded in compelling the butchers, bakers, brewers, and others, to deliver them, at stated periods, considerable quantities of meat, bread, and beer. This had risen to such an amount as to furnish a trade, in which a number of petty shopkeepers were engaged. When the town was cleared of beggars, the imposition ceased, as a matter of course, and the tradesmen who were thus benefited voluntarily engaged to supply daily certain quantities of the articles in which they dealt to the military workhouse. Arrangements of a simple and satisfactory kind were made for the receipt of these contributions, and of the broken victuals and stale bread, that would otherwise have been wasted in families.

Such were the sources from which the means of supporting the poor, who had formerly subsisted by beggary, were derived. In a town of sixty thousand inhabitants, they amounted to about twenty-five thousand dollars annually; and, by the great economy and skill in providing occupations for such as were able to work, this sum was found sufficient to maintain the twenty-six hundred mendicants, who were arrested in the city of Munich alone.

It was a task of no small difficulty to reduce so chaotic an assemblage of persons, who had never yielded to any control, to a state of good order. The firmness and decision, with which all the preparatory measures were taken, showed the futility of resistance; but for some days great confusion prevailed. By degrees, however, they were classified, first in reference to such work as any of them had been accustomed to perform; and as this method, among such a mass of inveterate idleness and dissipation, soon failed, the remainder were arranged according to sex, and, as far as possible, age, in separate halls, in each of which instructors in simple branches of manufacture were placed.

It is impossible to follow Rumford further in the history of the steps, by which he brought the military workhouse of Munich from the condition of a tumultuous assemblage of idle vagabonds, to that of a prosperous and thriving manufactory. It is clear, that he brought to the task not only the highest degree of administrative talent, but the deepest knowledge of human character. The great object of all his measures was, to elevate the subjects of his salutary discipline in their own opinion, and thus to render them worthy of the esteem of the community. The paupers, although arrested in the first instance, were not treated as criminals, but dismissed, on parole, to their former lodgings; nor were they afterwards shut up in the establishment, but permitted to proceed, as workmen, to any other manufacturing establishment, daily, to their allotted tasks. So far from compelling them to wear any distinctive dress, they were restricted to their old clothes, with proper precautions for the sake of cleanliness, until they had merited, by their industry, the privilege of receiving the uniform of the establishment. The distinctive dress was thus made a badge of honor, instead of a mark of disgrace, and was so considered, not only among the inmates of the workhouse, but by the public. It became necessary, in the first instance, for the purpose of instruction, to separate husband from wife, and parents from children; but so soon as the parents were found worthy of being trusted, the children were placed under their direction, and thus the halls of the establishment were speedily occupied by family groups.

As the capacities of the laborers developed themselves, distinctions were drawn between them. The best workmen were separated from the others, and separate apartments assigned to them; and thus, in every possible way, it was attempted to restore feelings of self-respect, and the desire of independence. The suppression of the mere annoyance of beggary would have been no small exploit; but, in this case, his measures also put an end to a vast amount of petty theft and forced contributions of the most outrageous description. The mendicants were not merely withdrawn from the eye of the public, to be supported at its cost, but were taught to earn their own livelihood, and many of them fitted to return, as industrious laborers, to a society of which they had been the pest. Thus, beginning with twenty-six hundred, the numbers working in the establishment were reduced, in the course of five years, to fourteen hundred. The establishment, which, for the first year, cost the community about twenty-five thousand dollars, at the end of six years, after paying wages to such as had shown themselves worthy of it, and supporting all who were prevented from begging, had yielded a profit of forty thousand dollars. A strong proof of the beneficial results of the system of training pursued in the military workhouse, is to be found in the feelings of the subjects of his charity towards himself. Rumford, during his personal superintendence of the establishment, was seized by a dangerous illness, upon learning which, its inmates went in procession to the cathedral, where, at their request, divine service was performed, and public prayers offered for his recovery; and four years afterwards, when the news of his being ill at Naples reached Munich, they voluntarily set apart an hour each evening to join in supplications for his restoration to health. No one can read his own history of these transactions without being satisfied, that the heart of Rumford was teeming with

Christian charity and the most disinterested benevolence.

The cost, which, as has been seen, was incurred in maintaining the beggars assembled in the military workhouse at Munich, was very small; and when the items are analyzed, the proportion of this cost, which was expended in food, is so trifling as to appear almost incredible. This result was reached by a careful study of the economy, which a scanty pay had taught the Bavarian soldier to practise.

At the time when Rumford entered the service of the Elector, the pay of the private soldier was no more than about three cents a day; under his administration, it was raised to about four cents. Out of this, he was compelled to purchase every article of food, except bread, of which a ration of a little more than two pounds was issued to him. The bread was made of unbolted rye-flour, and, although coarse, was wholesome and palatable.

When we compare this scanty allowance with the rations of our own army and navy, we should fancy, that the condition of the Bavarian soldiers must have been miserable in the extreme; but, so far from this being the case, they are described as "the finest, stoutest, and strongest men in the world, whose countenances show the most evident marks of health and perfect contentment."

The secret of this extraordinary fact lies in the art of cookery, which the Bavarian soldier appears to have carried to the highest pitch of perfection, if that consists in making the greatest quantity of agreeable and nutritious food out of the smallest quantity of the raw material. Their skill had been so successful, that the soldier was enabled to subsist on two thirds of his scanty pay, and, in addition, to save five sixths of his ration of bread, which he sold.

In order that he might make himself acquainted with this system of economy, Rumford required reports of their housekeeping from the sergeants, who superintended the messes into which the army was divided. The details of these are published in his essays, and have become the text of those, who, from benevolent motives, have undertaken to provide food for the poor, in all civilized countries. Rumford himself, struck by the remarkable character of the results, conceived that the water, which was used in converting the animal and vegetable matter into soup, actually became of itself nutritious. Physiologists, however, have reached the true explanation. The quantity of matter required to supply the waste of the body, at all ages, and furnish the material for the growth of the young, is small, compared with the actual capacity of the digestive organ; while the latter is not satiated, nor the appetite satisfied, unless it receive a certain degree of distention. A quantity of warm liquid, holding so much nutritious matter in solution as to render digestion necessary, will fulfil the latter object, as well as an equal bulk of solid food; while the necessity of expelling the excess, above the actual wants of the system, may, in the latter case, be productive of evil.

Military men, who have, in service, had an opportunity of comparing the relative effects of food cooked in different modes, when circumstances rendered it difficult to be procured, are well aware of the fact, that it goes much further when used in the preparation of broths, than when exposed to the naked fire in roasting or broiling. The former method, however, requires a certain degree of skill in the preparation, or its advantages may be lost; for animal food, if suddenly exposed, or rapidly brought to the boiling temperature, becomes coated with an insoluble substance, which effectually prevents its becoming either tender or palatable, and at the same time hinders the water from taking up the soluble parts. It is not, then, without reason, that, while the armies of Napoleon were in the height of their career of victory, it was ranked among the highest requisites of a soldier, that he should be able to make good soup; and the French troops lived luxuriously upon rations on which the carnivorous Englishman would have starved.

The allowances of the Canadian *voyageurs*, in the employ of the Hudson's Bay Company, show, perhaps even in a more striking manner, than the example of the Bavarian soldiers, how small a weight of solid matter is sufficient to maintain man in a high state of vigor and efficiency; but the experience of that laborious service exhibits one fact, of which Rumford was not aware, namely, that the strength of men laboring almost without cessation cannot be kept up without animal food, and that the fat is its most portable form. A few ounces of the latter substance, properly combined with farinaceous matter, will suffice for the daily ration, while one of our countrymen would feel the cravings of hunger if furnished with a pound of clear pork, and permitted to broil or fry it.

In imitating the plans of Rumford for feeding numbers of persons at a small expense, one remark of his is too important to be passed by; and yet it is to be feared, that, while all his other proposals have been carried, in some cases, beyond the proper point, this has been, in a great measure, neglected. "It is a maxim," says he, "as ancient, I believe, as the time of Hippocrates, that *whatever pleases the palate nourishes.*" The Bavarian soldiers, cooking in rota tion for themselves, did all in their power to render their viands agreeable to their tastes; but in the preparation of the soups *à la Rumford,* intended for gratuitous distribution, little pains have been usually taken to accomplish this, in reality, important object. However carefully prepared and seasoned, food of this description ceases to be palatable when it becomes lukewarm, and thus loses its best qualities when not consumed near the place where it is prepared, unless it is re-heated.

In connection with the preparation of food in such manner as to diminish the quantity required for sufficient and agreeable nourishment, Rumford directed his attention to the consumption of the fuel employed in cooking it. The Bavarian soldiers cooked their food in earthen vessels, over an open fire; and the average weight of wood employed in the process was ten elevenths of the whole weight of the prepared dishes. Aware that in this way much of the heat must be lost, both by radiation from the burning fuel, and in the ascending currents of air, he, when he undertook to carry his methods into effect in the kitchens of his military workhouses, placed his boilers over furnaces of masonry, and enclosed them in flues, through which the smoke was compelled to circulate, before it entered the chimney. By this method he succeeded in reducing the consumption of fuel to one fifteenth part of the weight of the cooked food.

The methods and principles, which he thus developed, were afterwards carried into effect in innumerable charitable and penal establishments, and have even been partially introduced in the kitchens of private houses. In the latter, however, there are many circumstances that must forever prevent the entire adoption of Rumford's plans of culinary apparatus. Thus, for a great part of the year, in temperate climates, a fire of some description is a necessary of life, and the fire which heats an apartment may be made to perform all the culinary processes of families of moderate size. Even should it be attempted to perform the heating and cooking by separate fires, although economy of fuel would certainly be attained, yet the additional care and attention, if not labor, which would be necessary, might more than counterbalance that advantage. A stronger objection to the adoption of Rumford's kitchen apparatus is to be found, in England and the United States, in the national tastes for meat cooked by broiling or roasting.

When Rumford busied himself in endeavoring to introduce his plans for saving fuel into England, he was speedily made aware of this difficulty. Determined to overcome it, he studied the rationale of the process of roasting, and the cause of the difference between meat prepared in that way and by baking. He soon discovered the manner in which contact of air affects the former process; and saw, that, could he direct a current of air over meat while in the act of baking, he might give it all the characters acquired by roasting, while, in addition, a large quantity of nutritious matter, which passes off or is decomposed, might be collected and rendered useful.

The principle being thus ascertained, he contrived an iron oven, in which, by means of pipes heated from the furnace beneath, and another passing to the chimney, he could direct a current of heated air over the surface of the meat when the cooking was nearly completed. This oven fulfilled all his expectations; but it was, in addition, susceptible of a still more important application. No one has ever tasted bread prepared in close iron ovens, without being aware of its great inferiority to that baked in the brick ovens of professional bakers. The difference arises from the fact, that, while the thoroughly dried brick rapidly absorbs the vapors of water and alcohol, which arise from the bread, these remain, in the close iron vessel, to render the paste sodden; but, in an iron oven constructed upon Rumford's plan, the vapors are more completely removed than in one of brick, and, by proper management, bread of even better quality may be baked.

While Rumford's boilers and stewpans, set in flues over close furnaces, have excited so much attention, and come into such frequent use, it appears extraordinary, that his oven, so well adapted to more than one important use, should have been in a great degree neglected. We, in truth, know of no instance, in the innumerable forms of cooking-ranges with which the records of our patent-office is loaded, and in all of which an oven forms an essential part, where the principle of Rumford has been adopted; nor has it attracted greater attention in England, to meet the wants of which country it was more especially designed.

We have seen the measures, by an energetic application of which, Rumford banished from Bavaria the pest of beggary. When he subsequently, as we shall see, resumed his residence in England, in 1795, he found that country in some alarm at the increasing price of bread; a fear, which, a few years afterwards, was realized in a scarcity almost amounting to famine. This impression in the public mind led him to publish the account of his experience in Bavaria, and of the means he had there carried into effect for economizing food, and the cost of preparing it. He also gave to the world his ideas in relation to the fundamental principles of establishments for the poor. These are so worthy of continual study, by all those, who, from position, or feelings of benevolence, are led to seek to ameliorate the condition of their less fortunate fellows, that an analysis of the essay in which they are contained can hardly be considered tedious, particularly in a country where the continual influx of the indigent, from foreign countries, threatens to create among us all the evils from which Europe has so long suffered, evils of which the growth among us is so rapid, that our means of resisting them have uniformly failed to keep pace with the exigency.

1. The first principle, which he lays down, is, that "no laws can effectually provide for the relief of the poor without the voluntary assistance of individuals," because the sympathies, by which alone the vicious can be reclaimed and the desponding excited to exertion, cannot be commanded by force.

2. The arrangements for the purpose must be such as to command the confidence of the public. This can only be insured by engaging in the scheme persons from the middling classes of society, as well as placing at its head those most elevated in station, and possessed of the greatest wealth; by having the duties of ad-

ministration performed without fee or reward; by the complete publicity of all the records of receipt and expenditure, and accessible registers of the names and residences of all who receive relief; and, finally, by conducting the business in such a manner, that it may be seen to be successful.

3. He combats the opinion, that to support the poor in part by voluntary subscription, must necessarily be attended with a heavy expense; showing that, so far from this being true, it must in the end, be attended with a saving, not only to the public, but to individuals, it being probable that, in any case, half the sum annually extorted by beggars would be sufficient for the support of the poor of all descriptions. In proof of this, he cites the fact, that, in Munich, the sum given to beggars alone was more than three times as great as the amount required for the comfortable support of all the poor collected in the military workhouse.

4. However large a city may be, there should be but one establishment, one committee for the general management, and one treasurer; so that, although it would be necessary to divide it into districts, under the superintendence of local committees, there should be a single fund, and no more than one account of receipts and expenditures.

5. While sums must be given weekly in alms to some, while to others an allowance of food and clothing may be given, the most valuable mode of relief is, to furnish, at cost, from public kitchens or stores, cooked food, clothing, or fuel, in order to prevent the applicant from becoming a burden on the public.

6. All money given in alms, in such manner as not to induce habits of industry, cannot fail to operate as an encouragement to idleness and immorality; while, to bring the idle to seek or earn subsistence by labor, force can never be effective. It may be absolutely necessary to have recourse to punishment; but this should never be done until good usage has been tried and found unavailing. To the improper or careless use of rewards and punishments he attributes the prevalence of poverty, misery, and mendicity, in the countries where they abound, and particularly in Great Britain, where " the healthfulness and mildness of the climate, the fertility of the soil, the abundance of fuel, the numerous and flourishing manufactures, the extensive commerce, and the millions of acres of waste lands, which still remain to be cultivated, furnish the means of giving employment to all its inhabitants, and even to a much more numerous population." " Providence," says he, " ever attentive to provide remedies for the disorders, which the

progress of society occasions in the world, has provided for idleness, as soon as the condition of society renders it a vice, but not before, a punishment every way suited to its nature, and calculated to prevent its prevalency and pernicious consequences. This is want; and a most efficacious remedy it is for the evil, when the *wisdom of man* does not interfere to counteract it, and prevent its salutary effects."

The method of applying the preceding principles is next developed in the form of "proposals for forming, by subscription, an establishment for feeding the poor, and giving them useful employment." They are supposed to be issued by some person high in the public confidence, and begin with a pledge that no person "shall find means to make a job" of the establishment. The mode of organization is then pointed out, to be performed at a meeting of the twenty-five persons who stand highest on the subscription list, who shall choose by ballot, out of the subscribers at large, a committee of five persons, to superintend the execution of the plan. The first part of the plan, in order, is a public kitchen, to furnish food, at low prices, to such poor persons as may be recommended by any of the subscribers for assistance. The nature of the food, and its price, are then set forth, of four different descriptions and qualities. It is then proposed, that four eating-rooms shall be provided, in each of which no more than one of the four varieties of food shall be served up, and that, in addition, rooms neatly fitted up, kept constantly clean and well warmed, shall be provided, in which the persons who frequent the establishment shall be permitted to remain during the day, and whither they shall be encouraged to bring their work.

The establishment, thus far, being no more than a cheap public house, provision is next made for charity, by means of tickets to be issued to the subscribers, half yearly, until their value shall reach half the amount of their original subscriptions, each of which tickets will not only entitle the bearer to admission, but to a portion of food. The latter portions of the essay are chiefly occupied with an examination of the modes, by which profitable occupation may be given to the persons who frequent the establishment. But, as much must depend upon the circumstances of the country in which it is situated, it would be useless to enter into the details of a plan, which appears to have been drawn up in reference to the state of society in England.

It is not possible to examine the principles laid down by Rumford, as the basis of establishments for the aid of the poor, without being struck by the profound knowledge of human nature which they exhibit; nor to compare them with those, which appear developed in the poor laws of England and the United States, without becoming aware, that the latter, instead of acting to remedy the evil of pauperism, seem as if planned to perpetuate it. Rumford endeavors to sustain the natural desire for independence, while the poor laws endeavor to destroy it altogether.

In his Bavarian workhouses, the avowed object was the suppression of mendicity, and the subjects of his benevolence were already degraded by the practice of beggary. His efforts were therefore directed, not only to maintain, but to elevate them. The application of his principles to those in indigent circumstances, but above the condition of beggars, might prevent their falling into it. · It will easily be seen, that, in an establishment of the form indicated in the proposals, of which an abstract has been given, it might be rendered impossible to distinguish between those who received alms and those who supported themselves.

The only question which admits of doubt is, how the kind and description of food is adapted to the circumstances of all countries; and here we cannot but be of opinion, that the desire of generalizing what was peculiar in its advantages in Bavaria, had generated in his mind an attachment to one particular system, far from being suited to universal application. In this system, soup is the grand and distinguishing feature; and it has taken such firm hold of his own mind, that it would appear, to a careless reader of his essays, that without it his principles must fail, just as Owen had reached the conclusion, that the social system, of which he has been so strenuous an advocate, could not be successful in a structure of any other shape than a parallelogram.

Now, to the greater part of the Anglo-Saxon race, soup, if not an abomination, will never be received as the staple of more than one daily meal; while tea and coffee, whose use Rumford reprobates, with their accompaniment of sugar, have become necessaries of life. But, whatever have been the prejudices and arguments of medical men and others against the use of these articles, no one, who has had the experience of their good effects, and particularly of those of tea, under circumstances of fatigue and exposure, can fail to be aware of their immense value to those worn down by labor and benumbed by cold. Soup, therefore, cannot be made the panacea for poverty and vice, either in England or the United States.

So, also, the part of his system, which consists in the establishment of eating-rooms, was not thought applicable in England, where females of good character are never to be seen in public houses, although admirably adapted to the forms of life on the continent of Europe, in the cities of which a considerable part of the population take their meals at the *restorateurs.*

In the severe winters of the northern part of the United States, it may also be doubted, whether shelter during the day would be sufficient, and whether it would not be necessary to provide the means of lodging a part of the poor, at least during the inclement season. While, therefore, the principles of Rumford's charitable establishments are coëxtensive in their application with the crime and poverty that afflict so large a portion of the human race, the details are limited, in their successful application, to the country which gave them birth, or those where the people have similar habits.

In spite of these differences in the merits of the principles and details, the latter, being more dwelt upon by him, received the greater share of public attention, and soup-houses became the fashionable mode of distributing charity in London, Paris, and the cities of the United States. In Paris, this description of food was well adapted to the habits of the people; but in England and America, it was received with grumbling, or rejected, by all who could in any other mode obtain food. One reason, no doubt, was, that it was considered sufficient to make the food nutritious, without attempting to make it pleasing to the palate. We know of those who, with the benevolent motive of setting an example of its use, purchased it at the public establishments, but were prevented from giving it a second trial, on account of its insipidity and utter want of all the agreeable qualities of food.

This defect is far from inherent; for the soups of Rumford, whether containing none but vegetable matter, or a mixture of animal substance, may be easily rendered as delicious as the most costly preparations of the French kitchen, of which some of the best productions are no more than *soupe maigre*, whose very name is so offensive to an Anglo-Saxon ear.

Finally, Cobbett, whose native English prejudices in favor of steaks broiled on the coals were as prominent as his political repugnance to English aristocracy, preached, in his unequalled idiomatic style, a crusade against the soup-houses, and exclaimed against the refinement of cruelty exhibited in feeding Englishmen upon bones and potatoes. As in many of his other works, the falsehood of his premises is so masked by the plausibility of his arguments, that the effect upon the popular mind was almost irresistible.

Contenting himself with the mere name of bones, as sufficient to excite a popular clamor, he purposely left out of view the fact, that bones contain, weight for weight, a greater portion of nutriment than the flesh of animals; while, on the other hand, seizing with avidity on the chemical fact, that potatoes exhibit, on analysis, little else than the elements of water and insoluble earthy salts, he chose to avoid the conclusion, that the latter substances, which he stigmatized as *dirt*, are the very principles by which that vegetable is approximated, in its qualities, to animal food, for which, if in sufficient quantities, it may serve as a substitute, for the very reason that both possess the earthy phosphates and sulphates. The philippics of Cobbett had the double effect of disgusting the poor with the food offered to them, and of exciting, in the minds of the charitable, a doubt how far their benevolence was judiciously applied.

CHAPTER VII.

Opposition he experienced in Bavaria. — Military School at Munich. — Projects for improving the Breed of Horses and horned Cattle; and for diminishing the Evil of Usury. — Landscape Garden at Munich. — Monument erected in it. — He returns to London. — His Improvements in Fireplaces. — Remedy for the Smoking of Chimneys.

It has been seen to what a height Rumford rose in the favor of the Elector of Bavaria, and how elevated a rank he attained in his service. The very eminence, which he attained, carried with it its inconveniences and troubles. It can readily be conceived how ungraciously an old and proud nobility could have brooked the advancement of a stranger to the very highest posts in the state, upon which they had been accustomed to look as their own exclusive right, and with what discontent they regarded the intrusion of one, who could with difficulty prove his right to a single escutcheon, into an aristocracy, where a blank in the full number of sixteen quarterings was considered a blemish. The officers of the army, in particular, must have viewed with jealousy and envy the promotion of a foreigner over their heads. Rumford himself speaks of one of his plans being thwarted by "the malicious insinuations of persons, who, from motives too obvious, took great pains to render abortive every public undertaking in which he was engaged." Strong, however, in the implicit confidence of the Prince, and secure of the gratitude of the body of the people, he bore bravely against the clamors of the privileged classes, until all his measures for reorganizing the military force, and improving the condition of the people, had been at least fairly tried, and, in most cases, brought into a state of successful operation. The reorganization of the army being completed, his attention was next directed to securing to it a supply of intelligent and well-educated officers. For this purpose he proposed, and, under the auspices of the Elector, undertook, the establishment of a military academy at Munich.

In other European countries, military schools exist, composed of two classes of pupils. One of these pays for its education; the other is composed of the sons of those, who have, by military or civil service, deserved well of their country, yet are so poor as to require aid to give their children a good education. The latter receives its education gratis. The Polytechnic School is, perhaps, the most perfect in its arrangements for securing the harmony of these very distinct classes, of any that has yet been established. The very condition of admission to an examination, to prove whether the candidate is qualified to join that seminary, is the deposit, in advance, of a half year's fee; and those who pass the examination, if entitled to gratuitous education, make their claim through a department of the government entirely foreign to the administration of the school.

Rumford's mode of insuring harmony was different. He proposed, in addition to these two classes, to introduce a third, namely, one intended to bring forward such youths of the lower classes of the people, as were known to have shown evident signs of uncommon talents. To accomplish this object, all civil and military functionaries were invited to recommend subjects for this class, and were not confined to any particular rank of society, but the children of the very lowest, if possessed of the requisite qualifications, were as readily received as those of the highest. The six years during which this establishment was conducted under the auspices of Rumford himself, could hardly have been sufficient to give the scheme a fair trial; yet within that short period, several instances of uncommon genius were called forth from very obscure situations.

His next attempt was one intended to improve

the breed of horses in the Bavarian territories, where, although great numbers were bred, they were of a race so inferior, that the higher classes sought theirs from Holstein and Mecklenburgh; while those suited for the army, and particularly for the artillery train, were hardly to be procured. The method, by which he proposed to effect this desirable object, was, to purchase mares of the best races in foreign countries, and to distribute them among the farmers, attaching no other conditions to the loan, than that of a care in the preservation of the quality of their progeny, and of replacing the original animal, at its death, by another of approved quality. The animals thus placed with the peasantry were not to be reclaimed by the government, except in the case of the army taking the field.

Such conditions might well be considered as advantageous; yet it was found difficult to induce the farmers of Bavaria and the Palatinate to receive the mares, and no more than two or three hundred were thus placed. It was the intention of Rumford to import and distribute several thousand; and as he was unable to effect as much as he had intended, the ardor of his zeal for improvement was not satisfied.

His attempt to improve the breed of horned cattle was less ambitious in its extent, and was, in proportion, more successful. Upon forming the pub.ic garden at Munich, to which we shall presently refer, he was enabled to comprise, within its circuit of six miles, a small but excellent grazing farm. This was stocked with thirty of the best cows, that could be procured from those places on the continent most celebrated for fine cattle; and the stock was kept up to its numbers by new importations. The calves were distributed through the country, by selling them to any person, who would engage to rear them, at the same price which the butchers were in the habit of giving for the purpose of slaughtering them. The benefit he thus conferred on Bavaria was not limited to the influence of the establishment itself, but, so soon as the value and beauty of the new breeds became apparent, several of the nobility, and some of the most enterprising of the farmers, sent to Switzerland, and other countries, for cows and bulls to improve the native stock.

The next measure to which we shall refer, is one of which we must consider the benefit as rather problematical. The public functionaries of Bavaria were but poorly recompensed for their services, and yet strove to vie with their richer social equals in luxury and dissipation. Hence a frequent anticipation of the receipt of their salaries by borrowing on their pledge, for which advances the most exorbitant usury was often paid. To relieve the distress thus occasioned, Rumford proposed to make loans, on orders for salaries and pay, from the funds lying idle in the military chests. The plan was carried into effect, and at a rate of interest not more than one twelfth of what was frequently charged. If, however, the cause of the distress lay in improvidence, and the expenditure of more than the actual income of the parties who sought the loans, we cannot see that the relief could have been more than temporary.

In the immediate vicinity of Munich was a large extent of waste land, which had formerly been a hunting-ground of the Prince; and although the game had long since been extirpated, and the forest had disappeared, it was still the property of the Elector. Rumford, who had in England imbibed a taste for the art of landscape gardening, of which that country was, at the time, almost the sole seat, proposed to render this profitable by converting portions of it into a *ferme ornée*, while other parts were laid out in walks and drives, for the recreation of the inhabitants of Munich. The circuit of the grounds was six miles, around which a road was constructed, embellished at intervals with picturesque cottages and dwellings, that were occupied by the tenants who cultivated portions of the ground, or those employed in superintending and taking care of the grounds.

To diversify the features of the ground, a space was excavated, which, filled with water, formed a beautiful artificial lake, while the earth removed from it was employed to form a mount. To accommodate the citizens in search of recreation, a public coffee-house was erected, and committed to the charge of a respectable keeper, while edifices intended for embellishment afforded seats at the best points of view.

After Rumford left Bavaria, the principal nobility and inhabitants of Munich chose to express their gratitude for his exertions in procuring them this place of recreation, by erecting a monument to commemorate his agency, on which they also caused to be recorded his services in rooting out mendicity and founding institutions for education.*

The different successful projects to which we have referred occupied the whole attention of the ten best years of Rumford's life; for he had entered the Bavarian service when little more than thirty, and had completed all of which we have spoken in 1794, when he was in the forty-first year of his age. The labor, both mental and bodily, which he performed, was enough to shake the firmest constitution; and he had, at the

---

* The monument is of a quadrangular form, having two principal fronts, opposite to each other, ornamented with

same time, to contend with much opposition. Under these labors and anxieties, his health at last sank, and he was compelled, for a time, to withdraw from public business. To obtain relief, he asked leave of absence from the Elector, for the purpose of making a tour in Italy, which was granted him; but even in that climate he did not find a remedy, and was, while at Naples, in actual danger. On his return to Bavaria, after an absence of sixteen months, he was still un-

---

basso-relievos and inscriptions. On one side is an inscription in the German language, of which the following is a literal translation.

"Stay, Wanderer.
At the creative Fiat of Charles Theodore,
Rumford, the Friend of Mankind,
By Genius, Taste, and Love inspired,
Changed this once desert Place
Into what thou now beholdest."

On the opposite side of the monument, under a bust of Count Rumford;

"To him,
Who rooted out the greatest of public Evils,
Idleness and Mendicity,
Relieved and instructed the Poor,
And founded many Institutions
For the Education of our Youth.
Go, Wanderer,
And strive to equal him
In Genius and Activity,
And us
In Gratitude."

able to resume the duties of his department, and obtained a further leave of absence, for the purpose of visiting England, which he reached, after an absence of eleven years, in September, 1795.

Rumford was well received by his former acquaintances in London; and the fame of his benevolent exertions in Germany, not to mention the lustre of the rank he had attained, speedily drew towards him a great share of public attention. He was called to give his counsel in all schemes for the improvement of the condition of the poor, and his advice was sought in many cases of merely private interest. To escape from the labor to which such applications subjected him, he determined to publish the results of his experience, and the records of his labors, in a series of essays. These have furnished the materials whence the account of his exertions in Bavaria has been chiefly drawn; but, as the publication proceeded, many new subjects presented themselves, and his opinions in relation to them are included in the same work.

Rumford had been born and brought up in a country, where the aboriginal forest had not disappeared; where trees were looked upon as enemies; and where it is a probable tradition, if not a positive truth, that the back-log of the wood fire was occasionally drawn in by a yoke of oxen. In England, he had seen an almost equally extravagant consumption of coal. In Germany, on the other hand, densely peopled, where no mines of mineral fuel were worked, and where the supply of trees, in the forests, was hardly adequate to the various demands, he had found a system of economy, in the application of heat, that must have excited his admiration. On his return to England, among the various subjects submitted to him was the evil of smoky chimneys; and he seized this occasion, not only to remedy that annoyance, but to point out the means by which a very great saving of fuel might be effected, while both the healthiness and comfort of the apartments might be increased.

A prejudice existed in England, as it still does there, and has till lately in this country, against the use of stoves. Rumford, although his German experience had taught him on how little foundation this prejudice rests, knew it would be impracticable to change at once the habits of a nation. He had by this time made the effects of heat a subject of study, and had obtained a knowledge in relation to them beyond that of any living person, while it still further exceeded that of any former age. This knowledge he now applied, with the greatest success, to an object, which, however trifling in appearance, is one, that has a most important bearing on the comforts of civilized life. A vulgar proverb classes a smoky chimney as one of the three domestic evils, which assimilate the family hearth to the abode of tormented spirits; and that we no longer feel the adage in its full force, is to be ascribed to the labors of Rumford.

The most polished nations of antiquity had no other means of providing for the issue of the smoke of their fires, than by leaving openings in the roof. They indeed appear, in some instances, to have heated apartments by flues circulating beneath the floors, which must have terminated in a vertical funnel, thus forming an approximation to the chimney; but there appears to be no instance of the arrangement of an open hearth and vertical flue until late in the middle ages. Chimneys and fireplaces of the latter date are still to be seen in the kitchens and halls of baronial mansions; but the hearths were of great size, the arched openings wide and lofty, insomuch that they could be entered by persons standing upright, and admitted seats to be placed on each side of the fire. The latter, indeed, were the only places where the warmth of the fire could be enjoyed, without exposure to the currents of cold continually rushing to join the ascending column in the chimney. So imperfect were they in this original form, and so inadequate to heat large apartments, that the uncovered fire, with an opening in the roof to give exit to the smoke, continued to be used contemporaneously with their earlier forms; and relics of the ancient practice still remain in the halls of the colleges of Oxford and Cambridge.

Even when an increasing scarcity of fuel compelled less extravagant modes of applying it to be sought, the arched opening remained of large size, the fireplace of a depth equal in extent to its front, and the walls were carried back perpendicular to the latter. Fireplaces of this structure are still to be seen in old houses in the United States, capable of receiving a four-foot billet of wood unsawn, or are masked by masonry reducing them to less dimensions, upon the principles we shall presently have occasion to state.

In England, where coal had come into almost universal use as a fuel, the grates in which it was burnt were almost exact cubes, and were lined with cast iron on the sides and back.

Previous to the time of Rumford, Franklin was the only person who had taken a sound view of the waste and inconveniences attending the fireplaces of his day; and the stove, which he contrived as a remedy, is an admirable application of sound principles. The article which usually bears his name, however, either from an ill-judged economy in its structure, or because the principles of his invention were not attended to, wants the descending flue and the passage for the admission of external air to its hearth, the very points which contain the whole spirit of the contrivance; and thus the memory of Franklin has been made responsible for the very errors it was his chief object to avoid. The evils of the fireplaces, which continued in use in England and the United States until the early part of the present century, may be recollected by those whose age reaches fifty; and they are remembered with feelings in which shuddering and scorching are strangely combined, but which are almost unknown, and scarcely to be imagined, by the present generation.

The quantity of heat radiated from a fire being, if unaided by reflection, in proportion to the front of the burning fuel, the deep and rectangular fireplaces contained a body of inflamed matter, wholly without influence on the air, or walls of the apartment, and which produced no other effect than to heat the air previous to its ascent in the chimney. This useless body of fuel required much air to support its combustion, while the wide throat admitted it to be mixed with a large quantity from the apartment, causing a demand, indeed, for the heat of the excess of fuel, but requiring continual supplies of external air. Thus the air of the apartment, continually renewed in large quantities from without, was itself little affected by the radiant heat of the fire, and kept the walls and furniture at a low temperature. Fires, therefore, of greater extent in front than would now be required, were absolutely necessary to maintain a temperature of tolerable comfort; and while the parts of the body exposed to their radiant heat might be absolutely scorched, the opposite side, exposed to a current of cold air, might be suffering pain from the rapid abstraction of heat.

If the influx of external air were insufficient to supply the column ascending in the chimney, smoke infallibly entered the apartment, and it became necessary, in well-built houses, to open the doors or windows to cause its ascent, thus rendering the fire almost nugatory; while, even with this precaution, the eddies formed by the mixing currents of air often brought the gases, vapors, and soot, in puffs into the room. Chimneys which did not smoke were, therefore, the exception to the general rule; and the exposure of the surface of the body to cold currents generated the acute pains of rheumatism, while the frequent alternations of an increased and checked perspiration caused colds, to be followed, in regular course, by pulmonary complaints. In this state of things, Rumford undertook to remedy the manifold evils of the open fireplace.

Analyzing the action of the burning fuel, he

saw, that it was divided into two parts, one of which radiated into the room, while the other, giving increased temperature to the column of air in the chimney, caused it to rise. He saw, also, that, while the radiant heat was passing through the air in the room, it hardly affected its temperature, but, reaching almost undiminished the walls and other solid bodies, communicated warmth to them, and thence to the air in contact with them, which, thus caused to circulate, diffused the heat through the apartment. Every escape of air by the chimney beyond what was just sufficient to maintain the combustion of the fuel, was, therefore, a positive waste of heat; and it was clear, that the throat of the chimney should be no larger than should just allow the passage of that quantity, and that all the air entering it should have been previously caused to pass through the fire.

Next, as the radiation is proportioned to the extent of surface, he saw that any depth in the mass of fuel, beyond what is necessary to insure a perfect and rapid combustion, was useless; and, as the surfaces which contain the fire must be heated, and will also radiate, the sides of the fireplace ought not to be perpendicular, but inclined to the front. He had not yet reached, in his discoveries, the relation between the surfaces of bodies and their power of radiating heat. That relation remained to be investigated, in its full extent, by one whom his example and encouragement stimulated to the task; but a sagacity almost intuitive led him to reject the iron backs and jambs by which fireplaces were then surrounded, and propose firestone, or brick and unglazed tile, as the substitute. These bodies are possessed of surfaces that his follower, Leslie, has shown to be among the best of all radiators.

It is remarkable, that, although publishing, and probably writing, in England, the first of his published plans for the improvement of fireplaces is one for burning wood, and that in this he was more successful, in the application of his own principles, than in his second plan, which is intended for burning coal. We shall therefore take the former, as best suited to serve as an illustration of his methods. A fireplace, having a rectangular hearth four feet three inches in width, two feet three inches in depth, and three feet three inches in height, is diminished, by additional jambs and lintels, four and a half inches on each side and at top; half the depth is filled up with masonry, rising behind the lintel, so as to have a throat of no more than four inches in depth, instead of the sixteen inches, which had previously corresponded to the whole depth of the flue. The sides are enclosed by masonry inclined to the false back, at an angle of one hundred and thirty-five degrees; and thus no more than one third of the latter was left open.

The fireplace, which would have before received entire billets of cord-wood, and which was usually charged with them sawn in two, would no longer receive them, unless sawn into three pieces; and the entire charge could never amount to half of what, in the original form, was the least quantity by which an active combustion could be maintained.

We shall not enter into the description of fireplaces for coal, because his principles received, almost immediately after their publication, a degree of development in the United States, which they did not reach in his own hands, and have hardly attained in England up to the present day. His papers reached New York at a time when the sudden and unexpected growth of that city threatened the speedy exhaustion of all the forests within reach of its existing communications; where fire-wood had risen to a price unexampled before or since; and where, in consequence, an active importation of bituminous coal from Liverpool began to take place. This species of fuel was, in appearance and effects, when badly managed, utterly repugnant to the cleanly habits which the ladies of New York had inherited from their Dutch ancestors; but the necessity of the case was paramount; and where no other prejudices of established usage existed, it was as easy to introduce grates for burning coal set upon good principles, as upon bad.

It is due to the persons concerned in the introduction of the use of this description of fuel into the United States, and of Rumford's plans and principles for its cleanly and economic use, that they should be commemorated, while those who witnessed their experiments and efforts still live to record them. To fulfil this grateful task, we may therefore state that the first range for cooking with coal was imported and set up by William Renwick, in 1796; and that, in 1798, it was lined with fire-brick, in conformity with Rumford's principles, under the direction of Professor John Kemp, of Columbia College; that a Rumford kitchen was put up by Isaac Gouverneur in 1798; and that parlor grates were planned, and the details of their setting pointed out to the mechanics who executed them, by David Gordon.*

From these germs, by insensible and almost forgotten steps, have been derived the innumerable plans of cooking ranges, with which the

---

* This gentleman, who returned to Europe in 1808, became distinguished as an engineer, and particularly for his mode of rendering gas portable, for the purposes of illumination.

records of our patent-office is loaded; the kitchens of our charitable and penal establishments; and the almost perfect forms of grates in which we burn anthracite coal.

In fireplaces on Rumford's principles, less than half the fuel will radiate into the room as much heat as was formerly done by the old ones; but, the quantity of air passing up the chimney being much diminished, this amount of radiant heat produces a much greater effect on the temperature of the room, and the currents, before so annoying, become insensible. Thus we may, in fact, procure an equal degree of warmth in our dwellings with less than a fourth part of the wood, or bituminous coal, consumed by our fathers. Our obligations to him, however, go much further; for, except upon the principles which he was the first to develop and explain, it would have been impossible to burn anthracite coal in an open fireplace.

The success, which attended the Rumford fireplaces, formed the ground of the only objection which was urged against them. Reduced from the original dimensions no more than has been described, and thus burning half as much fuel as before, it was complained that they made the rooms too hot. He therefore took the pains to show how easily the walls, ceilings, and floors of a room might be cooled; although he justly remarks, that nothing can be more perfectly ridiculous than the embarrassment of a person on account of his room being too warm, when the remedy is so simple and obvious, that to point it out might be considered as an insult to his understanding.

The structure of fireplaces recommended by Rumford, and of all which imbody a correct application of his principles, is, in addition to the saving of fuel, a certain and infallible remedy for a smoky chimney, except in the case where its top is commanded by buildings or other objects more lofty than itself. Even in this case, his methods will do much to diminish the frequency and amount of the evil, if they cannot remove it altogether. There can indeed be no doubt, that the persons, who make a trade of curing smoky chimneys, have, in almost all instances, applied their ingenuity to the wrong part of the structure, and that, in ninety-nine cases out of a hundred, everything that they propose to themselves, by apparatus applied to the top, may be effected by the simple step of giving a proper form, and sufficiently contracted dimensions, to the parts in the immediate neighborhood of the fire.

If, then, the legends of antiquity have for thousands of years commemorated, as a benefactor to the human race, the fabled personage who stole fire from heaven, to apply it to the service of man, may we not claim equal honors for him, who stripped it of the shadowy and unclean mantle in which it had ever since been invested, and made its use compatible with a degree of social refinement long rendered inaccessible by the fuliginous cloud, which floated under the roofs and pervaded the halls of our ancestors?

CHAPTER VIII.

His Visit to Dublin. — Further Improvements in heating Boilers. — Heating by Steam. — Discussion in Relation to the Heating of Dwellings. — Ventilation of Apartments. — Warm Bathing. — Renewal and Continuance of his Communications with the United States.

Soon after Rumford's return to England from Bavaria, he was invited by Mr. Pelham, at that time Secretary of State in Ireland, to visit that country, for the purpose of giving his advice to various charitable establishments. This invitation was accepted; and, in compliance with it, he proceeded to Dublin in the spring of 1796. This visit gave him an opportunity of putting in practice a number of economical arrangements, indicated by his previous experience, but which had not yet been proved in their most complete form.

We have seen, that, in the military workhouse at Munich, he had reduced the consumption of fuel to no more than one fourth of what was expended by the Bavarian soldiers in cooking with an open fire. This great saving, however, was far from satisfying his hopes. The kitchen of that establishment was therefore twice pulled down and rebuilt. He was, in the mean time, engaged in experiments upon the manner in which bodies of different kinds convey heat, and had reached a number of most important inferences, at variance with the opinions received at the time, but which are now so familiar, that, when we shall refer to these discoveries, it will almost excite surprise that they could have been left to be investigated at so modern a period as that in which Rumford lived. We shall have occasion to refer to these experiments, and consider their philosophical bearing, when we shall see how important a space they fill in the general theory of heat.

They were undertaken by Rumford principally with a view to their direct application to the heating of boilers; and in this he was eminently successful. Thus, while a pound of wood, in his first close fireplace at Munich, produced as much heat as four pounds burnt in an open fire, in his last form of a close fireplace, a single pound went, on one occasion, as far as eighteen pounds consumed in the open air. This important result was gained by applying the heat, as far as practicable, from beneath. The fireplace was of about half the diameter of the bottom of the boiler; the flame was caused to circulate in a flue surrounding the fireplace, and another single flue was carried from the first around the lower part of the side of the boiler, before it entered the vertical chimney. The flame of the fuel, which was pine wood, was exhausted before it entered the last flue, in which the smoke was as far cooled as it could be, without too much diminishing the draught of the chimney.

For larger quantities of liquid, he proposed rectangular boilers, with one direct and two return flues, all beneath its bottom; and he found no advantage whatever from flues passing along the sides.

In Dublin, he superintended the fitting up of a laundry for the Dublin Society, intended to serve as a model for those of private gentlemen's families; of a boiler, as a model for those of bleachers; and of a kitchen, for the House of Industry. In the latter establishment he first put into practice the method of heating by steam and the waste heat of the fire employed in cooking. He also furnished a plan for heating with steam the building intended for the meeting of the Irish House of Commons, a cottage fireplace, and a model of a perpetual lime-kiln. This was the first attempt at avoiding the inconvenience and waste of heat, which takes place in the ordinary intermitting kilns, and is, at least, in principle, better than any of the plans for the same purpose, which have since been constructed. Indeed, with some slight additions, which were made to it by Monteith, of Closeburn, it may be considered perfect.

One great object, which he had in view, was to consume all that part of the carbonaceous matter of the fuel, which is usually carried off in smoke; and for this purpose, he adopted the principle, which had been previously applied by Franklin in an iron stove, of causing the draught of air to pass downwards through the fuel after it had been perfectly ignited by an upward draught. On his return to London, he planned a kitchen for the Foundling Hospital, which was left unfinished at the time that he was suddenly recalled to Munich.

Having thus, in the order of time, recorded, the more important of the practical and economic inventions of Rumford, instead of following him to Bavaria, we shall proceed, in this place, to mention other investigations of a similar practical character, although belonging to a later period of his life.

The doctrine of latent heat, investigated in its widest extent by Black, and applied so successfully in a single case by Watt, had satisfied men of science that steam was capable of being applied to great advantage in boiling liquids of greater volubility than water, and in heating water up to the boiling point. A pound of water, converted into steam, was known to be capable of giving out heat that would raise from the temperature of freezing to that of boiling more than five pounds of water. All attempts, however, to apply this principle to practice had failed. Rumford, having ascertained the manner in which heat is conveyed from one part of a mass of liquid to another, pointed out the cause of the failure, and indicated the sure means of success. He showed, that it was necessary, that the steam should enter the vessel, containing the liquid to be heated by its condensation, at the lowest part; that the pipe which conveyed the steam should come from above; and that its vertical branch should be of such length, as to insure that the pressure of the atmosphere should not be able to force the liquid through it into the steam-boiler.

Rumford also pointed out the important fact, that when liquids are heated, or even boiled by steam condensed by mixture with them, wooden vessels will answer as well as those made of metal. The prodigious extent to which this mode of heating has been carried in almost innumerable branches of manufacturing art, together with its application to warming buildings, and in cookery, need only be referred to for the purpose of showing how great were the benefits this investigation of Rumford's has conferred upon human industry.

The plan of heating rooms and buildings by steam met with much opposition, in England, in consequence of the prejudice, as we must call it, which exists, not only in that country but in this, in favor of open fireplaces. This prejudice is combated by Rumford, in a very ingenious essay, by arguments which must be considered unanswerable. Admitting the necessity of pure air for the support of life and health, he shows that cold air is not necessarily purer than warm, and that those, who have been accustomed to live in apartments where immense open fires have caused violent currents of cold air to circulate, are in error in considering the equal and genial warmth of apartments heated by steam or stoves as close and unwholesome.

He then cites the universally admitted fact,

that it is dangerous to be exposed to a stream of cold air, and inquires whether this is not more likely to be injurious if one side of the body be heated by a fire, while the other is exposed to the chilling blasts.

Taking up the admitted fact, that coughs and catarrhs are caught in what are called warm rooms, he shows that the air of the rooms, heated by any number of open fires, or burning candles, may be in fact cold, and that this is the reason why the partial effects of their radiant heat are injurious to health.

There is no prejudice common to the people of England and the United States, that is more inveterate than the belief, that to live in warm dwellings renders men less able to bear exposure to cold out of doors, and none more senseless than that which regards as effeminate those, who resort to furs and warm clothing when they go abroad. In the more equable climate of England, the latter notion is not as prejudicial to the general health as it is in ours, where the extremes are so much greater, and the alternations more rapid; and he, who should remove this error from the minds of the people of the United States, would be a public benefactor. We are, indeed, by slow degrees, introducing a greater degree of comfort into our dwellings; but the prejudice against stove heat is still so strong, that it is only the necessity of economy that leads us to resort to it; and he, who, in our cities, would venture to clothe himself in fur, would be looked upon with surprise, if not with contempt.

To satisfy the people of England, that their opinions on this subject were erroneous, he quotes the examples of the Swedes, Russians, and Germans. No people are more strong and healthy than the two former; none less liable to colds and consumptions, although they keep their houses, throughout the winter of their severe climates, at a very elevated temperature. Referring then to the Germans, he states that the rooms of persons of rank and fashion are commonly kept in winter at the temperature of sixty-four or sixty-five degrees of Fahrenheit, both by day and night, while those of the peasantry are kept much warmer. In spite of this elevated temperature in their dwellings, and the comparative severity of the winter, the most delicate females find no inconvenience in going into the open air, frequent balls and operas, go on sleighing parties, and even spend a whole month of the coldest part of the year in a continued round of balls and masquerades.

If living in cold rooms, he says, really tends to give strength and vigor to the constitution, it might be expected that the dwellings of the inhabitants of the polar regions would be kept at a low temperature, while, on the other hand, the opposite fact is true, that the hottest dwellings are to be found in the coldest countries.

If exposure be necessary to harden the constitution, why does Providence furnish the animals, destined to live in cold climates, with warm natural clothing? And is not this provision of nature an example to man in the choice of his artificial covering?

That exposure to a cold climate is not required to enable persons to sustain its rigors, is shown by the well-known fact, cited by Rumford, that persons who have returned from India to England suffer little from cold during the first winter they spend in their new residence. The same fact has been observed in relation to the inhabitants of our Southern States, who spend a single winter at the north; but, since Rumford wrote, an experiment on a vast scale has been performed, which must be decisive of the question. Of the troops drawn from almost all parts of Europe, which composed the army with which Napoleon invaded Russia, the Neapolitans suffered least during the disastrous retreat, while the Poles, and natives of Northern Germany, were the most affected by the cold. Thus it would appear, that exposure, without adequate clothing, to the rigors of a cold climate, so far from hardening the body to bear it, in fact weakens the constitution, and renders it more susceptible of injury.

In respect to ventilation, the error is as great as in other directions. If a room be warmer than the external air, a very small opening near the ceiling, and another near the floor, will cause the air in it to change with great rapidity; and no apartment is so tight, that the doors and windows will not supply apertures for this purpose. But if a room be of the same temperature as the external air, nothing but a strong wind blowing into it will force out the air it contains. When, then, on a cold morning, we open our windows, as is the almost universal habit, we indeed let out the warm air the room previously contained; but in a few minutes all further circulation ceases, and we suffer all the inconvenience without a particle of benefit. And in respect to bedding and clothing, the only object of *airing*, as it is styled, is to remove noxious matter in the form of vapor; yet such is the force of popular belief, that it would incur the risk of ridicule to assert, that airing is far more effectually performed in a room well warmed with a stove, with no more than the chinks and crannies, which will exist in the most perfect building, than if every door and window were thrown open, and the temperature brought down to that of the external air. Rooms, however, heated by stoves, or steam, may be easily rendered uncomfortably warm, and particularly if occupied by numbers of persons. For this there is a sure, safe, and immediate remedy; it is only necessary to open a small portion of the upper part of one of the windows, and the lower part of another, and a gentle and moderate circulation will take place, that will carry cool and fresh air to every part of the room.

One other objection to stove and steam heat, which was not opposed to Rumford's plans at the time, but is of more recent discovery, does in truth exist. The relations of the air to moisture are so changed, that what at the lower temperature would be considered as actually damp, becomes, at one more elevated, comparatively dry. The same quantity of vapor, indeed, exists in both; but the difference between the actual temperature and the dew-point, on which the relative dampness or dryness depends, is increased by the whole increase of temperature. Thus the moisture of the surface of the body may be carried off faster than it can be supplied; the skin will, in consequence, become parched, the mouth and throat affected by thirst, and symptoms almost febrile ensue. Nothing, however, is more simple than the remedy; a small quantity of water kept boiling in the apartment, by the same means by which it is heated, will supply the necessary quantity of moisture to the air.

"If, then, man has been less kindly used than brute animals, by being sent naked into the world, without a garment to cover and defend him from the inclemency of the seasons, the power which has been given him over FIRE has made the most ample amends for that natural deficiency; and it would be wise in us to derive all possible advantages from the high prerogative we enjoy."

A school of physicians in England had formed a theory of the effects of bathing, upon what was observed to take place in animal membranes, when acted upon by hot or by cold water. In the former case they become flaccid, in the latter rigid. Hence it was inferred, that cold bathing was bracing and invigorating, while warm bathing was relaxing and debilitating. Still there were diseases in which warm bathing was admitted to be salutary; but it was thought that it could not be resorted to without great precautions.

Under the direction of a physician of this school, Rumford visited Harrowgate, in Yorkshire, to drink the waters and bathe. He, in the first instance, in conformity with established usage, took the warm bath in the evening, and then went immediately into a bed, which had been previously well warmed, to prevent, as was said, his taking cold. So far from receiving benefit, he found that, on the nights when he took the bath, he was unusually restless, and evidently feverish. By the advice of an intelligent gentleman, who was a fellow-lodger, he changed his plan, and took the bath at midday, about two hours before dining; and, instead of passing from the bath to bed, employed the interval in his ordinary pursuits. Up to this time, he had bathed only once in three days, but finding himself stronger, as well as less sensible to cold, and his appetite better, on the days he bathed, he next had recourse to the bath every second day, and, observing increasing benefits, he, in opposition to the advice of his physician, took the bath daily.

The results of this actual experiment on his own constitution were so different from the received theory, that he thought them worthy, as they no doubt were, of being published, for the purpose of combating a popular error. His experience showed that, so far from being relaxing, hot bathing was invigorating, as all who have given it a fair trial must know. It might be added, that cold bathing is a severe shock, which it requires a strong constitution to bear without injury; and is, in fact, only beneficial as a violent exercise, under circumstances that often render it salutary. After citing his experience, he discusses the question of the increased liability to taking cold supposed to be incident to warm bathing, refuting the notion in his own case, by exposure purposely incurred, and citing the practice of the Russians, who proceed from a bath of the vapor of boiling water to throw themselves into water of the temperature of ice, or actually roll themselves in the snow, without injury.

This disquisition of Rumford's on warm bathing fell almost unheeded on the ears of the people of England. Fourteen years after its publication, there was no public bath in any of its cities, except London. Those, who desired to use one for luxury or health, were referred to the hospitals, as the only place where it could be obtained; and, except an annual dip in the ocean by those who could reach it, it was asserted, by their own writers, that the bodies of the great mass of the English people went unwashed from the cradle to the grave. We fear that the same might have been said of our own people, with the exception that the example of the French emigrants of St. Domingo had introduced public baths into all our great cities, at least twenty years earlier than they were generally adopted in England. Such was the effect, which an unfounded medical theory produced on the habits of two great nations, which count themselves, and in other respects perhaps justly, as more scrupulously cleanly than any others. One fact may not be unworthy of being cited, which is an extension of those attained by Rumford, namely, that a bath may be taken without danger in the coldest weather, if it be as hot as can possibly be borne without distress.

We have thus completed a brief and perhaps insufficient sketch of the economic, practical, and philanthropic labors of Rumford. We have purposely reserved his scientific investigations, although many of them were undertaken merely in the view of their application to the subjects of which we have treated, for another portion of this memoir.

There appears to be no means of ascertaining when Count Rumford resumed his intercourse with his relations and friends in America. The earliest letters, which have been preserved, bear date at Munich, in January, 1793. It is evident, however, that these are not the commencement of his correspondence with his mother and Colonel Baldwin; for we learn by them, that he had previously made arrangements for his daughter residing with her grandmother, and provision for their comfortable support.

When he reached London, in 1794, he desired his daughter to join him, with which *invita-*

tion she complied early in 1796; and when he returned to Munich, she accompanied him.

All his subsequent communications with his connections in the United States appear to have been governed by the utmost kindness and liberality. On the fortune of his wife he had acquired certain legal claims, and, in particular, the estate by courtesy for the duration of his own life. Even had he felt any delicacy in enforcing these rights against her children by her first marriage, for his own advantage, none such need have existed, had he acted on behalf of his daughter, who was as equitably one of her mother's heirs as any of her other children. This heritage he however abandoned, as well as his own claims, preferring that she should derive her fortune from his own exertions, rather than take a share in an estate which would have been grudgingly allowed her. On only one occasion does he appear to have shown anything like displeasure in his communications, and that was under the influence of an impression that the Rolfs, instead of feeling grateful for his forbearance, had the intention of making a charge against him for the support and education of their half-sister. Thus we have not only reason to consider him as an affectionate son and parent, but as governed, in his domestic relations, by feelings of the highest and most liberal character.

CHAPTER IX.

He revisits Bavaria. — Is appointed Chief of the Council of Regency. — His Success in maintaining the Neutrality of Munich. — Appointed Minister of Bavaria at the Court of St. James, which refuses to receive him in that Capacity. — Invited to return to the United States. — Establishment of the Royal Institution. — Death of the Elector Charles Theodore. — Influence of that Event on his future Plans. — Bids Adieu to Bavaria, and visits Paris. — Marries Madame Lavoisier, and fixes his Residence at Auteuil.

WHEN Count Rumford returned to London from Dublin, he received intelligence which caused him to set out immediately for Germany. In the war waged against France, the German empire, in its federative capacity, was a member of the coalition with Austria, Prussia, and England. The several states of the empire, therefore, sent their contingents to the armies acting in the Netherlands, and on the Lower Rhine, without actually joining, as allies, with their whole force. When, at the close of the campaign of 1794, Prussia abandoned the coalition, and made a separate peace with France, the Electors of Bavaria and Mayence, with several other German princes of less consequence, issued a manifesto setting forth that they had only taken arms for the purpose of defending the territories of the Germanic body, and not with any view of interfering with the internal affairs of France. Their contingents, however, were not withdrawn; and thus, under the extraordinary system which then regulated the affairs of the Germanic body, they were, as its members, at war with France, and yet desired to preserve the neutrality of their territories.

During the campaign of 1795, although the republicans were at first successful, yet they did not penetrate to the Rhine until September, and, after having crossed it, were forced back before the close of military operations. But in the spring of 1796, Moreau crossed the Rhine at Strasburg, and, making his way through the Black Forest, marched to operate against the hereditary dominions of Austria by the valley of the Danube. It was thus rendered evident, that the electorate of Bavaria was to be the seat of war; for, while it lay directly in the road of Moreau towards Vienna, an Austrian army, left by the Archduke Charles to check the advance of the French towards Vienna, while he was moving to attack Jourdan on the Lower Rhine, was retreating before the army of Moreau, and disputing every inch of ground.

When Rumford reached Munich, the state of affairs had become so critical, that the Elector was on the point of abandoning his capital. This he did only eight days after Rumford's arrival, having first appointed a council of regency, at the head of which Rumford was placed. Within a few days, the French army forced the passage of the Lech, and defeated the rear-guard of the Austrian army at Friedberg. The latter fell back to the line of the Inn, and attempted, in their retreat to the new position, to pass through Munich. They, however, found the gates of that city shut. Crossing the Inn, they established themselves on the right bank, and, occupying a height which commanded the city, erected batteries. Irritated at the closing of the gates of Munich, and other acts growing out of confusion and alarm, the Austrian general threatened to fire upon the town; while, on the other hand, the French army was pressing on in pursuit of them, and it was probable that its commander would resent any hospitality afforded to their enemies. In this juncture, in virtue of the powers conferred upon him by the Elector, Rumford assumed the command of the Bavarian forces, and, by his firmness and admirable conduct, succeeded in causing the neutrality of Munich to be respected. That city was thus saved from being made the seat of a contest between the two armies, or subjected to a bombardment for refusing entrance to one or the other.

The inhabitants of Munich were fully satisfied, that it was to him alone that their security had been owing, and he received the most unequivocal testimonies of their gratitude.

Moreau, although victorious, and superior in force to the Austrians in his front, found it inexpedient to advance beyond the line of the Inn; for the Archduke Charles, having defeated Jourdan, and forced him to recross the Rhine, was speedily left at liberty to operate on his flanks and rear. He therefore commenced his celebrated retreat, and, evacuating the Bavarian territory, left the way open for the return of the Elector to his capital.

Equally sensible with his people of the important services of Rumford, he conferred new honors upon him, and, among the rest, placed him at the head of the general police of Bavaria. What appears to have been most grateful to the feelings of Rumford, the Elector permitted him to settle one half of his pension on his daughter, and extended its term to the duration of her life.

Two years more were spent by him in Bavaria, in important public duties, during which he found time for various philosophical investigations. In these pursuits and labors, his health, which had been reëstablished in England, was again impaired, and he found that it would be necessary again to seek that climate, which he had, by experience, found so well adapted to his constitution. To manifest his esteem, and place him in a position worthy of his services and talents, the Elector furnished him with credentials, by which he was named the minister plenipotentiary and envoy extraordinary of Bavaria, near the court of St. James.

Under the English rule of unalienable allegiance, Rumford found, on his arrival in London, that he would not be received in his diplomatic capacity. That court had, although with much repugnance, been compelled to receive those whom it considered as its rebel subjects, as the representatives of their newly-gained sovereignty. This might have appeared a warrant for the recognition of a native of the country, whose independence was acknowledged, as the minister of another power in the circles of the court; for there was nothing to prevent him from being recognized as a citizen of the United States, and being named by them as their representative in England. The court of St. James, however, insisted on considering him as a British subject, and thus disqualified to be the representative of a foreign nation.

This refusal could not have failed to be mortifying; but Rumford received at the very time a compliment, which must have been a full compensation. There was, as has been stated, no obstacle to his return to the United States, where the simple oath of fidelity to the constitution would have qualified him for any office in the gift of the people; but his name and fame had begun to attract the notice of his countrymen, who looked upon him with feelings of patriotic pride. Rumford's attachment to his native soil had, in the preceding year, been manifested in a most decided manner; for he had directed the transfer of five thousand dollars United States three per cent stock to the American Academy of Arts and Sciences, to serve as the foundation of a prize; and his character was thus brought prominently to the notice of the existing administration, which, in consequence, paid him the compliment of a formal invitation to revisit his native land. Thus assured, not merely of immunity, for that was guarantied to him by the laws, but of an honorable reception, Rumford for a time entertained serious intentions of taking up his residence in the United

States. With this view, he requested his friend Baldwin to look out for a "little quiet retreat" in the vicinity of Boston. His views of a residence are thus expressed.

"As I am not wealthy, and prefer comfort to splendor, I shall not want any thing magnificent. From forty to a hundred acres of good land, with wood and water belonging to it, if possible, in a retired situation, from one to four miles from Cambridge, with or without a neat comfortable house upon it, would satisfy my wishes.

"I should want nothing from the land but pleasure-grounds, and grass for my cows and horses, and an extensive kitchen garden and fruit garden. I should wish much for a stream of fresh water, or for a large pond, or the neighborhood of one.

"I need not tell you how much it would increase my enjoyments to live in your neighborhood. My daughter is quite enchanted with the scheme, and never ceases to urge me to execute it as soon as possible, and on her account I am anxious to engage in it. I wish to leave her a home, something immovable that she may call her own, as well as the means of subsistence at my death; and I am not surprised nor displeased to find that she prefers her native country to every other. To own the truth, I am quite of her opinion on that subject."

This plan of retirement, however, was not destined to be carried into execution. Six months after the date of the letter we have quoted, he writes again to Colonel Baldwin, from London, March 14th, 1799, in the following terms.

"I will not attempt to describe the painful disappointment I feel at being obliged to give up all hopes of seeing you, and the rest of my dear friends, in America, this year. A small pamphlet, which you will receive with this letter, will acquaint you with the reasons, which have induced me to postpone my intended voyage; and you will, I am confident, agree with me in opinion, that I have done right in sacrificing the pleasure that voyage would have afforded me to the more important objects to which my attention has been called. I beg you would be so kind as to give my dear mother the earliest notice of this change in my plans; and that you would, at the same time, endeavor to give her just ideas of the very great importance of the undertaking in which I have been called upon to give my assistance, and show her how impossible it was for me to refuse that assistance, especially as it was asked in a manner so honorable to myself. And as the success of the undertaking will be productive of so much good, and will place me in so distinguished a situation in the eyes of the world and of posterity, you will, I am persuaded, find little difficulty in persuading her, that I have done perfectly right, and in reconciling her to the disappointment she will naturally feel at not seeing me arrive in America at the time appointed."

The enterprise to which he refers in this letter was that, which a short time afterwards received the patronage of the King of England, and is known as the "Royal Institution." Of this Rumford may be considered as the real founder; and it, from its very beginning, had a most important influence on the state of science in that country, which it has not ceased to exert up to the present day. In its very earliest stage, it drew Thomas Young from the practice of medicine back to the physical and mathematical pursuits in which he was so distinguished; in its progress it called Davy from obscurity, to take the first rank among the chemists of Europe; and, not to mention his successor Brande, it is still made illustrious by the researches of Faraday.

The objects of the Royal Institution, as set forth in its charter, were to form "a public institution for diffusing the knowledge and facilitating the general introduction of useful mechanical inventions and improvements, and for teaching, by courses of philosophical lectures and experiments, the application of science to the useful purposes of life."

To accomplish these objects, thirty thousand pounds sterling were raised by subscription, in addition to a considerable income derived from annual contributors. At its opening, in March, 1800, Rumford thus speaks of it.

"The number of our subscribers now amounts to nine hundred and thirty-eight, among which are two hundred and sixty-five who have paid fifty guineas each. Our prospectus, charter, ordinances, by-laws, and regulations, are now printing. The first number of our journals was printed a few days ago. By these publications the nature of our institution may be learned, and its tendency directly perceived. The plan of the institution has met with general approbation in every part of Europe. If it should not be copied in America, I shall be greatly disappointed."

To the Royal Institution Rumford gave the greatest part of his private collection of philosophical apparatus, and furnished it with specimens and models of all his own inventions.

The institution was established in a large house in Albemarle Street, purchased out of the subscribed funds, and in which large and convenient lecture-rooms were fitted up. An excellent library of scientific works was speedily collected, and has been ever since on the increase; to this access can be obtained with the greatest facility; and, in particular, mechanics and arti-sons were invited to make use of it without charge.

The influence of Rumford's mind over the early proceedings of the Royal Institution may be seen by the list of the committees appointed by the managers at one of their first meetings, in March, 1800; for by far the greater part of the subjects referred to them were those, which had already occupied so much of his own attention.[*]

---

[*] These committees had for their duties the following objects.
1. The experimental and scientific investigation of the processes used in *Making Bread*;
2. The art of preparing cheap and nutritious *Soups* for the poor;
3. The improvement of *Cottages* and *Cottage Fireplaces*;
4. The construction of *Stoves* for warming dwelling-houses;
5. The improvement of *Kitchen Fireplaces* and *Kitchen Utensils*;
6. The improvement of *Household Furniture*;
7. Experiments on the effect of the various processes of cookery on the *Food of Cattle*;
8. The improvement on the *Kitchen Fireplaces*, and kitchen utensils used on shipboard;
9. The improvement of *Lime-Kilns*;
10. The effects produced by mixing clay and other substances with coal-dust and cinders, in forming *Fire Balls*, to be used as fuel;
11. The improvement of mortar and cements;
12. The construction of *Cottages* in Pisé work;
13. The improvement of useful *Machines* of all descriptions;
14. The manufacture of *Iron* from its ores.

After a lapse of more than forty years, the Royal Institution still continues to render valuable services to the British public. It has, however, undergone changes in the pursuits of its managers, who no longer apply, as a body, to scientific investigations. Their journals, therefore, changed their form, from a record of the papers read at the meetings, to that of a scientific periodical, which, conducted by Brande, and enriched with the "Astronomical and Nautical Collections" of Young, was the most valuable of the kind in Europe. The lectures, merely popular in the first instance, took, in the hands of Davy, a high scientific cast, and the Royal Institution still ranks as the first school of chemistry in the United Kingdom.

While Rumford was thus engaged in planning and carrying into operation this important project, an event occurred, which again changed the course of his eventful life. The Elector Charles Theodore, in whose favor and confidence he stood so high, died in 1799. Although his successor was the same Maximilian Joseph, of Deux Ponts, who had been the means of introducing him to the former prince, and although he was not insensible to the merits and services of Rumford, yet this event made it apparent, that he was no longer to look upon Bavaria as a home. As is usual in monarchies, the opponents of the administration of which Rumford had been so important a member, had sought to acquire an influence over the presumptive heir, and in this they had been successful.

Rumford, therefore, saw that a residence in Bavaria, ruled by opponents, if not actual enemies, would be uncomfortable, even if it were not pain enough for one of his active habits, both of body and mind, to remain unemployed. The political relations of the electorate were also changed by the accession of a new sovereign. Bavaria had at first endeavored to preserve a neutrality between the opposing arms of France and Austria, as far as she could consistently with her duty to the Germanic body. But this, in the very nature of things, was impracticable, and, being compelled to choose of which he should become the ally, Charles Theodore selected Austria. Hence the mission of Rumford to England, where, although not received formally as ambassador, he acted as a political agent; and, in the campaign of 1800, the Bavarian troops were in English pay. The defeat sustained by the allied forces at Hohenlinden, and the occupation of the electorate by the armies of France, probably satisfied Maximilian that the policy of his predecessor, of which Rumford, if not the proposer, had been an active instrument, was injudicious. We therefore find him, from that time until the German people rose in a body against Napoleon, and compelled their princes to change their political relations, the firm ally of France.

This new state of things presented itself to Rumford, when, after the peace of Amiens, he revisited Bavaria. Here, although graciously received, he found he was no longer to be employed; and, after assisting in the reorganization of the Bavarian Academy of Sciences, on a plan "which united munificence truly royal with utility of every kind," he bade a final adieu to the electorate. After spending several months in travelling in Germany, Italy, Switzerland, and France, he reached Paris, in the neighborhood of which he was destined to spend the remainder of his useful and bustling life. Of these travels we have not been able to obtain any record, except the single notice, that, in August, 1803, he was at Berne, whither he had returned from an expedition to the glaciers of the Oberland, and was about to proceed to visit those of Savoy.

At Paris he was received with all the honors and distinctions to which his scientific fame and personal merits entitled him, and he probably was struck by the very great difference in the relative standing of men of science in that country and in England. He could not but be aware, that he had owed his success in English society, and the influence he had exerted over some of its public institutions, more to his title and high military rank, and the fact of his bearing the diplomatic credentials of the Elector of Bavaria, than to his own high qualities. He saw, that, in England, rank was necessary to make science influential, while in France, at that time at least, scientific eminence was a sure road to the highest distinction. With his knowledge of English society, he might have doubted whether, returning under circumstances that ill-disposed persons might have considered as of disgrace, he would be as well received, and take as high a stand in scientific circles, as he had before done.

His daughter had left him, and returned to America, about the time that he gave up his design of visiting the United States; and it would appear, that the idea of a rural retirement with her in the neighborhood of Cambridge had been abandoned. He probably found, when his public avocations were at an end, like most men who long for leisure while oppressed with business, that retirement is more onerous than labor. Whatever may have been his projects for his future life, they were decided, as the course of his early years had been, by a matrimonial connection.

In the scientific circles of Paris, Rumford met

with a lady, who, if past the bloom of youth, was not without attractive qualities. This was the widow of the celebrated Lavoisier, who, endowed with an ample income, and honored in bearing the name of her lamented and distinguished husband, filled no small space in the society of the French capital. The relict of Lavoisier must have been an object of interest to Rumford, who had pursued so many objects analogous to those, which had attracted the attention of that founder of the modern school of chemistry; and this interest appears soon to have ripened into a mutual attachment. We know, at least, that, in July, 1804, he wrote out to his daughter to obtain the certificates of his own birth, and of the death of his first wife, which were, by the French law, necessary as preliminaries to a contract of marriage; and to his mother he wrote at the same time, "the lady I am to espouse is four years younger than myself, and is of a most amiable and respectable character." As soon as the certificates were received, he was united in wedlock to Madame Lavoisier. Immediately after his marriage, he took up his residence in the villa at Auteuil, which had been the property of her former husband, and the scene of so many important discoveries in physical and chemical science.

CHAPTER X.

Loss of his Papers. — Further Experiments on the Force of Gunpowder. — Experiments on the Gases; on the Absorption of Moisture; on the Light yielded by Combustion; and on colored Shadows. — His Discoveries in Relation to Accidental Colors. — His Experiments on the chemical Effects of Light.

Having brought up the history of Rumford's life to the time when he fixed his permanent residence at Auteuil, we shall now recur to his scientific investigations and discoveries, which it will be more convenient to consider collectively, than it would have been to introduce them in the strict order of time.

To judge from those, which he was enabled to publish, the loss which the world sustained when he was robbed of his papers, must have been very great. He speaks of this loss in a communication to the Royal Society of London, in the following terms.

"Since writing the above, I have met with a misfortune which has put it out of my power to fulfil my promise to the Royal Society. On my return to England from Germany, in October, 1795, after an absence of eleven years, I was stopped in my post-chaise, in St. Paul's Churchyard, in London, at six o'clock in the evening, and robbed of a trunk which was behind my carriage, containing all my private papers, and my original notes and observations on philosophical subjects. By this cruel accident, I have been deprived of the fruits of the labors of my whole life, and have lost all that I held most valuable. This most severe blow has left an impression on my mind, which I feel that nothing will ever be able entirely to remove."

The promise to which he refers, as made to the Royal Society, is to communicate to them his experiments on the strength of various materials, which were begun soon after his first arrival in London, and were continued and completed, while the most ample means, furnished by the Elector of Bavaria, were at his command. The direct object was to obtain facts by which his reform in the structure and equipment of the Bavarian artillery might be guided. No record remains of any of these experiments, except a single statement in relation to the strength of wrought iron.

The communication, to which the above account of the loss of his papers is attached, is one on the force of gunpowder. The experiments form a part of those which he performed in the Bavarian arsenals; but, luckily, he had communicated them to the Royal Society before his departure from Munich; and their record thus escaped the fate of his other papers.

The experiments of Robins and Hutton, as well as those of Rumford himself, had limited the action of gunpowder, upon a military projectile, to a force of one thousand atmospheres. There were, however, various cases in practice, where the explosive force appeared vastly to exceed that limit. Thus, in the blasting of rocks, in the action of military mines, and in certain accidents that occasionally take place in firing both cannon and small arms, the effects appear prodigiously greater than can be accounted for by an action of no more than that number of atmospheres. Rumford, having ascertained by experiment, that gunpowder is almost always thrown out of the muzzle of the piece, without being ignited, and that an appreciable time is required for the complete inflammation even of a single grain of gunpowder, was led to ascribe the difference in the two classes of effects to the fact, that while a ball is moved before any great portion of the gunpowder is ignited, the charge of a mine, or one employed in blasting a rock, is so strongly resisted, that the whole of the gunpowder is converted into an elastic fluid, before the motion, which its action finally produces, begins.

The proposition that no motion is produced *per saltum*, but that a body must go through all the degrees from rest to the velocity it finally receives, is as old as the true mode of considering the laws which govern the action of forces; but it was not well understood at the time that Rumford made his experiments, that time was required for an impulse to be communicated from particle to particle, until the whole mass of a body began to move. One fact, affording a positive proof of this principle, had, however, been observed by Hutton, namely, that a ball from a cannon strikes the mark as surely, when the piece is suspended as a pendulum, as when it is firmly fastened down. This happens, because the motion communicated by the reaction of the gunpowder has not been propagated throughout the whole mass before the ball leaves the muzzle; and although this time is so short as not to be detected by our senses, it may be accurately calculated when the initial velocity of the bullet is known.

Another fact, illustrative of the same principle, is the parting of a rope when attached to a shell thrown from a mortar, in the apparatus proposed for relieving persons in stranded vessels; and, these illustrations of the principle having become familiar, Montgolfier planned the valves of his hydraulic oven in conformity with it; and in this instrument the times which it takes the stream to regain its velocity after being checked by the valve, and for the valve to acquire that which the current is capable of giving it, are sufficiently long to be the subject of definite observation. When, therefore, gunpowder, instead of acting upon so small a mass as cannon balls, exerts its force upon heavy masses of rock, masonry, or earth, the first impulses will not have been communicated throughout the bodies, until every particle of the powder has been converted into an elastic fluid; and, as the product of the combustion is by its gaseous nature capable of filling, even at ordinary temperatures, several thousand times as great a space as the solid whence it is generated previously occupied, and its elastic force is, besides, vastly increased by an elevated heat, the effects, of which we have spoken, are no longer to be wondered at, nor are they inconsistent with those so far inferior, which are manifested in the firing of artillery.

The apparatus which Rumford planned for the purpose of ascertaining, by experiment, the force exerted by gunpowder confined until the whole had been inflamed, is most ingenious. The receptacle for the powder was a bore, one quarter of an inch in diameter, and about two inches deep, formed in a solid mass of wrought iron. This capacity was no more than sufficient to contain twenty-eight grains of gunpowder. As the elastic fluid might have escaped by an ordinary vent, an ingenious arrangement was adopted for communicating heat to the gunpowder through the metal, by means of a red-hot iron ball. The muzzle was closed by a thick plate of wrought iron, and, to prevent corrosion, the surface was coated with gold. A plate of oiled leather was interposed, to prevent any escape of the elastic fluid, until the plate should be lifted from its place; and the plate was loaded with a weight, which, in the largest charges, was a brass twenty-four pounder, resting upon it, and confined to a vertical motion by guides. This twenty-four pounder weighed eight thousand and eighty-one pounds, and, to omit the experiments performed with weights of less magnitude, was lifted by the explosion of eighteen grains of gunpowder, but by no less charge.

Rumford from this experiment concluded, that the force thus exerted by the elastic fluid was equivalent to a force of nearly thirty thousand atmospheres, or fifteen times as much as it exerts in setting a cannon ball in motion.

On filling the chamber with gunpowder, the strong wrought-iron body in which it was formed burst. By calculations, founded on his own experiments on the strength of that material, he inferred that the force then exerted was equivalent to fifty-five thousand atmospheres, and, in spite of the strictures of Hutton, we see no reason to doubt the accuracy of the inference.

In these experiments Rumford succeeded in reaching the explanation of phenomena before anomalous, and rendered the service of artillery more safe, by pointing out a cause of danger, which, if suspected to exist by practical men, was denied by those who derived their science from the researches of Robins and Hutton.

These investigations of Rumford's are mentioned first in order, because, although made at a comparatively late period, they are the sequel of the earliest experiments in which he was engaged, those performed at Woburn, and of the first paper of his which was published in the "Transactions of the Royal Society" of London. Between the date of the latter and that of the experiments on confined gunpowder, he had devoted much attention to a variety of other subjects. While the researches of pneumatic chemistry formed the prominent object of the attention of men of science, Rumford instituted a set of very ingenious experiments in relation to the oxygen separated from water by various substances. These, although of value at the time, have ceased to merit the notice of the existing age of chemistry, in consequence of the vast strides which that science has made in the interval; they may, however, be still quoted as a model of accurate philosophical investigation, and particularly in the caution with which he excluded the possibility of being misled by any preconceived opinion or admitted theory.

His next experiments had relation to the quantity of moisture, which different substances are capable of absorbing without exhibiting indications of its presence. The direct object was to ascertain the fitness of different substances for clothing in damp situations and climates; and although experience had in some measure settled upon woollen, as best adapted for the purpose, these experiments explain the reason of this preference, and render what was by some considered as merely fanciful, a well-established philosophical principle. Wool, by these experiments, gained in weight, after being exposed for three days in a damp cellar, more than sixteen per cent, while cotton gained less than nine per cent, and linen little more than eight per cent. Hence the value of woollen clothing to persons exposed to wet, or, when worn next the skin, to those in whom, by climate or labor, a copious perspiration is excited, is obvious. It is now admitted, that flannel is even more valuable as an under-garment in hot than in cold climates, although those, whom experience has taught that a blanket is a more agreeable covering in summer than linen, are still considered as indulging in fanciful notions.

The establishment of the Military Workhouse at Munich led Rumford to a series of researches on a subject that has not as yet been referred to. The apartments of that institution being open till a certain hour of the night, economy of light became a matter of nearly as much importance as that of either food or fuel. He could find no facts in relation to the quantity of light emitted by burning various substances, in the different ways which were then practised, in the works of any of his predecessors; and, as by the adoption of methods of an inferior kind, he might subject the establishment to unnecessary expense, he saw the necessity of obtaining a novel order of facts before he finally adopted a plan of illumination.

The question evidently divided itself into two separate considerations. 1. The relative quantities of light given by oil, and tallow in lamps and candles; and, 2. The comparative cost of the substances giving equal quantities of light. The first of these considerations could only be solved by means of some accurate measure of the relative intensity of the light; and no instrument previously contrived for this purpose was of any value. His first step, therefore, was to contrive a *photometer*.

The principle which he adopted was, that the equality in the intensity of two different lights falling upon the same object, is determined by the shadows cast by bodies which interrupt them being of equal depth; the equality of this depth can be judged of by the eye, particularly when the shadows are brought into optical contact, for then no line of division will be visible. If the lights which thus cause shadows of equal depth are at the same distance, each emits an equal quantity of the luminous principle; but, if they be at different distances, then the quantity of light emitted must be in the ratio of the squares of the respective distances.

With this apparatus, constructed upon the above principle, he performed a number of interesting and valuable experiments. By means of these he obtained results as yet unknown in science, as well as many important practical inferences. He showed, that light is not sensibly diminished in passing for moderate distances through the air; he determined the quantities of light lost in passing through plates of glass, and by reflection from glass mirrors, and determined the relative quantities of different substances consumed in giving an equal degree of illumination. Applying this latter set of experiments to the question, which had led him to undertake the investigation, he settled upon the Argand Lamp, as the best and most economical mode of illumination, stating, in particular, that a given quantity of light furnished by wax candles cost, in Bavaria, nine times as much as when furnished by a lamp of that construction fed with rape-seed oil.

He also determined, by experiments with this apparatus, that flame is perfectly transparent, and permeable by the light of another flame; and that the quantity of light is not proportioned to the quantity of heat furnished by the combustion of a given quantity of a given combustible body, but depends also on the briskness of the combustion. He subsequently, by the union of these two principles, succeeded in the construction of a lamp, which gave more light than had ever before been produced artificially. Adopting the idea of Argand, of a hollow cylindric wick, exposed, on both surfaces, to a current of air rendered more rapid by a chimney, he arranged a number of wicks in the manner of concentric cylinders; passages for air were left between these, as well as within the innermost cylinder, and on the outside; and all were enclosed in a tall glass chimney. The flames of these wicks mutually exerting their heat, while the light from within has a perfectly free passage through the flames more distant from the centre, form an arrangement by which a mass of light may be produced, limited only by the power of the materials of which the lamp is made to bear the intense heat without fusion.

A lamp upon this plan was constructed under his directions, after he took up his residence near Paris, and completely fulfilled the expectations he had formed of its performance. So brilliant and overpowering was its light, that it is said that the artist employed in its construction was unable, after lighting it for the first time, to find his way home, but was compelled, by its effect on his eyes, which prevented them from recovering the power of seeing in a faint light, to pass the night in the Bois de Boulogne. Remarkable as were the effects of this lamp, it did not attract the attention it evidently merited; and we know of no instance where it came into use. It was, however, intended by the late Mr. Hassler, to employ it for night-signals, in the survey of the coast of the United States; and one lamp, as a model, was actually constructed under his directions. In the long interval which elapsed between the beginning of this survey, and its efficient progress, the *heliostat* of Gauss had been invented, which, making observations practicable by day, rendered night-signals unnecessary; and this lamp was not brought into use.

The same principle has, however, been applied, with the utmost success, to gas-lights; but the lamps do not bear the name of him who discovered it, but of Bude, who introduced it into use.

In the course of his experiments with his photometer, he, on one occasion, desired to compare the intensity of the light of a candle with that of the sky. On comparing the two shadows, both of which were thrown on the same piece of white paper, he found the one, whence the daylight was excluded, of yellow color, while the other was of a most beautiful blue. The fact, that shadows cast by objects in daylight sometimes appear of a blue color, had been recorded, and partially explained, by writers on optics. Of this fact Rumford had, at the time, no recollection; and, if he had, the particular course of his investigations would not have been influenced by it. It might, at first, appear, that the color of one of the shadows was owing to the natural blue hue of the sky, as that of the other was due to the yellow color of the flame of the candle. But he found that the same contrast existed, when the light, instead of coming directly from the heavens, was reflected from the roof of a house covered with new-fallen snow. His final conclusion, after a great variety of experiments, is, that the different colors, which the several shadows appear to exhibit, is in fact "an optical deception, owing to contrast, or some effect of other real and neighboring colors upon the eye;" and thus the solar shadow appeared blue, because the light of the candle was actually yellow.

Conceiving that he had established this as a principle, he next proceeded to investigate the effects produced by the contrast of the local colors of bodies. He first showed that the view of any decided color will call up, in a neighboring colorless object, the impression that it is colored of such a hue as, when mixed with the actual color, will constitute white light. Proceeding further, he ascertained, that, whenever two such colors are placed side by side, the contrast is not only the strongest, but also the most agreeable that either of them can produce with any color whatever. Such colors, in the language of opticians, are called *accidental*, or complementary, to each other, and lists of them are now to be found in all works on the subject of light and vision.

Intent always upon the practical applications of his discoveries, he saw, that in this principle lay the more or less agreeable nature of the contrasts of colors employed in dress and in furniture. It is, therefore, applicable to ladies' garments, to military uniforms, and to the decoration of apartments. What is called good taste in dress may, therefore, be attained by a strict attention to philosophic rules; and the choice of a gown, or a ribbon, will be successful, or not, according as it is consistent or repugnant to immutable laws of nature. To exhibit the application of this principle, he arranged according to it the colors of the furniture of his house, the agreeable effect of which was striking to all who visited him.

In further prosecution of his experiments on light, he undertook the examination of the chemical effects attributed to it, and particularly of its action in reducing the oxides of silver and gold. Although these investigations have long been superseded by others more extensive and numerous, and in particular by the brilliant applications of this action in the hands of Daguerre and Talbot, we may still cite some discoveries which he made while prosecuting them, and which deserve to be remembered. These were the facts that gold and silver, when in solution, may be reduced by charcoal, ether, the essential oils, and gum. Had Rumford made no other physical investigations than those referred to in this chapter, his name would have been quoted as authority upon philosophic questions. They, however, form but a limited portion of his inquiries, and attracted a comparatively small degree of his attention, which, by the practical turn of his mind, was directed far more forcibly in another direction. In this, although confined to no more than a single object, he was so successful as to place his name in the list of those most distinguished for originality of thought and brilliancy of discovery.

CHAPTER XI.

He proves that Heat is not influenced by Gravitation. — Demonstrates that Liquids are very imperfect Conductors, and Gases absolute Non-Conductors of Heat. — Explains the Manner in which Heat is propagated by Fluids. — Explanation of many natural Phenomena. — Experiments on the Radiation of Heat. — On the Heat developed by Friction. — His Thermoscope and Calorimeter. — Prizes instituted by him. — Views of his Character. — His Death.

VARIED as were the philosophical investigations and discoveries, which we have already recorded, they were far less valued, by Rumford himself, than those in which he endeavored to determine the nature and study the effects of HEAT. Fire had been ranked, by one of the schools of ancient philosophers, as one of the four elements, of which all material existence was made up. The effects of heat, in expanding bodies, had been a subject of careful study from an early date in the history of the application of the inductive method to physical science. Black had discovered and stated the law of latent heat; and Lavoisier was engaged, when Rumford commenced his investigations, in examining the relations of bodies to specific heat. The actual nature of heat, although then and still unknown, was, notwithstanding, assumed, and made the foundation of two distinct and conflicting hypotheses.

The school of chemistry, whose authority was about to expire, had imagined to itself a material substance, which was called *phlogiston*, existing as a constituent part of all combustible bodies, and which, in issuing from them while in the act of burning, took the sensible forms of light and heat. Consistently with this hypothesis, bodies ought to be heavier, before they are burnt, than the products of their combustion, unless the phlogiston were, in fact, a principle of levity, in which case they ought to be lighter. The latter view of the subject is finely ridiculed by a satirical writer of the last century, who represents a pretender to science as astonished that the floor of his room was inflamed when he kindled a fire upon it. "It' ought not to have taken place," said he, "for heat always ascends." Lavoisier overturned this hypothesis, by showing that the products of combustion, when collected, are always heavier than the body before it is burnt, and that the gain in weight is owing to their having combined with one of the constituents of the air of the atmosphere. Anxious, however, to account for the light and heat, which are the important phenomena of combustion, he stated, that this constituent of air, oxygen gas, was a compound of a fixed base with the matter of light and heat; and to the latter hypothetical element his school gave the name of *caloric*. Davy, in more modern times, has shown, that the phenomena of light, which attend combustion, are included in the general law, that bodies, when heated intensely, become luminous; and that the cause of the heat lies in the intensity of the chemical action to which the changes effected during combustion are owing. He has, also, in addition, proved that flame is no more than an elastic fluid, heated to such a degree as to emit light.

In Rumford's day, the question between the phlogistic theory, and that of Lavoisier, could not be considered as decided, and various lofty names might be cited as those of adherents to the former hypothesis. Rumford saw that some important light might be thrown on the discussion, by ascertaining whether heat were possessed of weight, or not. He therefore planned an ingenious experiment, by which he showed, conclusively, that the existence of heat in a body neither increased nor diminished its weight, and, therefore, that heat neither gravitated, nor acted in opposition to gravitation. His experiment consisted in counterpoising a quantity of water with alcohol at ordinary temperatures. Both were then cooled down until the water froze, and it was found that they were still in exact counterpoise. The loss of heat by the alcohol was indicated by the lowering of its temperature, except so far as influenced by its capacity for specific heat; but the water, besides being affected in the same manner while it remains liquid, parts, in the act of freezing, with a quantity of heat amounting to one hundred and forty degrees. Taking the relations of water and gold to specific heat as a basis, he next showed that the former had, in freezing, lost as much heat as would have heated an equal weight of the latter to redness. In spite, however, of this enormous loss of heat, the water remained of the same weight, as proved by a balance of the utmost delicacy. We may therefore claim for Rumford the merit of having shown, more conclusively than any other person, that, whatever heat may be, it is not possessed of weight.

There is no mode in which bodies may be cooled more rapidly, than by immersing them in liquids. Hence it might be, and was, long inferred, that bodies of this class were good conductors of heat. In relation to gases, the apparent ease with which heat passes through them is such, that no one before Rumford's time doubted that they all, and air in particular, opposed no obstacle to its transmission. Some of the difficulties he experienced, in economizing the heat applied to boilers, led him to doubt the received opinion in respect to liquids; and an accidental discovery led him to be equally skeptical in relation to aeriform bodies. Yet so far was he blinded by preconceived opinions, that he was, as he states himself, "long incapable of seeing the most striking and evident proofs of their fallacy."

He had remarked, among others, two or three facts at complete variance with the received theory, that liquids are good conductors of heat. Thus he observed that baked apples retained their temperature for a surprising length of time; that, after the surface of a dish of thick mucilaginous soup became cold, the lower parts were hot enough to scald; and, finally, that the water in the Bay of Naples, flowing in waves over hot volcanic sand, was not sensibly warmed. Although the last fact finally excited his attention, and made him resolve to make experiments for the purpose of ascertaining its cause, his action was determined by the accidental observation of another phenomenon.

Having occasion to use, in some of his experiments, spirit thermometers having bulbs four inches in diameter, he was surprised at observing, that, when one of them was exposed to a heat as great as it was capable of exhibiting, the whole mass of liquid was thrown into a rapid motion of circulation, in ascending and descending currents. These currents were rendered visible by the accidental circumstance, that some fine particles of dust had entered the instrument before it was sealed.

His inference from this appearance was, that this motion was caused by the particles of the liquid *going individually* and in *succession*, to give off their heat, to the cold side of the tube, and that liquids were in fact non-conductors of heat. To prove this opinion, he conceived that he ought, in the first place, to inquire whether the propagation of heat through water were obstructed or not by rendering the internal motion of its particles difficult; and having still fresh in his memory the burning he had experienced in eating hot apples, he made them the first subject of his experiments. By a careful examination, he found, that nine hundred and sixty grains of stewed apples contained less than nineteen grains of solid matter, or not quite one fiftieth part of their whole mass, the residue being liquid, and chiefly water. Through a mass of this article he found that heat was propagated only about half as fast as through an equal bulk of water. On mixing the water with starch and eider-down, he found a similar result. He therefore considered it as demonstrated, that any thing by which the intestine motion of a body of liquid is impeded, lessens its power of propagating heat.

His next attempt was to exhibit this intestine motion in a striking and visible manner; and for this purpose he planned the experiment now so familiar in all courses of physical lectures, in which powdered amber is mixed with the water to which heat is applied from beneath. He then planned and performed the now familiar experiment, by which water may be kept in a boiling state over a body of ice, without melting any part of it, and compared it with the rapidity with which ice is melted when floating on hot water. By these and other experiments, varied with great ingenuity, he came to the conclusion, that all liquids must necessarily be non-conductors of heat; and, reasoning upon this fact, he was led to the remarkable conclusion, that water, at any temperature not below forty degrees, when it obtains its maximum density, will melt as much ice, in a given time, when the ice floats on its surface, as boiling water can; and this apparent paradox he demonstrated by actual experiment.

Pursuing this subject further, he showed that oil was as bad a conductor as water, and reached the still more remarkable conclusion, that mercury, while in a liquid state, is also a non-conductor.

He thus established the universality of the law, in relation to all fluids, which, in previous observations and experiments, he had found to exist in gases and vapors, namely, although they carry off the heat from bodies immersed in them, they do it not in consequence of their conducting property, but because, the density of the portions which are in contact with the heated body being rendered less, these portions rise, and are replaced by others, which, being heated in their turn, rise also; and thus a motion continues until the solid, and the fluid in which it is immersed, reach the same uniform temperature.

In these investigations, he, with his usual tendency to practical inferences, discovered the explanation of numerous natural phenomena, and reached several important useful applications of the principle.

Among other phenomena, he was enabled to explain the fact why very succulent vegetables are either annual in temperate climates, or die down to the root in winter; why those containing more solid matter, but whose sap is perfectly liquid, are deciduous; and why those whose juices are thick and viscid are evergreen, and bear intense cold.

Taking up the fact discovered by his friend, Sir Charles Blagden, that water has its maximum of density at about forty degrees, he saw in this a wise provision of Providence for preserving the liquidity of the lower part of masses of water in cold climates; for as soon as the water reaches that temperature, all downward motion ceases, and ice speedily forms on the surface; after which, in consequence of the bad conducting property of the water, however low the temperature of the ice may fall, little heat can be abstracted from the water beneath.

Pursuing his researches further, and citing an observation of De Saussure at the Lake of Geneva, he shows, that, had the constitution of the water been such, that its motion would have continued until it reached the temperature of thirty-two degrees, instead of stopping at forty degrees, the quantity of heat given out would have been sufficient to raise a mass of ice-cold water, as large as the lake, and forty-nine feet deep, to the point of boiling.

"We cannot," says he, "sufficiently admire the simplicity of the contrivance by which all this heat is saved. It well deserves to be compared with that, by which the seasons are produced; and I must think that every candid inquirer, who will begin by divesting himself of all unreasonable prejudices, will agree with me in attributing them both to the same Author."

The water of the ocean, on the other hand, is not only less easily frozen than fresh water, but does not appear to have, like it, a point of maximum density. Hence, as it cools and descends in high latitudes, it forms submarine currents, which set towards the equator, while counter superficial currents set from the equator towards the poles. In this necessary state of things, which was first pointed out by Rumford, he saw the reason why the ocean, always temperate at its surface, softens on the sea-coast the rigors of winter, warms by its currents the polar regions, and, at the same time, cools those near the equator.

Taking up the properties of air as a non-conductor, he explained the effects produced by confining it in such manner, that it cannot enter into the general circulation, as exhibited in the use of curtains, hangings, and double sashes to windows. In application of this principle to practical purposes, he contrived a double door for furnaces. Extending his views further, he saw, that in this property of air lay the value of the clothing with which nature provides the animals destined to inhabit warm climates; for, while the wool, fur, feathers, or down, with which they are covered, are of themselves among the worst conductors of all solid bodies, they, from their structure, enclose and confine air, which is an absolute non-conductor. In like manner, he showed that the loose and flaky structure of snow renders it a mantle, by which the earth is protected from the influence of the cold winds, and thus the seeds and roots of vegetables are preserved from destruction by frost. Not content, however, with his former inferences in relation to this property of air, he planned an *experimentum crucis*, which leaves not a doubt on the subject; and thus, while, in opposition to his inferences, we are now compelled to admit that liquids conduct heat, although far more slowly than the worst conductors among solid bodies, the fact, that air and gases are absolute non-conductors, is established beyond all possibility of cavil.

The latest of Rumford's investigations on the subject of heat had reference to the radiating power of different surfaces. That heat was derived from a fire in two different manners, had furnished, as we have seen, the basis of his plans for improving fireplaces. He now generalized one of these effects into the law of radiation equally in all directions, from bodies differing in temperature from those which surround them. He then showed, that the intensity of the radiation from different bodies of equal temperatures is very different; that it is less from bodies that reflect light than from those which absorb it; less from metals than from their oxides; and less from opaque and polished bodies than from translucent and rough bodies. The fact contained in the paper on this subject, which was at the time considered as most remarkable, was, that the same body may, at the same time, be a source of heat to bodies colder, and of cold to those warmer, than itself.

He finally shows, that those bodies, which radiate heat best, receive it most readily.

In these experiments and inferences, which were read to the French Institute in 1802, but not published until 1804, he anticipated the discoveries of Leslie, which, when impartially viewed, are no more than repetitions, in a more precise form, of those of Rumford, illustrated by a greater number of instances.

We thus see, that, while the investigations of Rumford, in relation to the subject of heat, were first instituted with a view to practical utility in the art of preparing food, he extended the results he obtained to the explanation of the more important and extensive operations of nature upon the surface of the globe, and in some cases, as in that of the submarine polar currents, predicted, what fifty years of subsequent observation have hardly yet exhibited in its full extent. We may in truth say, that, with whatever delight he dilates upon subjects often considered beneath the dignity of the philosopher, he has applied his discoveries with as much advantage to the general laws of terrestrial physics, as he has to useful purposes in public and domestic economy. Above all, in his inquiries he never lost sight of the most important object of science, its bearing upon the evidences of natural theology, and, at every new step in his discoveries, pauses to show in what manner they illustrate the power and wisdom of the Deity. After dwelling upon this subject, he goes on to say,

"But I must take care not to tire my reader by pursuing these speculations too far. If I have persisted in them, if I have dwelt upon them with peculiar satisfaction and complacency, it is because I think them uncommonly interesting, and also because I conceived they might be of use in this age of *refinement* and *skepticism*.

"If, among barbarous nations, the fear of a God, and the practice of religious duties, tend to soften savage dispositions, and to prepare the mind for those sweet enjoyments which result from peace, order, and friendly intercourse, a belief in the existence of a Supreme Intelligence, who rules and governs the universe with wisdom and goodness, is not less essential to the happiness of those, who, by cultivating their mental powers, have learnt to know how little can be known."

One only of his more important inquiries remains to be mentioned. The fact, that heat is developed by friction, is among the oldest of recorded physical phenomena. On the discovery of the law of specific heat, it was, without inquiry, included among the cases which could be explained by means of it. Rumford saw reason to doubt this conclusion, and by a well-planned and admirably conducted experiment, showed, that no change took place in the capacity of the body subjected to friction, and that heat continued to be evolved so long as enough of the body remained to admit of the action. This experiment and inference lay dormant, in its practical applications, for many years, but has recently been applied to heating large buildings with success and economy.

Besides the temporary apparatus with which his experiments were performed, he contrived two instruments, which are still considered as important parts of a philosophical apparatus. These are so well known that we need only mention their names; the thermoscope, and a calorimeter.

The former, which was slightly modified by Leslie into the differential thermometer, was made by him the basis of apparatus intended for the purposes of photometry, hygrometry, and atmometry.

Proud as he might be of his own discoveries in the science of heat, he neither felt envy of his contemporaries, nor was sensible of the dread that his most brilliant investigations might be superseded or eclipsed by his successors. So far from this, to encourage those who might desire to follow in the same path, he instituted prizes, amply endowed, to be adjudged by the Royal Society of London, and the American Academy of Sciences, for the most important discoveries of which light and heat should be the subject; and, with rare good fortune, was himself the first to whom the former of these prizes should be awarded.

Nor did his liberality stop here; but, by his will, he bequeathed the annual sum of one thousand dollars, together with the reversion of other property, to Harvard University, for the purpose of founding a professorship to teach "the utility of the physical and mathematical sciences, for the improvement of the useful arts, and for the extension of the industry, prosperity, happiness, and well-being of society."

Rumford's union with Madame Lavoisier does not appear to have been productive of any great degree of domestic felicity; neither does he appear to have rendered himself popular in the society of the French metropolis. Cuvier, in his eulogium, hints that the urbanity of his manners was not equal to his ardor for public utility, and that a certain degree of coarseness was evident in his conversations and conduct. He also accuses him of having been the benefactor of his species without loving or esteeming them, as well as of holding the opinion, that the mass of mankind ought to be treated as mere machines, and that their welfare ought not to be intrusted to their own free-will.

We cannot, however, assent to these disparaging views of his character. It is possible, and even probable, that he may have rebuked the principles of infidelity, then so prevalent in France, with a sternness worthy of his pilgrim ancestors; but the man, who, in youth, had captivated the affections of a most accomplished lady, and been singled out for unusual favors, by so good a judge of all that was becoming in a gentleman, as Governor Wentworth, who, in middle age, by his personal demeanor and carriage, attracted the notice of a Prince bred in the saloons over which Marie Antoinette, of Austria, presided, and had for years enjoyed the favor and personal intimacy of Charles Theodore, of Bavaria, could never, in the decline of life, when the habits and impressions of earlier years become indelible, have degenerated into coarseness of manner. Neither with the evidence before us of continual efforts in his charitable establishments to elevate the condition, and create a desire of honorable independence, in the subjects of his philanthropy, can we admit that it was any part of his theory or practice to treat men as mere engines, to be directed and set in motion by their superiors in intellect or in station.

His true character is rather to be inferred from his useful and philanthropic labors, and his numerous useful and scientific discoveries, than from the report of those who only knew him after his energy was impaired, and he had experienced disappointment and ingratitude. We, however, draw from the report of his French eulogist one prominent trait, which may not have been developed in the preceding pages; this was the love of order, and the strictest observance of method, in all his pursuits. This he called "the necessary auxiliary of genius, the only possible instrument of true happiness, and almost a subordinate divinity in this lower world." It is to this feature in his character, that we are to ascribe all his scientific attainments, and the high reputation he must ever hold in the eyes of posterity. From the time he landed in England, except a single short interval, until he bade adieu to Bavaria, he had been engaged in one continued series of important and engrossing employments, civil, military, and diplomatic; and yet, by a wise and skilful distribution of his time, he found leisure not only to devote himself to the most minute objects of domestic economy, but to enter into and accomplish philosophic investigations, that have become a portion of physical science, which no future discoveries can obliterate.

But while this love of method was the means of his acquiring celebrity, it is assigned as the cause of his death, when still in the fullest enjoyment of his mental and physical powers; for, being seized with a fever, he persisted in the pursuit of his usual routine of occupations and diet. His death took place on the 21st of August, 1814, at his villa, in Auteuil, in the sixty-second year of his age, depriving mankind of one of its most eminent benefactors, and science of one of its brightest ornaments.

APPENDIX,

BY THE EDITOR.

No. I.

Count Rumford's Donations to the American Academy of Arts and Sciences, and to Harvard University.

In the year 1796, Count Rumford, who was at that time in London, presented to the American Academy of Arts and Sciences, at Boston, five thousand dollars in the three per cent stocks of the United States, the object of this gift being, as expressed by the donor, in a letter to the President of the Academy,

"To the end that the interest of the same may be received from time to time, for ever, and the amount of the same applied and given, once every second year, as a premium to the author of the most important discovery, or useful improvement, which shall be made and published by printing, or in any way made known to the public, in any part of the continent of America, or in any of the American islands, during the preceding two years, on heat, or on light, the preference always being given to such discoveries as shall, in the opinion of the Academy, tend most to promote the good of mankind."

He further requested, that the premium "might

always be given in two medals, one of gold and the other of silver, and of such dimensions that both of them together may be just equal, in intrinsic value, to the amount of the interest of the aforesaid five thousand dollars."

Several years passed away without any discoveries being made, which seemed to meet the intentions of the donor. Meantime the fund continued to accumulate, but was useless as to the immediate objects for which it was given. That the general purpose of Count Rumford might, in some degree, be answered, by employing the proceeds of the fund for the promotion of the branches of science most nearly allied to those specified in his letter, the Academy at length applied to the legislature for permission to appropriate the income in a more general way, without adhering to the precise form of biennial premiums. An act was accordingly passed, authorizing the Supreme Court, sitting in chancery, to make a decree in conformity to the suggestions of the Academy.

By this decree, the Academy was empowered to purchase books and apparatus relating to light and heat, and to award payment for experiments, observations, lectures, and treatises on the same subjects, from the income of the fund, reserving always, however, a sufficient amount for procuring two medals, one of gold and one of silver, of the value of four hundred dollars, whenever any important discovery in light or heat should be made. By the application of the income upon these principles, about two thousand volumes on the physical sciences have been added to the library; and an apparatus for magnetic observations, and astronomical instruments, have been purchased; meteorological observations are taken, and a journal is kept, at the charge of this fund; and three thousand dollars have recently been appropriated to aid in purchasing a telescope for Harvard College.

By these examples it is evident, that such a construction has been put upon the decree of the Court, as to embrace the whole circle of the physical sciences. How far this construction comports with the views of the donor, who is very precise in defining his object, and the manner in which he wished the income to be appropriated, it would be useless now to inquire. It cannot be overlooked, however, that, if it is desirable to gain the confidence of other magnificent lovers of science, and encourage them to similar acts of liberality for specific objects, the Academy cannot be too cautious in adhering as strictly as possible to the letter and spirit of the instrument, in which the intentions of the donor are defined and prescribed.

Is there any probability, that it could ever have entered the imagination of Count Rumford, that three thousand dollars of his fund should be given away to aid in purchasing a telescope for an institution, with which the Academy is in no manner connected? Might not the money be granted with just as much propriety for erecting a college building, or any other structure, in which telescopes are used, or the sciences taught? In the instance of this fund, there are undoubtedly reasons why a liberal construction should be allowed; but there are also limits, which the Academy should be careful not to over-up, if it would impress the conviction upon the public of its being a faithful guardian of the trust. Has the Academy the power, can it be invested with the power, of bestowing the income of this fund upon another institution, or, in other words, of purchasing philosophical instruments, which are to become the property of such institution? At all events, if large appropriations are made for remote objects, common justice requires that these should be such as will in some way connect with them the donor's name, so that the real benefactor shall be known to the public.

During the fifty years, since the fund was given, one occasion only has occurred for awarding the premium. In 1839, two medals were granted to Dr. Hare, of Philadelphia, for his invention of the compound blowpipe, and his various improvements in galvanic apparatus.

The following are the amounts, which have been paid out of the income of this fund, for different objects, from the time of its origin to the month of May, 1844, as they are reported by Mr. J. Ingersoll Bowditch, the treasurer of the Academy.

Publishing Magnetic Declinations,	$230 00
Astronomical Instruments,	770 09
Meteorological Observations,	1808 55
Printing,	816 14
Medals,	606 00
Telescope, in part,	1200 00
Books, and charges connected with them,	7348 97
Miscellaneous,	208 80
	$13054 55

The present amount of the fund is $24504.

By his will, Count Rumford bequeathed to Harvard College one thousand dollars annually, and the reversion of other sums, for the purpose of founding a professorship, "to teach, by regular courses of academical and public lectures, accompanied with proper experiments, the utility of the physical and mathematical sciences, for the improvement of the useful arts, and for the extension of the industry, prosperity, happiness, and well-being of society." The amount of property, which came into the hands of the corporation, in 1815, after the death of Count Rumford, was about eleven hundred dollars annually, subject to a deduction of two hundred dollars a year, payable to the Countess, his daughter, in case she should fail to receive her annuity of two thousand florins from the court of Bavaria. The university was also to receive the reversion of about four hundred and forty dollars annually after the death of certain annuitants.

The Rumford professorship was accordingly established in the university, and went into operation in the year 1816. Dr. Jacob Bigelow was the first professor, who occupied the chair eleven years, and was succeeded by Mr. Daniel Treadwell. Hitherto this foundation has produced all the benefits, which the liberal donor could have anticipated. A course of lectures is annually delivered to the undergraduates and other students of the university. The aggregate amount of the fund at this time, according to the Treasurer's last annual report, is about twenty-nine thousand dollars. A valuable apparatus, consisting of machines, models, and instruments, suitable for illustrating the topics embraced in the lectures, has been added to the department.

There are other evidences of Count Rumford's generous spirit, the more interesting, as they afford pleasing proofs of his filial affection. His mother lived to an advanced age, and had several children by a second marriage. While he resided in Bavaria, he set apart for her five hundred pounds sterling, and remitted to her the interest annually, informing her that the principal was her own property. On this subject he wrote to her from London, November 1st, 1795, as follows.

"I have now come to a resolution to transfer the property I have destined for you into the American funds, and to send you a power of attorney for receiving the interest regularly, at Boston. Or, if you please, I will transfer the capital at once to you, and have it entered in your name, in the books of the United States. It will then be yours, to all intents and purposes, and you may dispose of it as you may think proper."

The amount thus transferred was five thousand dollars in the three per cent stocks of the United States. Again, in 1804, he writes from Paris.

"I know how much you interest yourself for all your children, and especially for those of them who have been unfortunate in the world, and who stand most in need of your assistance. Of the five thousand dollars in the American funds, which I desired you to dispose of among your children by will, you were so kind to my daughter Sally, as to bequeath to her one thousand. As I have made ample provision for Sally myself, I desire you would make a new will, and give to my sister Ruth, who, I hear, has been unfortunate in life, the thousand dollars in addition, which you had destined for Sally. My dear mother, I cannot refuse myself the pleasure of giving you a larger sum, to dispose of among those you love. I have five thousand dollars more in the American stocks, which I request you would dispose of among your children and grandchildren, by your will.

"It will give you pleasure to know, that I enjoy very good health. The air of France agrees with me better than the air of Germany, or that of England, and I am very happy here. I shall go to England and Germany occasionally, but my principal residence will, in future, be in Paris. It is not, however, my intention to become a French citizen."

He writes again, from Paris, July 22d, 1806. "I should be much less anxious on your account, my dear mother, if I knew that Sally was with you, to assist and take care of you. If more money should be wanted to make you both comfortable, than what I have hitherto furnished, I have written to Sally, to say, that, instead of eight hundred dollars, I am ready and willing to furnish one thousand dollars a year. It is my most earnest desire to make you as comfortable as possible, and that everything should be arranged as you like best."

Paris, December 1st, 1808. "You can hardly conceive how much I have your happiness and comfort at heart. Give my kind love to all my relations and friends. They will, no doubt, have nearly forgotten me; but I never can forget the place of my birth, and the companions of my early years. My life appears to me like a dream. I have been very successful; but, on the other hand, I have been uncommonly active and enterprising. It affords me the greatest satisfaction to think you are satisfied with the conduct of your son." In this letter he requests her to have her picture taken, "by one of the best limners in Boston," and to send it to him.

A deed of gift, for the ten thousand dollars mentioned above, was subsequently conveyed to his mother, and, in the letter informing her of this conveyance, he says, "I desire that you will accept of it as a token of my dutiful affection for you, and of my gratitude for the kind care you took of me in the early part of my life. I have the greatest satisfaction in being able to show my gratitude for all your goodness to me, and to contribute to your ease and comfort. I request that you will consider this donation as being perfectly free and unconditional, and that you would enjoy and dispose of what is now your property, just as you shall think best, and most conducive to your happiness and to your satisfaction, without any regard to any former arrangements you may have made at my request."

In conclusion he adds, "My health continues to be good, and I yet feel none of those infirmities of age, which sometimes render the evening of life painful. I have the satisfaction to think, that I have done my duty through life, and that is a great consolation to me, as I approach the end of my course. I shall never cease to be, my dear mother, your dutiful and affectionate child,

"BENJAMIN."

No. II.

Reasons assigned by Count Rumford for leaving his Country.

By the kindness of Mr. Joseph B. Walker, a few interesting letters, written by Count Rumford, respecting an important period in his life, have fallen into my hands since the preceding memoir was printed. They were directed to the Reverend Timothy Walker, of Concord, New Hampshire, the father of Count Rumford's first wife. Such extracts are here subjoined, as explain his reasons for leaving his residence in Concord, and ultimately his country.

"*December 24th*, 1774. The time and circumstances of my leaving the town of Concord have, no doubt, given you great uneasiness, for which I am extremely sorry.

"Nothing short of the most threatening danger could have induced me to leave my friends and family; but, when I learned from persons of undoubted veracity, and those whose friendship I could not suspect, that my situation was reduced to this dreadful extremity, I thought it absolutely necessary to abscond for a while, and seek a friendly asylum in some distant part.

"Fear of miscarriage prevents my giving a more particular account of this affair; but this you may rely and depend upon, that I never did, nor (let my treatment be what it will) ever will do any action, that may have the most distant tendency to injure the true interest of this my native country.

"I most humbly beg your kind care of my distressed family; and I hope you will take an opportunity to alleviate their trouble by assuring them, that I am in a place of safety, and hope shortly to have the pleasure of seeing them. I also most humbly beseech your prayers for me, that under all my difficulties and troubles, I may behave in such a manner, as to approve myself a true servant of God, and a sincere friend of my country."

"*Boston, January 11th,* 1775. As to any concessions that I could make, I fear they would be of no consequence; for I cannot possibly, with a clear conscience, confess myself guilty of doing anything to the disadvantage of this country, but quite the reverse.

"As Mrs. Thompson's company is almost the only thing, that can be any alleviation to my present troubles, and as my being absent from her is the greatest unhappiness of my present situation, I hope I shall be so happy as to obtain your consent to her leaving Concord."

His wife accordingly joined him, and remained with him for several weeks at Woburn. She returned to her father near the end of May. Meantime his case was examined by the committee of the town of Woburn. The following extract from a letter to Mr. Walker explains the result.

"*Woburn, August 14th,* 1775. When I was brought to trial, my friends, knowing in what a light my crime was looked upon by the populace, advised me to plead *not guilty.* I did so; but found, instead of quieting the disturbances, it only served to heighten the clamors against me, till, at length, I found it absolutely necessary that something should be done for my personal security. My friends advised me to leave the town till the storm should be abated, which they doubted not would be in a short time. I neither doubted the abilities nor scrupled the sincerity of my friends, and accordingly followed their advice. But the event has not proved equal to my expectations; for the storm, instead of subsiding, has increased, and the popular disturbances have grown into such a flame, as I fear nothing but my blood will extinguish.

"As to my being instrumental in the return of some deserters, by procuring them a pardon, I freely acknowledge that I was; but you will give me leave to say, that what I did was done from principles the most unexceptionable, the most disinterested, a sincere desire to serve my King and country, and from motives of pity to those unfortunate wretches, who had deserted the service to which they had voluntarily and so solemnly tied themselves, and to which they were desirous of returning. If the designed ends were not answered by what I did, I am sincerely and heartily sorry. But, if it is a crime to act from principles like these, I glory in being a criminal.

"As to the other 'known' and 'obnoxious facts' which you mention, namely, 'maintaining a long and expensive correspondence with Governors Wentworth and Gage,' I would beg leave to observe, that, at the time that Governor Wentworth first honored me with his notice, he was as high in the esteem of the people in general, as ever was any Governor in America; at a time when Mr. Sullivan himself was proud to be thought his friend. And as, from the first commencement of our acquaintance, till I left Concord, he never did anything, to my knowledge, whereby he forfeited the affection and confidence of the public, I cannot see why a correspondence with him should be obnoxious, or that the *length* or *expensiveness* of it should be thought an object of public attention, that merited public censure. It is true, Sir, I always thought myself honored by his friendship, and was ever fond of a correspondence with him; a correspondence, which was purely private and friendly, and not political, and for which I cannot find it in my heart either to express my sorrow, or ask forgiveness of the public.

"As to my maintaining a correspondence with Governor Gage, that part of the charge is entirely without foundation, as I never received a letter from him in my life; nor did I ever write him one, unless about half a dozen lines, which I sent him just before I left Concord, may be called a letter; and which contained no intelligence, nor any thing of a public nature, but was only to desire that the soldiers, who returned from Concord, might be ordered not to inform any person by whose intercession their pardon was granted them.

"But this is not the only groundless charge, that has been brought against me. Many other crimes, which you do not mention, have been laid to my charge, for which I have had to answer both publicly and privately. My enemies are indefatigable in their endeavors to distress me, and I find, to my sorrow, that they are but too successful. I have been driven from the camp by the clamors of the New

Hampshire people, and am again threatened in that place. But I hope soon to be out of the reach of my cruel persecutors, for I am determined to seek that peace and protection in foreign lands, and among strangers, which is denied me in my native country. I cannot any longer bear the insults that are daily offered me; I cannot bear to be looked upon and treated as the Achan of society. I have done nothing that can deserve this cruel usage. I have done nothing with any design to injure my countrymen, and I cannot any longer bear to be treated in this barbarous manner by them.

"And notwithstanding I have the tenderest regard for my wife and family, and really believe I have an equal return of love and affection from them; though I feel the keenest distress at the thoughts of what Mrs. Thompson and my parents and friends will suffer on my account, and though I foresee and realize the distress, poverty, and wretchedness, that must attend my pilgrimage in unknown lands, destitute of fortune, friends, and acquaintance, yet all these evils appear to me more tolerable, than the treatment which I meet with from the hands of my ungrateful countrymen.

"This step, I am sensible, is violent, but my case is desperate. I have nothing to expect from my enemies; and my friends are afraid to appear for me. I see no prospect of being able, either to return to Concord, or even to stay here much longer in peace and safety. A reconciliation upon honorable terms, is of all others the thing most to be desired; but you must allow me to say, that my present situation, notwithstanding it is thus dreadful, is to be preferred to a reconciliation, supposing it possible, upon the terms of my making an acknowledgment. The crime, which is alleged against me, that of being an enemy to my country, is a crime of the blackest dye, a crime which must, if proved against me, inevitably entail perpetual infamy and disgrace upon my name. If I confess myself guilty, will my enemies, will the world, think me innocent? Or, will even the charity of my very friends attempt to exculpate me when I accuse myself?

"Whatever prudence may dictate, yet conscience and honor, God and religion, forbid that my mouth should speak what my heart disclaims. I cannot profess my sorrow for an action, which I am conscious was done from the best of motives. If the event has proved contrary to my expectations, or if I can be persuaded that I have acted upon mistaken principles, I am ready, not only to express my sorrow, but to do it in the most open and public manner. But, till this can be the case, till I can be fully persuaded that I have really done wrong, I cannot be persuaded to acknowledge that I have done so.

"I am extremely unhappy to differ from you in opinion in anything, but more especially in an affair of so much consequence as the propriety of my returning to Concord upon the terms mentioned in your letters. But I hope that the reasons, which I have now given, added to the inimical disposition which the committee have lately shown towards me, will serve in some measure as an excuse for my not following your advice in this affair.

"I am too well acquainted with your paternal affection for your children, to doubt of your kind care over them; but you will excuse me if I trouble you with my most earnest desire and entreaty for your peculiar care of my family, whose distressed circumstances call for every indulgence and alleviation you can afford them. I must also beg a continuance of your prayers for me, that my present afflictions may have a suitable impression on my mind; and that in due time I may be extricated out of all my troubles. That this may be the case, that the happy time may soon come when I may return to my family in peace and safety, and when every individual in America may 'sit down under his own vine, and under his own fig-tree, and have none to make him afraid,' is the constant and devout wish of your dutiful and affectionate son,

BENJAMIN THOMPSON."

The Reverend Timothy Walker, to whom these letters were written, was the first clergyman, and one of the first settlers, of Concord. He commenced his pastoral duties in that place in 1730, and sustained the same charge fifty-two years, till his death, in 1762. He made three voyages to England, as agent for the inhabitants of the town in settling their difficulties with other claimants respecting the titles to their lands. His daughter, Sarah, married Benjamin Rolfe, one of the first settlers of the town, a man of education and talents, for many years one of its principal citizens, and often engaged in public affairs. After his death, which occurred in 1770, his widow married Benjamin Thompson. She died at Concord, in 1792, leaving a daughter, the present Countess of Rumford, who has for many years resided in Paris

LIFE

OF

ZEBULON MONTGOMERY PIKE;

BY

HENRY WHITING.

ZEBULON MONTGOMERY PIKE.

CHAPTER I.

His Birth and early Education. — Obtains a Commission in the Army. — His Promotion. — Appointed to command an Expedition up the Mississippi. — Departs from St. Louis. — Demoyne Rapids. — Speech to the Indians. — Remarks on the Indian Trade.

THE subject of this memoir was the son of Major Zebulon Pike, who had served in the war of the revolution, and who again entered the army of the United States, as a captain of infantry, in 1792, having, as the records of the Executive Journal state, " served with reputation in the levies" during the previous year. He was promoted to the rank of major in 1800. The family had resided for several generations in New Jersey, and numbered among its ancestors a Captain John Pike, who had a traditionary reputation as a gallant soldier in the Indian wars. In the organization of the peace establishment in 1802, Major Pike was arranged to the first regiment of infantry, under the command of Colonel Hamtramk.

His son, ZEBULON MONTGOMERY PIKE, was born at Lamberton, now the south part of Trenton, New Jersey, January 5th, 1779. While he was yet a child, his father removed with his family to Bucks county, Pennsylvania, where he resided for several years, a few miles from the Delaware River. He removed thence to Easton. Such advantages as the country schools afforded at that period were enjoyed by young Pike. For some time, he was under the tuition of a Mr. Wall, eminent in the neighborhood for his mathematical attainments. What progress his pupil made in this or other branches of study is not known, except from the fruits in after life. He is remembered, by some of his schoolmates still living, as a boy of slender form, very fair complexion, gentle and retiring disposition, but of resolute spirit. Instances are mentioned in which his combative energies were put to a test, which would reflect no discredit upon his subsequent career.

But his means of education must have been limited in their duration, if not in their quality; for, while yet quite young, he entered his father's company as a cadet. On the 3d of March,

1799, he received a commission, as an ensign, in the second regiment of infantry. He was promoted to the rank of first lieutenant in the same regiment, April 24th, 1800, and arranged to the first regiment of infantry in 1802.

While thus advancing through the initial grades of his profession, Lieutenant Pike was assiduous in supplying the defects of his education by the most earnest application to various studies, embracing, among others, the Latin and the French languages, and the mathematics. That he exhibited decided proofs of success in these exertions, may be inferred from the responsible duties to which he was soon called by the Commander-in-Chief, General Wilkinson.

The acquisition of Louisiana by the United States, under Mr. Jefferson's administration, imposed on the government a new and important duty. The vast country, which had been acquired, was almost unknown by the people to whom its sovereignty had now been assigned. It was highly proper, that efforts should be made to remove this general ignorance, at least in a degree. The public, it is true, in desiring the new territory, had wished for little or nothing more than the command of the Lower Mississippi, which was an indispensable outlet to the broad west, everywhere intersected by its tributaries. This opening, at all times liable to be closed while New Orleans remained in foreign hands, was now exclusively under the control of the United States; and the strong anxieties, and menacing agitations, which an occasional interruption of its free navigation had often spread through the region beyond the Alleghanies, were now suppressed, and without any cause for renewal. A fearful crisis had been averted. That privilege had been peaceably obtained, through negotiation by the government, which might, in a few years, have been violently seized by a mere section of the country in spite of that government, and at the imminent hazard of a foreign war. An unobstructed egress to the sea, and to the markets of the world, had been fully secured to the west, and the people were satisfied. Still, other duties remained for the government to perform.

Mr. Jefferson, mingling with his political feelings a love of science, and a desire to mark his administration by exertions to enlarge its boundaries, had a just appreciation of these duties. He determined to use the few means in his hands for this worthy purpose. The army constituted one of these means, the most convenient, as well as the most efficient. It did not furnish all that was wanting to fulfil those purposes in the best manner. At that early day, it embraced but few thoroughly scientific men. Why measures were not taken to supply this obvious deficiency, it is not known. There may have been a doubt whether any demand for extra means would be complied with. An administration, which came in under strong professions of economical reform, probably felt reluctant to ask an appropriation, which would generally have been regarded as contravening such professions.

The army had many intelligent as well as enterprising officers. Mr. Jefferson determined to avail himself only of such characters, in sending out leaders of explorations into the new regions which had been acquired, leaving researches of a higher order to subsequent and more prosperous years. Captain Merriwether Lewis, and Lieutenant William Clarke, both of the army, were selected by him to ascend the Missouri, cross the Rocky Mountains, and descend the Columbia to its mouth, and thus confirm, by more extended discoveries, the claim to that vast region, the initiation of which had been estaolished by Captain Gray. These two gentlemen proved, by the success of their expedition, how well qualified they were, in many respects, for the duty assigned to them; though there can be no question, that, had a few professionally scientific men been attached to the party, men who could now-a-days be obtained without fee or reward, the results would have been far more beneficial to the cause of knowledge, as well as more creditable to the country. It is believed, that Mr. Jefferson took much pains, even by personal teaching, to fit Captain Lewis, a kinsman, for observing Nature under her various aspects, and for bringing back other stores of information than those gathered up by the ordinary traveller; and the contributions he made to several departments of science were respectable and valuable. They were not, however, what they might have been, and ought to have been.

In projecting the expedition to the sources of the Mississippi, which was about contemporaneous with that up the Missouri, the President did not probably exercise any direct agency. General Wilkinson, of the United States' army, who then commanded on the Mississippi, appears to have selected the officer who was to conduct it. Pike had then attained the rank of First Lieutenant in the infantry. General Wilkinson, knowing his activity, energy, and perseverance, assigned to him the duty of conducting a small military party to the sources of the Mississippi, for the purpose of obtaining some knowledge of the upper parts of that great river, and of ascertaining the true position of those sources. Such information was desirable on many accounts. It would more fully develop the geography of the country; would open the great avenue to the north-western trade, thus far exclusively in the hands of the British, but now about to be assumed by our own people; and would manifest, in a palpable way, both to the Indian tribes there, and to the foreign traders among them, that the United States were the sovereigns of the country, and intended to be respected as such.

Probably General Wilkinson could not have made a more judicious selection, which was necessarily confined, by the size of the detachment, to the subaltern grades of the army. No scientific men, it would appear in this case, as in the case of Lewis and Clarke, were to be attached to the party. Lieutenant Pike had already displayed considerable literary proficiency, and was very ambitious of improvement. He was not qualified to act in any of the scientific departments, though he, no doubt, made strong summary efforts, when he knew his destination, to enable himself to collect hints and facts, that might be useful to them. The little time, however, he could have had for such a purpose, precluded, of course, any great success in such efforts. In his preface to his expeditions, he remarks, that he "literally performed the duties, as far as his limited abilities permitted, of astronomer, surveyor, commanding officer, clerk, spy, guide, and hunter." It is not to his disparagement, that he probably succeeded best in the five last capacities; and he made no pretensions to either botany, mineralogy, zoology, or ornithology.

It is not stated why he was sent alone into such a remote, little known, and, as there was much reason to apprehend, unfriendly country. Another officer, of a subaltern rank, would have much relieved the burden of the command, and increased the chances of beneficial results from the expedition. Its incidents often proved, that those results were sometimes in jeopardy through the want of such aid. Officers were at command, and it seems as injudicious as it was unnecessary to accumulate on the head of Lieutenant Pike the multifarious duties he enumerates, when a convenient distribution of them could so easily have been made. The party did not include even a surgeon, whose services, on such an enterprise, involving many and unusual exposures, were equally at command, among the medical gentlemen of the army; gentlemen who, by their education and studies, are supposed to possess many qualifications for investigating nature, besides their importance in case of diseases or bodily injuries.

It is not probable that Lieutenant Pike raised

any objections to the manner in which he was sent forth. It is more probable that his little experience suggested no doubt in his mind, as to his sufficiency for all the demands of the expedition; and it may also have been, that the very dependence upon his own resources, which his position implied, had a charm with his ardent spirit, and that he looked forward with as much pleasure to a gallant encounter with all difficulties, as to the more defined objects of his journey. It was not for him to judge, particularly where a prudent exercise of judgment might have bespoken self-distrust. It was for others to have determined the wants of the case, and provided accordingly.

Embarking with his little party, consisting of one sergeant, who proved a faithless soldier, one corporal, and seventeen privates, Lieutenant Pike left St. Louis, the 9th of August, 1805, in a keel-boat, seventy feet long, and with provisions for four months, (he was gone double that time,) to run all the hazards of an untried voyage up the Mississippi; more full of zeal to accomplish the objects in view, than thoughtful of those hazards, or of the many hinderances that were likely to beset his way.

This trip of Lieutenant Pike up the Mississippi was the first that had been made by any citizen of the United States; at least, it is not known that he had any predecessors. Adventurers may have previously ascended it in quest of furs; but their discoveries, if they made any, had not been made known to the public. Lieutenant Pike had, therefore, a fresh field of exertion. Whatever he should see and hear would be new to that public, which had but vague notions of the vast north-western interior. He kept a regular journal, which was published in 1808. This journal shows the distances made each day; the difficulties surmounted; the game killed; the British trading establishments found on the river; and the Indians, both tribes and scattered parties, met with. It deals very little in the descriptive.

Perhaps he had a dull eye for the picturesque. Few scenes are portrayed by him in that character, although it is now well known that the Upper Mississippi presents many that possess it in a high degree. No fault is to be found with this deficiency. His duties were specific; rather to observe man than nature, and courses and distances, than the aspects of a landscape. His ordinary journey was from twenty-five to thirty miles a day. Frequent accidents often made it less. At the season he started, the waters were likely to be at their low stage, when the current is comparatively moderate. His greatest embarrassment arose from the numerous channels, which are formed by the many islands in the river. It was difficult, if not impracticable, without experienced guides, to choose the right one. Determining by chance, or by deceptive appearances, he was sometimes obliged to retrace his course, and more often found himself gaining a point by a wearisome circuit, the more direct and much shorter route having been missed. These several hinderances made his ascent slow and toilsome, and it required much management and energy to keep up the cheerfulness and confidence of his followers. All this Lieutenant Pike evinced; and he succeeded in getting to the foot of Demoyne Rapids on the 20th of August.

These rapids are a formidable obstacle in the course of the Mississippi. They are about "eleven miles long, with successive shoals extending from shore to shore," and are about three quarters of a mile wide. He had "not a soul on board who had passed them;" still, he determined at once to attempt to surmount them, and had already made half, and the most difficult half, of the ascent, when he was met by a small party, which had come down to assist him up. This party was headed by an agent, who had lately been sent to the Sacs and Foxes, then settled at the head of the rapids.

He made a speech to these Indians, informing them "that their great father, the President of the United States, wishing to be more intimately acquainted with the situations and wants of the different nations of the red people, in the newly acquired territory of Louisiana, had ordered the General to send a number of his young warriors, in different directions, to take them by the hand, and make such inquiries as might afford the satisfaction required." He also wished them to point out such sites as they might think proper for trading establishments, and informed them that no traders must be among them without licenses from the United States.

Leaving the rapids of Demoyne after a short stay, Lieutenant Pike met, a few miles above them, three Mackinac boats, which had come by the way of the island of that name, at the head of Lake Huron, laden with goods for trade with the Indians. Few stronger evidences of a spirit of gainful enterprise could be produced, than were exhibited by boats like these, and their cargoes. The goods in these Mackinac boats had all come from England. They had reached Canada by the way of the St. Lawrence, and they left the ships at Montreal, ascending thence to Lake Huron, by the route of the Ottawa and other waters linked together by various portages. They were next transferred to the description of boats met by Lieutenant Pike, and, after passing Mackinac, and ascending the Fox River, they descended the Wisconsin into the Mississippi; a lengthened transportation, which involved a labor and expense that can be judged of only by experience; though any mind may conjecture the many hundred per cent that thence accrued upon the goods. All was summed up at the end of the trip, and worked into the price for which they were sold.

Every day that was added to the protracted journey, every tedious portage that was made, portages sometimes thousands of yards in length, and over which each package had to be carried,* every accident that led to damage or delay; all these were elements that entered into the price, swelling it to an inordinate degree, and making the simple knife, obtained in the cutler's shop for a few shillings, cost the Indian, when he stuck it into his belt, a nominal sum that would have procured him, under common circumstances, a handsome sword; while the plain *stroud* (petticoat) of the squaw, consisting of a yard and a half of coarse blue cloth, by the time it was swathed around her waist, brought her hunter lord in debt to an amount that

---

* These packages are made up to weigh from fifty to one hundred pounds, and slung from the forehead.

would almost have decked out a white woman for a city ball.

These high prices would have led to ruinous extravagance among the Indians, had there not been a correction for the evil, in customs that prevailed in the aboriginal trade. Few Indians made their hunts in advance of the sale. It was not their custom to procure skins by their own means, and then offer them for an equivalent in goods. Had such a provident custom prevailed, the traffic would have been carried on upon terms of greater equality. But the Indian must have his outfit before he goes out. He will hunt for food when hunger presses; but beyond this no voluntary exertion will go. It was, therefore, necessary that the trader, in order to overcome this habitual indolence, should offer some excitement, deal out certain goods in advance, to be repaid in furs, at the end of the hunt.

This system, the offspring of necessity, led to "credits," which led to extortion and wrong. The trader, seeing his property about to be borne off in various directions, dependent for a return upon the industry of a lazy race, or upon ideas of honesty that were exceedingly vague or lax, or upon a success that might not attend the best efforts, believed that no security could be found for adequate returns but in a price that provided for extraordinary losses. Hence the *couteau de chasse* was charged like a gilded rapier, and the coarse *stroud* as if it had been a rich brocade.

The foregoing details show that the prices, at which the goods thus taken into the Indian country were sold, must have been exorbitant in a high degree, and that the simple Indians were a prey to cupidity and extortion, that had no limits. But there was another custom among the Indians, which partly counterbalanced these great wrongs, and enabled them, in some degree, to outwit the unprincipled trader. At the end of the hunt, the hunter brought in the fruit of his exertions, the furs he had collected. If these paid his debt, which was not often the case, the account was squared; if an arrearage remained, as was generally the case, no reasoning nor threats could convince the red man that the responsibility held over to another season, and that his obligations survived the hunt. When that hunt terminated, and the furs obtained by it had been fairly rendered, he considered the account as cancelled. Whether it was balanced, or not, was a question he did not undertake to answer.

One of the objects Lieutenant Pike appears to have been instructed to keep in view while on his trip, was, the investigation of these evils of the Indian trade, and to ascertain where proper trading establishments could be fixed, which were intended to correct them. These establishments were, of course, to be made under the patronage of the government. They were afterwards actually made under the "factor" system. In a benevolent spirit, the United States enacted that certain stores should be conveniently placed within the Indian territory, where factors, having a salary, and no interest in the trade, were to keep on hand a constant supply of articles suitable for the Indians, which were to be exchanged with them for peltries, the articles bearing only a fair cost, all expenses included, and the peltries being received at a fair rate. Government thus, out of kindness to the Indians, became a trader, and a competitor with individual traders.

The theory was as promising as it was benevolent; but, like many theories, it did not fulfil expectation when put in practice. It is true, that, under it, the Indian was sure of a just equivalent for such furs and peltries as he brought in. This assurance was spread abroad by agents, and was generally known and understood. But an important consideration had been omitted in the calculations, that suggested the arrangement. Most of the Indians are improvident, and leave the morrow to take care of itself. The future causes them no anxiety. It is the present moment, with its gratifications or its wants, that occupies, almost exclusively, their minds; the former exhausted with blind avidity, the latter borne with passive endurance. They seldom lay up the means of providing themselves with the small equipments of a hunting expedition. While they used the bow and arrow, it was different. Then a few hours' exertion of their own hands provided all that was necessary. But the moment a gun was put into their hands, their dependence upon the trader was secured. They must have ammunition, or their guns were more useless than the bow and arrow; and they could obtain this only upon credit.

Hence the United States factor, who had a knife at a few shillings, and a stroud at not many more, and powder and ball at a fair rate, but who could sell for cash only, or its equivalent, would find his shelves nearly as full at the end of the season as at the beginning; while the individual trader, who sold on credit, though he might sell at an enormous profit, at a thousand per cent above his government competitor, would empty his shelves in a few weeks. Besides, no system can work well, unless it be managed well. The factor was expected, by the law, to be honest and disinterested; and he was often so. Still, he was in a remote part of the country, and beset by temptations, and dealt with a people, that were supposed to be unable to tell tales that could be understood. The system was abandoned, after a vain experiment of a few years.

On the 24th of August, Lieutenant Pike, while hunting on shore, lost two of his dogs. Two men volunteered to go in search of them, who, not returning in due time, were left behind, to make their way by land, and rejoin the boat at some point above. This was likely to be a hard case, as it proved to be. The banks of the Mississippi are not easily followed. A boat may be ascending by a channel that is often removed some miles from one of the main shores. And the *bottoms*, that is, the alluvial grounds, which form the islands, and most of the immediate banks, are but little lifted above the level of the waters, and mostly covered with a rank and dense growth of trees and underbrush; while the bluffs, or higher grounds, considerably elevated above the bottoms, are intersected by sharp and deep ravines, which render them nearly impassable within view of the river.

The Rock River Rapids were ascended on the 28th. They were not as extensive or difficult as those of Demoyne; still, as the party was without guides, much embarrassment, and some hazards, attended the ascent. Lieutenant Pike made a short delay there for his two missing men; but hearing nothing of them, and hoping that they would join him at Prairie du Chien, he continued his route, and reached Dubuque's mines on the 1st of September.* Mons. Dubuque, the proprietor under the Indians, received him with hospitality, and answered all his questions relative to his operations, and the quantity of lead he obtained. The mines there, at that early date, "produced from twenty to forty thousand pounds per annum, the ore yielding seventy-five per cent."

At this stage of his journal he remarks, that he found all the Indians distrustful of the Americans, the men holding them "in great respect, conceiving them to be quarrelsome, and much for war, and also very brave." This reputation he seemed to think not disadvantageous. The British traders, no doubt, were the authors of it, probably not anticipating that any benefits would arise to the Americans from its being entertained by the Indians. Somewhere about this time, Lieutenant Pike received on board his boat a Frenchman, who wished to proceed to Prairie du Chien, and who could speak the Indian lan-

---

* The two men did not rejoin Lieutenant Pike until the 1st of September, having, in the mean time, "been six days without any thing to eat, except muscles." They had been found by a trader, who sent them forward, and probably saved them from perishing.

guage. In the next meeting with the Indians, he most naturally found much advantage in being able to make himself understood by them.

To have sent him on an errand among these tribes, without so indispensable an assistant as an interpreter, seems to have been as unaccountable as extraordinary. Under such circumstances, it required little effort, on the part of the British traders, to render his party and his designs the subjects of unfavorable suspicion. Indeed, had these persons been perfectly neutral and silent respecting him, Lieutenant Pike could hardly have expected a favorable reception from those to whom he could not make his designs and sentiments intelligible. The first question put by these Indians, that is, whether he was "for war, or going to war?" showed the misapprehensions that were preceding him on his journey. Being at this time able to comprehend these questions, and to answer them satisfactorily, through his chance interpreter, he found himself at once the object of friendly attention.

CHAPTER II.

Arrives at Prairie du Chien. — Council with the Indians. — Falls of St. Anthony. — Hunting Excursion. — Reaches Red Cedar Lake and the Sources of the Mississippi. — British Trading Establishments. — Returns to the Falls of St. Anthony, and thence to St. Louis.

THE party reached Prairie du Chien on the 4th of September. This place had been long occupied by the French, being at the junction of the Wisconsin with the Mississippi, and on the route of Father Marquette, when, some time before the close of the seventeenth century, he was the first white man that ever floated down the upper waters of that noble stream. It had been a convenient trading point, and was still little more than the residence of Indian traders. Lieutenant Pike found several of them established there; among them a "judge," and "a captain of militia," under what jurisdiction he does not state. In his letter to General Wilkinson from this place, he says, that he was there obliged to change his unwieldy craft for two lighter boats; and that he had selected, in the neighborhood, "three places for military establishments." *

---

* One of these selections is the site of the present mili-

Leaving Prairie du Chien on the 8th of September, Lieutenant Pike, provided now with an interpreter, resumed his upward route. In passing a Sioux village, where a chief, called La Feuille, lived, the party received a salute after the manner of the Indians, that is, by discharging guns, loaded with ball as well as with powder, over the heads of the honored guests. Where the saluting party is shifting and desultory, and more or less excited by ardent spirits, some hazard seems to attend the compliment, particularly when, as Lieutenant Pike says they did in his case, some of the marksmen endeavored to show how near they can come to the boats without hitting. The chief here mentioned was the head of most of the bands of the Sioux on the river. He told Lieutenant Pike, that "he had never been at war with his new father;" and expressed a hope, that he should always be at peace with the United States.*

---

tary post at Prairie du Chien. While stopping there, Lieutenant Pike says, his men joined with the villagers in jumping and hopping, and beat them all. Many years subsequently, while stationed at the same place, we recollect that an officer of the army often challenged the Indians at a trial of skill with the bow and arrow, and invariably carried off the palm. This was beating them with their own weapons, on their own ground; though they might have said, that archery had gone out of use with them since guns had been introduced.

* This distinguished chief, who was called *Wabasha*, is

Lieutenant Pike, as we have before remarked, deals sparingly with the descriptive, either because his mind was too much occupied by his multifarious duties, or his eye was not led by his taste to dwell on the beauties of nature. His journal gives the reader but a faint idea of the features of the country through which he passed. In speaking of the scenery above Prairie du Chien, he alludes to, and dismisses from his journal, one of the most striking characteristics of the Upper Mississippi, in the following brief and not very expressive sentence. "Hills, or rather prairie knobs, on both sides." There is a singularity, with some mixture of grandeur, in the aspect of the banks of that part of this river, which is here sketched so slightly. From

---

Indian, stood at the head of his tribes many years thereafter. We saw him in 1820. He then said, he had never been at war with his father, though many of his young men, contrary to his advice, had been led away in the war of 1812. He was a small man, and had a patch over one eye; still, with a profile that was said to bear a strong resemblance to that of the great Condé, he impressed every beholder with respect. While with us at Prairie du Chien, he never moved, or was seen, without his pipe-bearer. His people treated him with reverence. Unlike all other speakers in council, he spoke sitting, considering, it was said, that he was called upon to stand only in the presence of his great father at Washington, or his representative at St. Louis. He was not a warrior. He said the Indians could prosper only by being at peace with each other, and with the whites.

the Falls of St. Anthony, some few hundred miles downward, the Mississippi winds through a bottom, which is generally two or three miles in width, and which is one or two hundred feet below the common level of the country.

Precipitous bluffs, often of a fantastic shape, and generally so denuded as to show the rocky strata on which they rest, form the banks of this bottom, through which the stream meanders amid many islands clothed with a dense mass of trees, and here and there a prairie without any vegetation except rank grass. From some of these high bluffs, or "knobs," as Lieutenant Pike rather inaptly calls them, the eye can often range up and down over this immense channel, once, perhaps, filled with a stream proportioned to its capaciousness, as far as its glance can reach, the "Father of waters" dwindling in the distance to the width of a blue ribbon; though, at periods of inundation, he sometimes spreads himself from bluff to bluff, as if he had, in former days, been accustomed thus to spread out the broad folds of his mantle.

At Prairie la Crosse, Lieutenant Pike observed "some holes dug by the Sioux, when in expectation of an attack, into which they first put their women and children, and then crawl in themselves. They were generally round, and about ten feet in diameter; but some were half moons, and quite a breastwork." These small redoubts probably explain the origin of many low mounds and lines, which frequently appear on the banks of the Mississippi, and its tributaries. They are generally upon a much smaller scale than similar remains found in other parts of the interior; remains that cannot be accounted for by such an inadequate cause as the custom here mentioned. The soil of these prairies on the Mississippi is loose and friable. A tomahawk, a knife, or even a wooden ladle or shovel, with the hands, could excavate one of these defences in a short time. Small parties, thus ensconced, have been known to make successful resistance against superior numbers. The prudential warfare of the Indians, which is careful of life, and forbids open attacks, where victory, though certain, may be purchased dearly, renders these extemporaneous fortifications most available.*

On the 13th of September, the party reached *La Montagne que trempe à l'eau.* This remark-

---

* It is somewhere related by Mr. Schoolcraft, that a party of traitor Chippeways went out against the Sioux, under a vow not to return without scalps. They were unexpectedly attacked on a prairie, and eleven of them killed; when the twelfth succeeded in making for himself one of these burrows, and kept his enemies at bay until he could escape. Thus saving his life, and returning without a scalp, he was rejected and spurned by his relations and friends, until a scalp restored him to his standing.

able hill, which looks as if it had been violently separated from its kindred bluffs at hand, and shoved out into the river, has long attracted the attention of travellers. It is not far from Lake Pepin, which Lieutenant Pike reached on the 16th. This lake is merely a large dilatation of the Mississippi. Boats are there more than usually exposed in high winds. Lieutenant Pike's boats ran some risk in crossing it during a storm.

The party came to the St. Peter's on the 21st., where Lieutenant Pike held a council with several chiefs, whose tribes owned the lands in that region, and succeeded in obtaining a cession of one hundred thousand acres, worth, as our negotiator remarks, two hundred thousand dollars, for which he gave presents to the chiefs estimated at about two hundred dollars.* This was certainly driving a good bargain. In his letter to General Wilkinson, he says the purchase was made "for a song." But it is probable, that the Indians' estimate of the value of the land, that is, two cents an acre, was, at the time, as near the true value as that of Lieutenant Pike, which placed it at two dollars an acre.

Remaining at the mouth of the St. Peter's

---

* Fort Snelling stands on this purchase.

long enough to finish this negotiation, and to explain to the Indians the objects and policy of the United States with respect to them, Lieutenant Pike, having made a change in his craft better suited to the difficulties of the navigation above, reëmbarked his party, to ascend the river to its source. The Falls of St. Anthony, just above the St. Peter's, were passed around by a portage. These falls do not appear to have much attracted the notice of Lieutenant Pike, whose journal describes them as an impediment in the way of his progress, rather than as a beautiful and somewhat grand feature of the Mississippi. He states their perpendicular height to be about sixteen feet.

The party, being above the falls, recommenced its ascent, and found the navigation much embarrassed by ripples, rapids, and shoals. To a person less determined to advance, the river, no doubt, as Lieutenant Pike remarks, " would have been deemed impracticable." It was often necessary to wade, forcing the boats along, nearly the whole day. On the 16th of October, snow having fallen so as to cover the ground, he began to think of forming a winter station, where his boats, with a suitable guard, could be left behind, while he, with the rest, continued on in such a manner as better agreed with the season. Some of his men began to show symptoms of sickness, arising from their excessive fatigue and exposure; and he determined to form this establishment at once, on a spot which was two hundred and thirty-three miles above the Falls of St. Anthony. Accordingly, selecting a place which was convenient to trees suited for huts, and for constructing canoes, he came to a halt on that day.

From that date until the 28th of October, all hands were employed in hunting, erecting huts, and carving out canoes, the snow falling frequently. Two small canoes having been completed, they were launched, and loaded, in order for a departure, when that which contained the ammunition accidentally upset. This mishap induced Lieutenant Pike to defer his departure until another canoe could be made of a larger size, and less liable to such accidents. In the mean time, the wet ammunition was dried in the sun, but with a loss of five sixths of the quantity. This was a serious and irreparable misfortune, being still further aggravated the following day, by an attempt, rather an imprudent one, we should think, "to dry the powder in pots," which ended in an explosion, with a new loss of powder, but, fortunately, with no other injury.

While waiting for the completion of the new canoe, he enclosed his huts with pickets, in which, he says, he could have "laughed at the attack of eight hundred or a thousand savages." These finished, and feeling impatient to be moving, but still unprepared to start, his "books being packed," he found himself "powerfully attacked with the fantasies of the brain, called ennui;" during which state of his spirits, he says, he could easily conceive why persons in "remote places," fly to the bottle for relief. Lieutenant Pike, under such temptations, chose the better part of flying to the prairies at hand, and engaging in a few days' hunt after elks and buffaloes. He was then in a region where these animals herded in large numbers, and, while employed in the pursuit of such of them as were wounded, but continued to retreat some time after many balls had been lodged in their bodies, he found his mind braced up, and every cloudy humor chased from the brain. Indeed, no hungry and fatigued hunter ever complained of the megrims. The most chronic case of hypochondria would be cured by one wild chase on the western prairies. It makes the blood course through the veins with railroad speed, and the spirits do not lag behind. If it be made in the saddle, both horse and rider seem to be winged; if on foot, as Lieutenant Pike was, and the animal be wounded, miles shorten into furlongs, and furlongs into steps, until the game be overtaken.

The hunting party, led off by such ardent pursuits in different directions, got much scattered; some of the men lost their way, and considerable time was consumed in collecting them, and the game they had killed, at the camp. Ice had made in the river; and the cold had increased to such a degree, that many of the hunters returned frostbitten.

Having left his sergeant, and the invalids of his party, Lieutenant Pike started for the source of the Mississippi, on the 10th of December, taking one canoe, and some sleds, which would become necessary as soon as the river closed. The sleds were made to carry about four hundred pounds weight each, and to be drawn by two men, harnessed abreast. This was a new and hard duty for the men; but they appear to have cheerfully given themselves to it, their leader setting them an example in all species of endurance. The party moved at first by both methods, some of the men dragging the sleds, while others conducted the canoe. Both methods were beset with difficulties, the canoe often having to be lifted over and out of obstructions, and the sleds as often having to be drawn on the bare ground. Lieutenant Pike had a double task to perform. Generally, he walked ahead in pursuit of game, made fires, and occasionally retraced his steps, sometimes to extricate the canoe from shoals or rocks, sometimes to urge on the sleds, impeded by constant embarrassments.

The progress was necessarily slow, not amounting, on an average, for several days, to more than five miles a day. A serious accident happened to one of the sleds, which, in moving near the river, upset, and threw its load into the water. It bore Lieutenant Pike's baggage, and most of the ammunition. All the cartridges were destroyed, and some pounds of choice powder, which he had for his own use. This was truly a heavy disaster. The subsistence and safety of the party depended on its ammunition. Hence any large and unlooked-for diminution of it was a cause for distress and apprehension. Fortunately, the major part of it, notwithstanding this loss, was still in good order; else the expedition must have ended where the accident occurred.

A *cache* was made of a part of the stores. Much fresh meat had been obtained in hunting, and it was necessary, either to throw that away, or leave behind some of the pork and flour on hand, which would keep good until the return of the party. The *cache* is an expedient of the forest life. A hole is dug, and the articles intended to be left are deposited in it, carefully wrapped in skins, when it is covered, and various devices are adopted to conceal the place, since robbery would almost certainly follow a discovery. In the present instance, a fire was kindled immediately over the hole, which gave the spot the appearance of an ordinary encampment. The Indians, being aware of the extreme acuteness of their brethren in detecting signs of such deposits, are very adroit in removing all such signs. Canoes, with all their contents, are sometimes thus concealed beneath the surface of the earth, without leaving a mark which would betray to the most scrutinizing eye the locality. Much time and care are necessary, of course, to effect such a cautious work. But the Indians do everything with deliberation.

The canoe being now abandoned, all the baggage was put upon the sleds, which often broke, or got out of order, and the advance of the party was still slow and toilsome. On the 22d of December, Lieutenant Pike remarks, "Never did I undergo more fatigue, in performing the duties of hunter, spy, guide, and commanding officer; sometimes in front, sometimes in the rear, frequently in advance of my party ten or fifteen miles." On the 26th, he "broke four sleds; broke into the river four times; and had four carrying-places." He made, that day, only three miles. This day's incidents is a sample of most of the daily occurrences and mishaps. It required no ordinary spirit to persevere, under such discouraging circumstances. But, as the weather became colder, and the ice stronger, and the snows more abundant, the party moved on with greater ease, and with accelerated speed. Twenty miles were then occasionally passed over in a day.

On the 1st of January, 1806, he saw signs of Chippeways, whom the interpreter had led him to suspect of hostile designs towards the party. This was probably a Sioux prejudice, that nation and the Chippeways being irreconcilable enemies. At this time the interpreter repeated his caution to keep the party together. "But, notwithstanding this," says Lieutenant Pike, "I went on several miles further than usual, in order to make discoveries; conceiving the savages not so barbarous and ferocious, as to fire on two men, (I had one with me,) who were apparently coming into their country trusting to their generosity." Fortunately, this confidence in the generosity of the savages was not put to the test, which might have proved, that more discretion would have been the better part of his duty. When the Indians have a hostile design, they do not throw away any chances of success, which superiority of numbers gives them. A party was soon after met, consisting of four Chippeways, one Englishman, and one Frenchman. All was friendliness.

Lieutenant Pike's tent caught fire during the night, and was consumed, with much of his clothing and effects. Three small kegs of powder were in the tent; but, luckily, did not explode. The cold was now so severe, that "some of the men had their noses, others their fingers, and others their toes frozen." The party reached Sandy Lake on the 8th of January, where they were received in a British trading establishment, which had been there for some twelve years; and though in latitude forty-seven, potatoes were there raised. Fish and wild rice were also abundant. He states the price at which certain articles were sold at that station; namely, flour, at fifty cents a pound; salt, at one dollar a pound; pork, eighty cents; maple sugar, fifty cents. These prices would make flour cost nearly one hundred dollars a barrel; salt, nearly three hundred; pork, about one hundred and fifty. The expense of transporting these articles to that remote place, over such a route, must have been enormous; still, it may readily be supposed that the profits were more so.

He resumed his course for Leech Lake, on the 20th of January, which he reached, after great fatigue and privations, in twelve days. He found there another British trading establishment, and met with a hospitable reception.

At this place he addressed a letter to Mr. M'Gilles, the head of the North-West Company in that quarter, in which he stated the views of the United States' government, and the restraints which must be imposed on all who traded with the Indians within the acknowledged boundaries of the United States, requiring, very properly, that no flag should be hoisted within the same, but theirs. The traders evinced no disposition to contravene these requisitions.

Lieutenant Pike also visited Red Cedar Lake, which was then considered one of the sources of the Mississippi, and he held councils with the Indians of those regions, in which he explained the objects of his visit among them, and gave them fully to understand that they were thenceforward under the rule of the United States, and must look to them accordingly. It was, undoubtedly, important to the general government, that some such manifestation of its sovereignty should be made in that quarter; and, probably, no one could have made it with more spirit, dignity, and effect, than Lieutenant Pike. The Indians appear to have respected him, and to have shown a disposition to conform to his suggestions, as to their new duties. But it was obvious that any impressions he might make, during his short stay among them, would be transitory, as long as the traders among them were of a character to be liable, at any emergency, to mislead them by adverse influences. It might not be necessary, in order to promote their own interests, or the designs of their own government, that these traders should at all times exert such influences. But the time was likely to come, and it did come several years after Lieutenant Pike's visit, when they could be, and of course would be, exerted to the injury of the United States.*

He perceived the only effectual guard against such consequences, and, in his communications to his superiors, after his return, recommended its adoption by the government; that is, to establish military posts at certain points, with a view to displace, in a tangible manner, the old jurisdiction, and make the new one respected. The flag is an emblem that carries with it some moral authority, even among Indians. He made it respected, and made it exclusive, while he was in the Indian country; but he well knew that the only mode of making it permanently respected, and permanently predominant, was to raise it on a fort, garrisoned by troops, who could

---

* During the war of 1812, the warriors of this remote region were persuaded, nothing loath, to join in the contest, taking side with Great Britain, and assisting, most efficiently, in many battles, fought on grounds which were more than fifteen hundred miles from their usual wigwams.

protect it from insult, and see that it was supreme in its neighborhood. The times, however, were not, perhaps, propitious for any such recommendations. Certainly they were not adopted until years of costly experience, in the waste of blood and treasure, had convinced the whole country of their necessity.

Lieutenant Pike felt much exultation at finding himself at the source of the Mississippi; not that he regarded himself as a discoverer, but because he would, probably, present to the American public the first true account of its position. It had been evident that great misapprehensions prevailed on this subject. Even the high contracting parties of the treaty of 1783 had but vague notions respecting it. The postulates relating to it, in that treaty, were altogether erroneous. Lieutenant Pike returned, no doubt, with a belief that he had identified the true source. Other "true sources" have been found by subsequent travellers, and the last has gone a little beyond his precursors, and thus fancied himself entitled to the merit of being called the Bruce of the Mississippi. This may be; but it is probable that all have been right. It would be difficult to determine which branch of a large tree extends furthest from the parent root. It may be equally, or more so, to determine which of the many head branches of the Mississippi, that have been discovered, is the most remote from the Gulf of Mexico; and the initial gush of its waters undoubtedly varies. A wet season may open many small tributaries to a small lake, which had no existence in a dry season. Hence the spring traveller, and the traveller of the summer solstice, may have different descriptions to give, and yet both be correct.

Having fulfilled his purposes at the headwaters of the Mississippi, Lieutenant Pike left them, on his return down the river, on the 18th of February; not precisely retracing his steps, as he wished to spread out his examinations, and he thus left behind many stores which he had deposited at Sandy Lake. He did not regard this as an inconvenience at the time, though subsequent events proved it to be such. But he found his *cache*, made the preceding December, all safe; and, thus recruited for his journey, he continued on, and reached his stockade, where he had left his sergeant and a small party, a few months before. This sergeant had proved faithless to his trust, and, during the absence of his commanding officer, had used up, in the language of the journal, "all the elegant hams and saddles of venison, which had been preserved for the commander-in-chief and other friends," and had made way with all the whisky, including a keg for Lieutenant Pike's "own use," and had also sold a barrel of pork.

This was a hard case, as no punishment of the delinquent could restore the missing supplies, which were the more necessary now, since the deposit at Sandy Lake had been left behind. Nevertheless, he was reduced to the ranks; and the party resumed its course down the river, on the 7th of April, having been obliged to await the breaking up of the ice, in order that it might embark in boats. The Falls of St. Anthony were reached on the 10th. Meeting at the mouth of the St. Peter's many Indians, who had assembled in expectation of his coming, he made further explanations of the views of the United States' government, and received from most of them satisfactory evidences of a friendly disposition.

During this intercourse with the Indians, their strongest and most incessant demand always appeared to be for whisky, or ardent spirits; and Lieutenant Pike was prepared to answer it on all suitable occasions, notwithstanding the faithlessness of his sergeant at the winter stockade, whose depredations on this article of the stores left in his charge probably excited more regret at the time, than is now felt by those who look at his journal.

When the United States were about beginning their relations with these remote tribes, it would have been well to adopt, in the outset, a rule of intercourse, in this respect, corresponding with the benevolent intent of their laws, which were designed to suppress the use of ardent spirits among the savages. Had the first public messenger to them appeared without any of this deleterious supply, they might at once have been made to comprehend the policy and wishes of their new father. This messenger, thus unfurnished, might not have found himself as welcome at all times, nor been able to relieve his wants so readily, as if he held in his hand this potent wand, which opens all doors, and answers all demands. Still, he would have stood consistently before them, as the representative of a government, which professed a wish and design to rescue them from the effects of this great evil.

It may be doubtful whether any law, any lets or hinderances, can shut out this bane from the forest, which must always be accessible to the devices of cupidity. No guards nor penalties can keep out individual enterprise, which has a wide frontier for its operations, and where impunity is more probable than detection, and where the penalties that follow the violation of the laws are as feathers in the balance with a successful evasion. But government can at all times mark its own intercourse by a strict adherence to the spirit of its laws and policy. Its officers and its agents might have been, from the beginning, prohibited from administering any fuel to this consuming fire. So far, at least, the country could have been consistent, and would have been blameless.

The party reached Prairie du Chien on the 18th of April, and St. Louis the 30th, having been absent eight months and twenty-two days.

CHAPTER III.

Expedition to the Sources of the Red River.— Leaves St. Louis and ascends the Missouri in Boats.— Osage Indians.— Pawnees.— He reaches the Head-Waters of the Arkansas River.— Hunting Buffaloes.— Disasters and Sufferings of his Party among the Mountains.— He builds a Fort.— Taken by the Spaniards, and conducted to Santa Fe.

LIEUTENANT PIKE was not allowed to remain long inactive. The satisfactory manner in which he had accomplished the objects of his expedition up the Mississippi led General Wilkinson to select him, not many months after his return, for another and more arduous and important expedition. The primary object of this second expedition, as Lieutenant Pike's instructions set forth, was to restore certain Osage captives, recently recovered from the Pottawatimies, to their homes on the Grand Osage. The second object was to effect a permanent peace between the Kansas and Osage nations. The third object was of a more considerable magnitude, according to General Wilkinson's statement. It was "to effect an interview and establish a good understanding with the Yanctons, Tetans, or Camanches." As this attempt was to lead him to the head branches of the Arkansas and Red Rivers, where he would find himself "approximated to the settlements of New Mexico," he was required "to move with great circumspection, to keep clear of any hunting or reconnoitring parties from that province, and to prevent alarm or offence."

He was moreover instructed "to remark particularly upon the geographical structure, the natural history and population of the country" through which he passed, and "to collect and preserve specimens of the mineral and botanical worlds; to regulate all his courses by the compass, and distances by the watch; to ascertain the variations of the needle, the latitudes with exactness, and to employ his telescope in observing the eclipses of Jupiter's satellites." These were certainly ample instructions, and implied an expectation of large results. Whether the outfit was in accordance with these multifarious duties, it is not stated. If he had occasion to note the accumulation of his tasks in the previous expedition, far greater had he in this; but a professional gentleman, Dr. Robinson, was connected with his party this time, as a volunteer, who would be likely to relieve the commanding officer of a part of his burden. Another lieutenant was also attached to the party; which consisted, besides, of one sergeant, two corporals, sixteen privates, and an interpreter. The Indians accompanying it were fifty-one Osages and Pawnees

Embarking at St. Louis, on the 15th of July, 1806, Lieutenant Pike proceeded up the Missouri in two large boats, and about the middle of August reached the Osage country, where the redeemed captives were restored to their relatives and friends. Thus the first object of the expedition was fulfilled.

Leaving his boats and the water route at the Osage towns, he prepared for a land route. On the 1st of September, he set off, having some thirty Indian warriors to accompany him; and on the sixth day, he crossed the ridge that divides the waters which run into the Missouri on one side, and the Arkansas on the other. The view from this ridge he describes as being sublime, the prairie rising and falling in regular swells, as far as the eye can reach.

He came to the Pawnee towns about the 1st of October, and found the Indians rather unfriendly. Spanish predilections were strong among them, and it was with reluctance they consented to substitute the American for the Spanish flag. When he left the Pawnee towns to proceed onwards, threats were thrown out that the Indians would forcibly prevent the march of the party, and it required all his firmness and prudence to avert their hostile designs. It is probable, that nothing but the spirit and determination he evinced in his intercourse with them, and particularly his indifference to all their unfriendly manifestations, saved his little party from being destroyed among those remote and suspicious bands.

It was at these towns that he found indisputable evidences of a recent visit by a detachment of Spanish or Mexican troops, amounting to about three hundred. He attributed the reception he met with to the influences this strong party had left behind. It was natural that the Indians, who judge by appearances, should have held in much higher respect a nation that exhibited before them such marks of its power, than one whose first assumption of sovereignty over them was enforced by such insignificant means; the one nation long known; the other then known, perhaps, for the first time, except through vague and unfriendly reports. Lieutenant Pike was obviously becoming surrounded with difficulties and hazards, as he advanced into this wide-spread interior, filled with strong and warlike bands, under such adverse contiguity and associations. But he permitted nothing to delay his progress, or check him in the fulfilment of his instructions; and his character and conduct imposed a restraint on the hostile Indians near his path.

He reached the Arkansas River on the 18th of October, at a point where the stream was not more than twenty feet wide, when he first struck it, though the rains of the two following days spread it over a bottom of four hundred and fifty yards in width. Here Lieutenant Wilkinson was detached, according to instructions, in canoes made on the spot, with seven of the party, to descend the Arkansas to the military post on its lower waters, taking with him twenty-one days' provision.*

---

* Lieutenant Wilkinson reached that post on the 9th of January following.

After passing the Arkansas, Lieutenant Pike first notices the wild horses; those animals, which probably descended from Cortes's Andalusians. In their wild state, they appear to be the wildest of wild animals. Snow and ice then also made their appearance; an early day for that latitude, if the position of the party had not been in a highly elevated region. Buffaloes were in abundance. Lieutenant Pike represents them as covering the face of the country. Three thousand, he thinks, were often in one view. Of course his party were not in want of provisions. Much salt was also observed; the best condiment for their fresh meat.

On the 15th of November, the blue peaks of the Mexican mountains were descried; and, two days afterwards, a number of Pawnees came upon the party, and were guilty of some rudeness; stole a few articles, and would probably have proceeded to extremities, had not Lieutenant Pike showed a determination to resist any further encroachments.

He was now ascending the branches of the Arkansas, and, near the heads of them, he threw up a small breastwork for the protection of his men, and then proceeded, with Dr. Robinson and two privates, towards the mountains, which had been so long in view, in order to ascertain more truly their character and position. During this excursion, he endured much suffering from cold and exhaustion. Snow and ice continually impeded his progress, and one of his men became frost-bitten. He ascended one of the peaks with great toil, whence he had a view of the Grand Peak, some fifteen miles distant. His measurements determined the altitude of the latter peak to be more than eighteen thousand feet above the level of the sea.

His movements, after his return to his party, were, for some days, in a wilderness of mountains. His object was to gain the Red River. The horses were daily giving out, and everything was in doubt and perplexity. The courses of the streams were not such as he had been led to anticipate, and the trace of the Mexican detachment, which he had been endeavoring to follow to within a suitable distance of Santa Fe, now eluded his search amid the snows that covered the ground. His party suffered the more from the inadequacy of their clothing. Lieutenant Pike himself, when ascending the mountains crowned with perpetual snows, had on only summer clothing.

At last, giving up all pursuit of the Mexican trace, and having reconnoitred the country from a high ridge, he resolved to bear south-west, supposing that such a course would enable him to strike the head-waters of the Red River.

He at length came to a river, which was taken to be that river, and the party continued to follow its course, partly on the ice, which frequently gave way, and partly on the banks, which were broken and precipitous, and destructive to the few horses that remained, now worn down with extreme fatigue and want of provender.

On the 4th of January, 1807, finding himself beset with embarrassments, in want of subsistence, and uncertain what course ought to be pursued, he divided his party into subdivisions of two men, each with a sled, and with directions to follow in the same track. Those who preceded were to leave, in some conspicuous place, all the surplus meat collected. This arrangement, he supposed, would enable the more active to succeed better in their hunts, and thus relieve those who were sinking with discouragement and exhaustion. Dr. Robinson and one private led the way, Lieutenant Pike following alone. Their course was along the banks of the stream, which were very precipitous, and were ascended with extreme difficulty, whenever the weakness or broken state of the ice drove them to the land.

Some days of fruitless fatigue, and nights of extreme suffering from cold and abstinence, were passed by the party in this segregated state, Dr. Robinson and Lieutenant Pike making unwearied exertions to obtain food when a reunion took place; the latter having ascertained, by observations from an elevated ridge, that the party was still in the neighborhood of the Arkansas, and not far from the spot it had left about one month before. This proof, that so much time had been vainly spent in painful wanderings, depressed the spirits of the men, and greatly perplexed their commander.

At last, after due deliberation, he determined to construct a small place of defence and deposit, where the horses, part of the baggage, the interpreter, and one man, might be left; while the rest, loaded with the remaining baggage, and crossing the mountains on foot, should seek out the Red River; sending back a party to bring up the rear, as soon as that object had been attained. In pursuance of this plan, all were set diligently to work, some in raising a block-house, some in hunting; and, on the 14th of January, the party destined to move on, consisting of twenty persons, set out on its search, each one, officer and doctor, as well as the rest, carrying a weight of about seventy pounds. This was a Roman soldier's load, and it required a Roman's spirit of endurance to bear this and the other heavy burden of ills, that weighed down the body and mind of most of the detachment.

On the 17th, having wet their feet, and the

night becoming very cold, nine out of the party found their feet frozen in the morning. This misfortune embraced the two hunters of the party. The next day, two of the best men, who were uninjured, were sent out in quest of game, while the commander and Dr. Robinson, who were also uninjured, took another direction, with the same object in view. These two gentlemen, though one buffalo was wounded with three balls, were unable to secure any meat the first two days they were out, making now four days of fast; and, worn down with hunger and fruitless strivings, they had sought a point of woods where they were likely to find their graves, when a buffalo fortunately passed by and was killed. This was a relief to the whole party, which else had probably perished, as no other success had been met with.

But, when it was determined to move forward again, it was discovered that two of the men were so much disabled by the frost, as to be without power of marching any further. This case presented a sad dilemma. It was necessary to move on, and these cripples must be left behind. All that could be done was done by Lieutenant Pike. He delayed one day, during which he provided everything in his power for their comfort and subsistence, taking with his party only one meal out of the stores on hand,

and then continued his journey. The snow was from two to three feet deep.

The second day after leaving these two men, having been unable to kill any thing, Lieutenant Pike and Dr. Robinson left the sergeant and the rest of the men to follow more at leisure, and pushed ahead, in the hope of providing something for their subsistence, the party being now utterly destitute. A violent snow-storm came on, which made all their exertions vain, and they lay down at night, overcome with hunger and fatigue, and painfully anxious for the men in the rear. The next morning, they had the satisfaction of finding them alive, though scarcely able to move through the drifting snows. To add to their despair, the buffaloes, their only resource, appeared to have quitted the plains, and it was necessary to pursue them into the mountains. It was under these discouraging circumstances, that one of the men uttered, for the first time, a loud murmur of discontent in the presence of Lieutenant Pike, who passed it by for the moment, intending to notice it at a more favorable season.

To pursue the buffaloes into the mountains, was a task beyond the strength of any of the party excepting Pike and Robinson, who undertook the task with all the strength and energy they had. Dr. Robinson succeeded in shooting one down, which saved the party. When this welcome relief had restored the men to some degree of health and spirits, Lieutenant Pike called the murmurer before him, and gave him a severe admonition, stating to him, that, while the sufferings which fell on the party were equally shared, there was no just cause of complaint, and that any new instance of such misconduct would be punished with "instant death." Such a threat may seem severe to those, who are unacquainted with the difficulties and perils, which surround a party thus removed from all coöperation and law, and where an absolute exercise of authority is necessary to its preservation.*

The extremity to which the party had been reduced determined Lieutenant Pike not to move again without some supply of meat on hand. Accordingly, he remained stationary until three buffaloes had been secured, a portion of which was

---

* We recollect to have conversed, a few years since, with a distinguished trapper, who had risen from his perilous labors among the Rocky Mountains to wealth and high political standing, on the subject of the customs which governed parties far beyond the pale of law and civilization. He said, such had a law onto themselves; that the leader inflicted even death, in a summary manner, in extreme cases, where the general safety demanded it. Judgment and execution were like the lightning and the thunderbolt. The necessity must, however, be strong, overruling, and inevitable.

left with another frozen man, who was unable at this time to move any further, but who was to be taken up when the other two were sent for. This most painful necessity of thus leaving his men scattered in the wilderness, in a crippled state, greatly aggravated the condition of Lieutenant Pike. After encountering many obstacles, he reached a stream, which, from its course, he concluded to be the Red River; upon which the party encamped in a joyful mood, supposing the uncertainty of their locality at last to be ended. A place of defence was planned, and to be constructed, in which four or five men could resist a *coup de main*, while the others went back for the unfortunate men left behind.

Several days were consumed in finishing this work, when Dr. Robinson, in pursuance of a previously concerted scheme, set out alone for Santa Fe. This extraordinary journey, undertaken in such an unprotected manner, and without any distinct idea of the bearing and distance of that place from Lieutenant Pike's present encampment, showed a spirit of enterprise and hardihood, that rendered Dr. Robinson a worthy coadjutor of his principal in this perilous expedition. It appears, by a note of explanation by Lieutenant Pike in his journal, that a claim on some merchant of Santa Fe had been put into his hands to collect, should a fitting opportunity for doing so occur. It was transferred to Dr. Robinson, who was to make it a pretext for a visit to the place, and a cover for observing its trade and resources, for the benefit of his countrymen. He regarded the excursion as a romantic adventure, and in that mood detached himself from the protection of his friend and commanding officer.

While Lieutenant Pike was thus engaged, and when on a short hunting range, with only one man in company, he was unexpectedly encountered by two horsemen, with whom, as it was too late to avoid them, he, after much shyness on their part, opened a parley. They proved to be a Spanish dragoon and a civilized Indian, from Santa Fe, who informed him, that Dr. Robinson had reached that place in safety, and had been kindly received by the Governor there. They showed a determination to ascertain where his camp was, and, being under an impression that it was on the Red River, and, of course, within the acknowledged boundaries of the United States, he thought it best to conduct them to it without hesitation. After making what observation they could, and without undeceiving Lieutenant Pike as to his actual position, they left him, saying that his camp was two days' journey only from Santa Fe.

Deeming it necessary, after this visit, to hasten

the completion of his defensive works, Lieutenant Pike, immediately after their departure, pushed on his labors with increased zeal. The next day, the party which he had sent back for the disabled men returned, bringing with them only the man last left, the other two being still unable to move. The latter were found in a very crippled state, some of the bones of their feet having come out. When once more left to their hard fate, they abandoned themselves to despair; though assured that every exertion would be made for their relief. And the commander immediately concerted measures for this purpose, by sending a party for his horses and the two men left with them, which was to take these men up on its return. A sergeant and one man volunteered for this arduous journey, which was more than one hundred and eighty miles out, and over two ridges of mountains covered with snow, besides being beset by unfriendly savages, and the hazard of perishing of want, as they took with them only ten pounds of venison.

Having established a watch for the return of any suspicious party, it was reported, on the 26th of February, that strangers were approaching. Soon after, two Frenchmen arrived, who said that the Governor of Santa Fe, hearing that some Indians were about to attack Lieutenant

Pike, had detached an officer, with fifty dragoons, for his protection; and that the detachment would be there in two days. It was soon manifest, that a part of this report was incorrect, as the dragoons, with about the same number of mounted militia, made their appearance in a few hours. The sentinel on post required them to halt at the distance of fifty yards, when the Frenchmen were sent out to inform the commanding officer, that Lieutenant Pike would meet him on the prairie at hand, and hear the object of his visit. The meeting took place accordingly, when Lieutenant Pike invited the two officers of the detachment to return with him into his fort, leaving the troops where they were. This arrangement was complied with, and the two Lieutenants accompanied him to his little block-house.

Lieutenant Pike was then informed by the commanding officer, that the Governor of Santa Fe, hearing that he had lost his route, had sent him to offer such assistance as might be necessary to enable him to reach the Red River, the navigable parts of which, for boats, were eight days' journey from Santa Fe. This was the first intimation that the party was not already on that river, and Lieutenant Pike was surprised to learn, on further inquiry, that his little fort was upon the Rio del Norte, within the bounds of Mexico. This explanation was followed by a polite hint, that the Governor wished to see him at Santa Fe, in order the more fully to understand the cause of his having thus taken military possession of Spanish ground. Regarding this as a step that could not be avoided under the circumstances, and having reason to think that the show of courtesy only disguised a peremptory order, he resolved, at once, to proceed to Santa Fe, to explain, personally, the cause of his involuntary intrusion upon the Mexican soil; having first required that an interpreter and an escort should remain at his station, to meet his sergeant and men who were expected from the other stations.

Escorted by the dragoons, he set out the next day for Santa Fe, which he reached on the 3d of March, having passed through several villages, one called *Agua Caliente*, and another San Juan, the former with a population of about five hundred, the latter, from one to two thousand. He found Santa Fe with a population of about four thousand five hundred.

CHAPTER IV.

Sent to the Interior of New Mexico. — Deprived of his Papers. — Returns to the United States through Texas. — Commendation of his Services by the Secretary at War. — Burr's Conspiracy. — Pike prepares a Narrative of his Expeditions.

THE Governor, after being convinced of his public character and honorable purposes, treated him with civility and hospitality, but informed him that both he and his papers must be sent to Chihuahua, to appear before the commandant general there. Lieutenant Pike protested against this compulsory diversion from his route, but left Santa Fe, under an escort, the 4th of March, 1807. His route soon led through a country, which was cultivated and populous. Many thriving villages were seen, and many caravans met, which showed the character of the business in that region. One of these caravans had fifteen thousand sheep, which were to be exchanged in the lower provinces for merchandise. Another caravan was returning from those provinces, having two hundred horses loaded with goods for New Mexico

Reaching the Passo del Norte on the 21st

of March, the party put up at the house of Don Francisco Garcia, who was a merchant and a planter. Lieutenant Pike mentions some of the possessions of this wealthy Mexican, among which were twenty thousand sheep, and one thousand cows. Soon after leaving this place, he saw a Mexican paper, which gave an account of Burr's conspiracy. This afforded a clew to the suspicions, with which his movements on the Mexican frontier had most naturally been regarded. It was not surprising that he should have been looked upon, as forming one of the ramifications of the revolutionary scheme, which that distinguished individual had projected.

On the 2d of April, he reached Chihuahua, where he was questioned, and his papers examined, with much scrutiny, by the commandant general, with whom, however, he fully asserted his dignity, and the rights that belonged to him as a citizen of an independent state. It was true, that he had been found, with a belligerent aspect, in the Mexican country; but his apology was ready, and, no doubt, acceptable; while he knew that the Mexican authorities had lately violated, in a similar way, the soil of the United States, for which no apology could be rendered. He very properly alluded to this circumstance, in his interview with the Mexican functionaries; not to vindicate himself, but to let them know that their want of scruple in this respect was well understood.

After a few days, it was determined by the commandant general that Lieutenant Pike should be permitted to return to his country, but without his papers, and also by such route as should be prescribed to him. He set off from Chihuahua, under an escort, for the province of Texas, thence to reach the United States' military post on the Lower Red River; having received an intimation, that he must make no astronomical observations, nor take any notes. The latter prohibition was dexterously evaded, his memoranda, set down at opportune moments, being stowed away in the gun-barrels of his men. This was a very safe place, provided there was likely to be no occasion to discharge the guns; and such a likelihood was very improbable.

The route lay through a country mostly cultivated, with many evidences of wealth. At one place, a proprietor had one hundred thousand sheep, cattle, and horses. The heat was intense; but, at all the *Haciendas*, the most delicious and refreshing fruit was found. As an instance of the arrangement of property in that region, in those days, he speaks of the Hacienda de Patos, belonging to the Marquis de San Miguel, who maintained fifteen hundred troops, to protect his vassals and property from the savages.

Passing through San Antonio, crossing the Brazos and the Trinity, and continuing his route by way of Nacogdoches, he reached Natchitoches on the 1st of July, 1807, having been absent on his tour nearly one year. It had been full of difficulties, dangers, and responsibilities; all of which he had met with energy, firmness, and discretion. His misapprehensions of the geography of the country, which led him to establish himself, in such a suspicious manner, on a foreign river, were excusable, bewildered as he was among mountains and streams that were likely to confuse all calculations. Still, it was natural for the Mexican authorities to regard his conduct, at first, as the result of a design, rather than a mistake, particularly when taken in connection with Colonel Burr's contemporaneous movements; and their treatment of him must be considered, under the circumstances, as having been marked by much moderation.

From the *Passo del Norte* to Nacogdoches, he passed through a country which has since risen to much notoriety as Texas. His visit was made some four or five years after the acquisition of Louisiana.

He does not appear to have seen any evidences, that the country deemed itself in any manner connected with that purchase. On the contrary, the population was thoroughly Spanish and Mexican in all its feelings and relations. He occasionally heard expressions that indicated dissatisfaction with the government, as it then existed, and which were a prelude to that revolution which overturned the metropolitan or European rule, without, however, having the remotest bearing upon an incorporation with Louisiana.

Lieutenant Pike was welcomed back to the United States, after his long and perilous tour, by all his friends, and by none of them with more cordiality than by General Wilkinson. In a letter addressed to him from New Orleans, that general says, "After having counted you among the dead, I was most agreeably surprised to find, by a letter from General Calcedo, (the commandant general at Chihuahua,) received a few days since, that you were in his possession, and that he proposed sending you, with your party, to our frontier post. I lament that you should lose your papers, but shall rely much on your memory; and although it was unfortunate that you should have headed the Red River, and missed the object of your enterprise, yet I promise myself that the route over which you passed will afford some interesting scenes." General Wilkinson adds, that it had been asserted that the enterprise, in which he had been engaged, "was a premeditated coöperation with Burr."

He was now promoted to the rank of Captain.

As soon as practicable, he digested his memoranda into a proper state for publication, and presented to the government, the following year, his "Geographical, Statistical, and General Observations on the Interior Provinces of New Spain," which, when published, were favorably received; together with a similar report of his expedition up the Mississippi. The Secretary at War, then General Dearborn, wrote to him on the 24th of February, 1808, and said, "I can with pleasure inform you, that, although the two expeditions you have performed were not previously ordered by the President of the United States, there were frequent communications on the subject of each, between General Wilkinson and this department, with which the President of the United States was, from time to time, made acquainted; and it will be no more than what justice requires, to say, that your conduct, in each of these expeditions, met the approbation of the President; and that the information you obtained and communicated to the Executive, in relation to the source of the Mississippi and the natives in that quarter, and the country generally, as well on the Upper Mississippi as that between the Arkansas and the Missouri,* and on the borders of

* There is probably a mistake here, as Pike did not visit the sources of the Missouri. Perhaps the Arkansas is intended. But we have copied General Dearborn's letter, as published in the Appendix to the Expedition.

the latter extensive river to its source, and the country adjacent, has been considered highly interesting, in a political, geographical, and historical point of view. And you may be assured, that your services are held in high estimation by the President of the United States; and if any opinion of my own can afford you any satisfaction, I very frankly declare, that I consider the public much indebted to you for the enterprising, persevering, and judicious manner, in which you have performed them."

This strong language is high praise from one, who was habitually chary of commendation. Nor was it undeserved. At the time Captain Pike explored those regions of our wide-spread interior, almost nothing authentic was known of them. More satisfactory information respecting the head-waters of the Mississippi, than was then in possession of the public, was highly desirable; and his narratives relating to them were read with interest. But his accounts of the Mexican territories were looked for with much more eagerness, and, when they came out, were received with avidity. The jealous policy of Spain had surrounded her provinces with guards and restraints, that rendered them almost inaccessible. Their condition and prospects were veiled from all foreign observation; and at the time Captain Pike obtained, through an unintentional aberration from his prescribed route, access to them, unusual attention was turned upon the Mexican country by the events of Burr's conspiracy.

This extraordinary transaction had awakened an intense curiosity respecting a region, which was known to abound with gold, and which precious metal was supposed to have been its ultimate object. The trial of Colonel Burr was beginning, or in progress, when Captain Pike returned, and was known to have visited the *El Dorado*, on which this individual was said to have fixed an eye of cupidity and ambition. Scarcely anything had been heard of Mexico since the conquest of Cortes, excepting vague reports of the unbounded wealth that flowed from its mines into the public and private coffers of Spain. It is not strange, then, that Captain Pike's tour through some of its provinces should have been regarded as a rare and most opportune work. His statements were, of course, founded on hasty and imperfect observations, it being obvious from his journal, that, from the time he left Santa Fe, until he reached the United States boundary, he was under a *surveillance*, and could take notes only by stealth. He could neither survey attentively what passed beneath his eye, nor inquire about that which he did not see, without exciting suspicion, and provoking rebuke. Still, with an acute eye, and a retentive memory, he appears to have gathered up many new and interesting facts, that were well received at the time.

From the brief analysis of Captain Pike's journal, which has been here introduced, it is evident that the whole party suffered greatly throughout the latter part of the route; and it was deemed a proper subject of recommendation to Congress, that some remuneration should be made to both officers and men. On the 7th of December, 1808, the Secretary at War made a special communication to the House of Representatives, in which their "meritorious services" were stated, with a view of leading to some such reasonable compensation. Although the subject was frequently brought before Congress in the shape of favorable reports, it does not appear that any act passed; and it is probable that General Pike fell in the field, while these arduous services of himself and his men were still unrequited. The neglect of himself may have weighed lightly on his mind, as the credit he had acquired must have gratified, and perhaps may have satisfied, his ambition; but the recollection of his followers, some of whom were probably crippled for life, even if they survived the abandonment to which they had necessarily been subjected, must have been a thorn in his generous bosom.

CHAPTER V.

War of 1812. — *Pike promoted to the Command of a Regiment.* — *Stationed on Lake Champlain.* — *Plan of Operations for the Campaign of* 1813 *on Lake Ontario.* — *Pike promoted to the Rank of Brigadier-General.* — *Remarks on the Military Operations.*

CAPTAIN PIKE was promoted to the rank of Major in the infantry in 1809, and, in the following year, to that of Lieutenant-Colonel in the fourth regiment of infantry. Being detained by services in the south-west, he was not with that distinguished regiment at the battle of Tippecanoe.

In 1812, the rupture with Great Britain, which had long been imminent, occurred, and an additional force was raised by Congress to meet the new demands for national defence, which that event produced. While still a Lieutenant-Colonel, the appointment of Deputy-Quarter-Master was conferred upon Pike, and in July, 1812, he was raised to the rank of Colonel of infantry, being soon after arranged to the fifteenth regiment. Among the most conspicuous, active, and ambitious of the young officers, who had attained that rank, he assumed the charge of that regiment, with great zeal for the service, and a strong desire to prepare it for distinction in the approaching campaigns.

General Dearborn, who had, while Secretary at War, well known, and often acknowledged, his merits and services in more subordinate grades, being now the senior Major-General of the army, and in immediate command on the northern frontier, where the fifteenth regiment was stationed, placed much reliance on Colonel Pike and his regiment. During the winter of 1812 and 1813, considerable preparation was made on both sides of the St. Lawrence and Lake Ontario for hostile movements. The operations of the preceding season had issued in little more than fruitless or idle demonstrations. Without any fitness for offensive action by their condition as to discipline, portions of the troops had been frequently thrown upon or over the boundary line, without any definite or attainable objects in view, raising the public mind with expectations only to depress it again with disappointment. Invasions of Canada were projected here and there, and even conquests of it confidently predicted, until army movements in that quarter excited little other feeling than distrust or ridicule.

While the rigors of winter still prevailed, Colonel Pike was placed by General Dearborn on Lake Champlain, with about twenty-five hundred

men, to be in readiness for any operations that
expediency might suggest. The war department had indicated objects for attack, such as
the Isle au Noix, Kingston, and other places,
which were regarded as within the means at
General Dearborn's command. This officer, however, although having numerically a large force,
had not been led, by the result of some small
trials that had been made of it in the face of
the enemy, to rely much upon its steadiness in
the hour of action. He well knew the character
of the militia, and that even his regulars were
such hardly more than in name. A block-house,
occupied by two companies of British militia and
a few Indians, had been surrounded by a large
force, consisting of some two regiments; still the
garrison made its escape, cutting its way through
our troops with little or no loss. A coöperating
party of Americans arriving soon after this escape, a scene of confusion is said to have ensued,
in which friends were mistaken for foes and fired
upon as such, and which showed how undisciplined and ineffective these troops were.

A few such unsuccessful and somewhat disgraceful experiments suggested the propriety of
abstaining from active operations for a time, until
the regiments were better fitted for the field.
Indeed, the precipitation of these hostile measures
on the frontier carried their own inevitable pun-

ishment with them. They could hardly have been successful, unless the enemy had been equally rash and unprepared; upon which no reasonable calculation could be made. The irruption of Major Forsyth, an officer of many high partisan qualities, was an exception, as he succeeded in crossing the St. Lawrence, and capturing some few troops and stores; but a retaliatory stroke immediately followed upon Ogdensburg, which, besides expelling Major Forsyth from the place, ended in captures and seizures that nearly balanced the losses and gains.

The war department, having determined to substitute, for these desultory and disjointed demonstrations and irruptions, the plan of a campaign that had more consistency, connection, and probable feasibility, laid down, early in the winter of 1813, a system of operations, which had for its first objects, on the St. Lawrence and Lake Ontario frontier, the reduction of all the British posts in that quarter. The capture of Kingston was pointed out as a leading measure. It was proposed to attack that place during the winter, provided the snow and ice threw no obstacle in the way. The latter, it was thought, would facilitate it; and thus a most important preliminary step would be taken in advance of the opening of the navigation. Many considerations favored such a plan. The winter garrison of

Kingston was supposed to be small, the season affording a probable security against any hostile designs.

Our troops at Sacket's Harbor were not of a number to cause alarm from that quarter, or lead to efforts to reënforce Kingston from below. The forces on Lake Champlain kept the British troops on the Lower St. Lawrence stationary there, as the threatening appeared to be directed below rather than above. By putting this command, consisting of more than two thousand men, in sleighs, it could be rapidly transported to the foot of Lake Ontario, before any counteracting movement could be made by the enemy. To be prepared for all emergencies, and for failure in the amount of transportation of this kind, Colonel Pike had shod his own regiment with snow-shoes, that they might be able to move on foot in any depth of snow.*

---

* Early in the spring of 1813, about the time that many officers were collected in Albany, on their route to the frontiers, a party of them was at Colonel Bomford's, where General Dearborn then quartered, when, allusion being made to Colonel Pike's new mode of shoeing his regiment, the Major-General undertook to exemplify the manner in which, while drilling the men thus shod, they were brought to the "'bout face," jumping up some ten or twelve inches from the floor, and coming down again, faced to the rear, with a shock (for he weighed some two hundred and fifty pounds) that greatly disturbed and endangered (as Mrs.

In pursuance of this plan, General Dearborn, some time in February, was concerting measures to throw, with promptitude, the Champlain troops upon the Upper St. Lawrence, and, at the same time, to concentrate other forces at Sacket's Harbor for coöperation. It was intended to remove his head-quarters suddenly from Albany to the latter place, a report being spread in advance, that fears were entertained for its safety; thus giving the concentration a defensive character, when its real objects were offensive. But, before these measures had been completed, General Dearborn became alarmed himself, as it appears from his despatches of the 3d of March from Sacket's Harbor; Sir George Prevost, the Governor-General of the Canadas, in the mean time, having abruptly prorogued the legislature then in session at Montreal, and moved up to Kingston with reënforcements, amounting, as General Dearborn writes, to several thousand men. This reversed the aspect of affairs, and General Dearborn confined himself to exertions for the security of Sacket's Harbor, giving up all hostile intentions against Kingston, until the fleet could be out in the spring.*

Bomford afterwards laughingly said) the china and other brittle wares in a closet below.

* General Armstrong, then Secretary at War, in his "History of the War of 1812," says, that Sir George brought

Colonel Pike was appointed, by the President,[*] a Brigadier-General, towards the last of February, 1813, and became the most prominent officer among the troops with which General Dearborn proposed to open the campaign. The general relied much on his zeal and gallantry, as well as other high qualities. In the despatch above referred to, General Dearborn says, "I should feel easier if Colonel Pike should arrive in season. I am in want of officers of experience."

The plan of attacking Kingston over the ice having been abandoned, the alternative presented by the Secretary at War then engaged all the attention of General Dearborn, that is, as soon as the fleet of Commodore Chauncy could sail from Sacket's Harbor, to reduce, in succession, the British posts on the borders of Lake Ontario. The Secretary at War had indicated these posts in the following order; "Kingston and York on Lake Ontario, and Forts George and Erie on the Niagara;" the attacks to follow each other according to that enumeration.

This order was not strictly followed by General Dearborn, who determined to make Kingston the last object of attack, instead of the first.

---

up few troops with him to Kingston, and countervailed his antagonist only by dextcrous and well-timed reports.

[*] The appointment did not go before the Senate in time to be confirmed before General Pike fell.

This change, however, did not vary the probable results. It was a question only as to what course would be most likely to bring into full and timely operation all the means on Lake Ontario necessary to produce those results. During the winter, while the force at Kingston was comparatively small, an attack on the ice might have been adventured with such troops as were at Sacket's Harbor, or within a few days' reach of it. Such an attack, avoiding, as it probably would have done, the harbor, would have left the fleet there, excepting its sailors and marines, nearly or quite inoperative; and the town once occupied, and the harbor defences taken in reverse, those defences, and the fleet itself, assailed in an unexpected and therefore vulnerable quarter, might have fallen an easy prey. But the proper season for this kind of attack having been permitted to pass away, it was probably deemed unwise to make an attempt with only the same forces, when the fleet of Sir James Yeo, let loose from the bonds of winter, and nearly ready for sea, greatly increased the strength of the place, and multiplied the chances of a failure on the part of the assailants.

Considering that the object to be attained was the capture of all the posts on Lake Ontario, and that, if this were done, the rotation of attack was of subordinate importance, General Dearborn concluded, after mature reflection, and consultation with Commodore Chauncy, to make York (Toronto) the first point of attack. It was obvious that the enemy's arrangements could undergo no change. He was inevitably held in suspense as to his opponent's purposes, and could form no safe conjectures respecting the direction that the threatened movement from Sacket's Harbor would take. It might be, with equal probability, towards Kingston, York, or Fort George. All were equally assailable. The greatest number of troops could be brought to bear upon the latter post; Kingston was the most convenient point of attack, and the most important object to acquire; while York was the weakest, and there success was the most certain. Under these circumstances, the enemy could not withdraw from any one of these posts any portion of its strength to reënforce another.

The probability was, that the attack would be made in the order indicated by the Secretary at War; not that it was likely there had been any disclosure made of the instructions of that functionary to the general in command. Obvious circumstances would lead to this conjecture. Kingston had been known to be marked as an object of attack for some months. Its capture, and the destruction of the warlike stores concentrated within it, would weaken the enemy more than any other success against him in Upper Canada. Indeed, such an achievement would sever the two provinces, and render the fall of all above that point an almost inevitable result. It was insuring the prostration of the branches, by cutting off the trunk.

This view of the case could not but be taken by the enemy, and determine him to reserve at that place a force adequate to its protection. York was, therefore, left to itself; also Fort George; neither of which places had large garrisons. The former had little defence from fortifications; but the latter was a work of considerable strength, and capable of making a stout resistance. It was, however, under our batteries, and exposed to many disadvantages. Both these places could easily be carried by such troops as might be readily brought to bear upon them; when the whole disposable force on the lake would be free for a movement on the more formidable post of Kingston. It is true, the delay might bring out the enemy's fleet. But that change of circumstances, without much augmenting his strength for harbor defence, might throw out a new chance of fortune against him, in the unfavorable issue of a naval action.

For these, and other considerations, General Dearborn marked out his course of operations to be, first, an attack on York; next on Fort George; then on Kingston; having, after the second step had been taken, the command of all the troops on the Niagara frontier, forming the major part of his force, and without which he could not venture upon the last place with ordinary chances in his favor. The troops he had at Sacket's Harbor, suited for offensive movements, did not much exceed two thousand men; and the reënforcements that were coming together about Niagara surpassed that number. Such a body as could be taken on board the fleet, some sixteen hundred, would be able to carry York. This initial step taken, a rapid transit could be made to the mouth of the Niagara, where some five thousand men would be in readiness to carry Fort George; when the whole body, by various means of water transportation, and prompt marches by land, could be concentrated at Sacket's Harbor for a strong attack on Kingston; or, if that were deemed unadvisable, for making a lodgment in the St. Lawrence below.

At this late day, many supposed faults may be detected in the campaigns of the war of 1812. The most obvious one, perhaps, is that of not having made a strong lodgment on the left bank of the St. Lawrence, somewhere between Kingston and Montreal. No one thought of attacking Quebec, and few thought of attacking Montreal, but Kingston was deemed attainable. Probably it was so during the winter; but the best chances melted away with the ice. It could, however, have been taken indirectly, at almost any time during the years 1812 or 1813, by the capture of Prescott. The enemy, aware of the importance of this point, had fortified it, but not strongly.

The possession of Prescott, with an intrenched subsidiary camp, would have put to eminent hazard the whole of Upper Canada. Once held by us, its recapture would have been a prime object with the enemy. All other operations would have been subordinate to it. The scope of the war would have been almost narrowed down to that point, until that recapture had been insured. Montreal and Kingston would have been partially denuded, had it been necessary, to effect this great and essential purpose; and we can hardly measure the sacrifices that must have followed. And, in the autumn of 1813, when General Wilkinson revived the operations of a campaign, which had been permitted to slumber throughout a whole summer, in expectation of his tardy coming, and committed, perhaps, the double error of not attacking Kingston, and of determining to attack Montreal, thus leading to a double failure, he might have easily secured Prescott, and ended the season with a substantial acquisition, whose advantages might have been incalculable in another campaign. But public opinion had been led to grasp at Montreal; and it was Montreal or nothing. It is well recollected which of the alternatives was ours.

CHAPTER VI.

Commodore Chauncy's Fleet embarks on Lake Ontario with Troops under the Command of General Pike.—Arrives at York.—The Troops land at that Place.—Major Forsyth and the Riflemen.—Attack upon York.—Death of General Pike.—Surrender of the Town to the Americans.—Remarks.

THE prospect held out by this plan of the campaign was certainly very promising. It had all such probabilities in its favor as could be commanded by those, who control only one side of the current of events. The force that could and would be brought to bear on each point of attack was ample, and left as little to hazard as prudence would suggest. The plan was founded on the best principles of strategy, and highly creditable to the generalship which dictated it. Had it been carried out with the spirit and perseverance with which it was commenced, there was every reasonable prospect of a successful issue. The causes of its failure were obvious; delays, without proper objects, after the capture of Fort George; and a change of command, wholly unnecessary and inexpedient, which led to the waste of nearly an entire season of inactivity.*

On the 25th of April, 1813, the navigation of the lake being fully opened, General Dearborn, agreeably to the settled arrangement, embarked on board the fleet of Commodore Chauncy, with about seventeen hundred troops, under the immediate command of Brigadier-General Pike. It was well known that Sir James Yeo had not then his fleet in readiness to come out. One of his vessels, which was necessary to put

---

* General Dearborn was withdrawn from command early in July, his successor being enjoined to rest on his arms until General Wilkinson should arrive from the south, except in cases which did not occur, and were little likely to occur. General Wilkinson reached Fort George some time in September, and resumed operations on the 1st of October. Thus nearly three months were utterly wasted by a body of some four thousand troops.

him upon a safe footing with his antagonist, had yet some week's work to be done upon it. No molestation, therefore, in the expedition was to be apprehended on the lake. Such an exemption was desirable; for, although Commodore Chauncy would not have avoided a combat under any ordinary circumstances, yet the crowd of land forces on board would, almost unavoidably, have much embarrassed his vessels in a fight.

On the 27th of the same month, early in the morning, the fleet reached the harbor of York, and measures were taken to land the troops at once. It was intended that the landing should be made at the site of the old French fort Toronto, where the grounds were clear, and the troops could have effected it under cover of the vessels; but, a heavy wind from the eastward prevailing at the time, the boats were driven a considerable distance to the leeward, and the landing was necessarily made at a point where some thick woods were at hand. General Sheaffe, who commanded at York, had about eight hundred men for the defence of the place; about one half of them regulars, the rest militia and Indians. As soon as the exact spot of disembarkation became certain, he detached some light troops to its vicinity, which, as soon as our advanced party, consisting of

Forsyth's riflemen, approached the shore, took a position in the woods hard by, whence they poured in a galling and destructive fire upon the party as it left the boats.

The riflemen were formed on the bank as promptly as possible, when the boats returned to the fleet for other troops. In the mean time, this gallant little band, assisted by some few other troops that were thrown on shore in other boats, sustained the brunt of the combat. The numbers in this initial struggle were about equal, and it became a fair and close fight, to be turned either way, as reënforcements should happen to arrive. The British light troops were choice men, and commanded by a brave officer.

Forsyth's men were undisciplined, but had seen some desultory service on the Ogdensburg frontier, and had unbounded confidence in their leader, who was rather an extraordinary man, and regarded as a most promising partisan officer. He had peculiar notions as to the manner of training men. The common rules of discipline were looked upon by him with the utmost contempt. All he seemed to require of those under him was, that they should be good marksmen, and ready to follow him. When out of action, he exacted almost nothing from them, leaving them mostly at free quarters, free will, and without any restraint, saving always, that, when they heard the sound of his bugle, a curved horn of about five feet in length, they should rally at once to his tent. The feelings of his men towards him were more those of children for a father than of soldiers for an officer. He was quiet and retiring in his manners, seldom out of his immediate camp, and was generally found seated on the ground with several of his favorite men around him, as if in a family group. But, in action, he became animated to enthusiasm.

At the time of this expedition, Major Forsyth was a fat man, probably weighing some two hundred pounds. The uniform of his men was green, and, at the time he landed, he wore a broad-skirted coat of that color, which was unbuttoned and thrown back, displaying a white vest spread over his ample chest, that afforded a mark for an enemy, equal to the chalked circle of a common infantry target. He had on his head a broad-brimmed black hat. Soon after the landing, the armorer of his regiment, a favorite of both himself and his men, was killed. The skill of this man was such, as enabled him to give the rifle its most deadly character; and the efficiency of the regiment was consequently supposed, both by officers and men, to depend much upon him. When he fell, every man felt as if a deed had been perpetrated by the enemy that demanded revenge, and the whole detachment, from Major Forsyth down to the most indifferent marksman, entered into the combat with a fierce spirit of retaliation, that, no doubt, contributed much to the obstinacy of the stand they made, and the unusual loss sustained by the enemy immediately opposed to them.

Taking to the woods in which the British light troops were posted, the riflemen, after their loose manner, placed themselves behind trees, and thus carried on the contest with their more concentrated, better ordered, and, therefore, the more exposed opponents. It is said that Major Forsyth continued, throughout the action, to move to and fro, armed only with a light sword, immediately in the rear of his men, pointing out, with an earnest solemnity that partook both of sorrow and anger, to one rifleman after another, some one of the enemy, and exclaiming, that he was the man who had killed the favorite armorer. This suggestion was almost sure to be fatal to the enemy thus specially branded with the guilt of having taken off the best man of the corps. The British light troops were nearly all left on the ground they first occupied, being too strong to retreat while the landing was only partially made, and too much exposed to stand before such expertness of aim, rendered so fierce and unyielding by one of the chance shots of an opening fight.*

Brigadier-General Pike landed, with the main body, as soon after the advance as practicable. The command on shore had been confided exclusively to him. General Dearborn was on board the fleet, but for the purpose of directing ulterior operations, rather than to assume any control over the attack on York. As soon as a sufficient force had disembarked, General Pike moved onward, the enemy's advanced parties

---

* The death of this officer was in harmony with his character. After the taking of York, finding that the official account of the action gave him little credit for the conspicuous share he had in it, he became sick and inactive, and kept himself in sullen seclusion among his own men, apparently determined that no services should be rendered, either by himself or his men, since they were so inadequately rewarded, or so unduly estimated. He did little or nothing the residue of that campaign. Having been promoted before the following campaign, he, on the Champlain frontier, was put in command of an advanced party, which was to engage the enemy, and then fall back, in order to draw him into an ambush. Lieutenant-Colonel Forsyth was the last man who was likely to fulfil such a plan. As soon as he opened the fight with the enemy, his instructions to fall back were either forgotten or contemned. His spirit could not brook a retreat, even for an ultimate advantage. He rushed on and fell, and lost, with his life, all the success that would probably have followed more prudence, or strict obedience of orders.

yielding and falling back before him, until they reached the redoubts which had been constructed for the main defence of the place. Having passed through a wood to the open grounds in front of those redoubts, he sent forward a detachment to attack them. One of them having yielded without much resistance, the column was halted, until some light artillery could establish their pieces beneath its cover, in order to open upon another, which still held out. As the troops were somewhat fatigued, the leading regiments were permitted to seat themselves on the ground, to await the effect produced by this artillery. General Pike had also seated himself, in like manner, with his staff around him, for a few moments' relaxation during the interval, when a magazine of the enemy exploded, and spread its ruins far and wide around.

This magazine was constructed of stone, and had a large quantity of ammunition within it; so large, that, when it took fire, its walls, broken into large fragments, were thrown into the air, where they hung for a moment, like a black cloud, over the troops within a circle of three or four hundred yards, and then descended, bruising, maiming, or crushing into the earth one half or more of those, who were within their baleful influence. The destruction was greatly augmented, without doubt, by the position in which the nearest troops were then found. Reclining on the ground, each man exposed to the falling masses an unusual surface, and the destructive effects were in proportion.

When those who were uninjured, or only slightly injured, began to look about, and endeavor to ascertain who had suffered in the disaster, it was soon discovered that their gallant leader, Brigadier-General Pike, was among the sufferers. Being seated, he had most naturally bent his body forward, as he saw the stones ready to descend, when one of the large masses fell on his back, and broke in upon the very springs of life. He survived only a few hours; long enough to be taken on board the fleet, and utter a few farewell words, expressive of affection for his wife and children, and of regret, so common to ambitious minds, that his career had been cut short just at its brilliant opening.*

---

* There were circumstances connected with this shocking explosion, which, when related after the first horrors of it had passed away, threw a smile over many a camp hour.

The time, which elapsed between the explosion and the descent upon the troops of the fragments sent by it into the air, although brief, admitted a moment's thought, in those who were self-collected enough to improve it, as to measures to ward off or diminish its violence. An officer of artillery, who was near one of his pieces at the time, dodged underneath the gun, stood there half-bent with his arms akimbo, and thus evaded a stone, which passed be-

After the fall of General Pike, General Dearborn landed as soon as practicable, and assumed the command; Colonel Pearce, a worthy and brave officer, having, in the mean time, as senior officer on shore, assumed a temporary direction of events. It was, of course, some little time before the troops recovered from the astounding shock which they had experienced, and it became known on whom this responsibility had fallen. This delay was seized upon, by the enemy, to set fire to a public vessel on the

---

tween his arm and his body, carrying away a patch of cloth from both the sleeve and the lapel. Another officer suddenly ensconced himself into an empty pork-barrel, which lay on its bilge at hand, thus sheltering the vital parts, while his legs got a severe bruising.

Another officer often told the manner of his escape; though the story was always listened to with many grains of allowance. Being nearly recumbent at the time, a tall and broad-shouldered soldier, in the confusion of the moment, stumbled at full length upon him, just at the opportune moment when the shower reached the earth, and received many severe contusions, which would have fallen on the officer beneath, had it not been for this fortunate interposition. And it was not until after the capture of Fort George, that this explosion ceased to haunt, like a dreadful spectre, the American army. While preparing for that capture, it seemed to be a settled conviction in the mind of the Commander-in-Chief, that explosions were to be the ordinary means of warfare with the British. On the point opposite Fort Niagara, and not far from Fort George, stood

stocks, and a magazine of military and naval stores; General Sheaffe withdrawing, unmolested, from the place, with his regulars, and leaving the local militia and the magistrates to propose terms of surrender. Such terms having been immediately sent out to Colonel Pearce, he most unwisely entertained them, and temporarily desisted from further movements, in consequence; although evidences were obvious enough, that undue advantage was taken of the interval by destroying public property, and making movements, which were forbidden under such cir-

---

a lighthouse, which was made of stone. The common impression was, that these stones were to be discharged upon our heads whenever we made the attempt to land; it being taken for granted, that we should land between that and a neighboring wood, as the open grounds there were completely commanded by the guns of our fort. Many British deserters came over during the month, which elapsed between the capture of York and Fort George. The question asked of each was, whether the lighthouse were *mined*. No answer intimated that it was; still it was determined to land at a safe distance from it, though the point chosen afforded the enemy an excellent cover, where his batteries could be silenced only by our vessels. After the landing had been effected, the lighthouse was approached by stragglers with much caution, until some one, more hardy or more curious than the rest, entering into it, found within its recesses, instead of a Guy Fawkes, some women and children, who had taken shelter there from the dangers of the day.

cumstances. It was too late to rectify this mistake when General Dearborn reached the ground, and he had only to secure such prisoners and such spoils as General Sheaffe had left.

The loss of the British by this event, in killed, wounded, and taken, was about five hundred men; while the loss on the American side, in killed and wounded, was three hundred and twenty. The greater part of the latter loss was caused by the explosion, which, at the time, was attributed to a murderous design, on the part of the enemy, to spread destruction among the assailants as widely as possible. Both General Dearborn and Commodore Chauncy, in their official accounts of the affair, laid this heavy charge upon the British. On the other hand, General Sheaffe states the explosion to have been the result of accident. It is known, that some thirty or forty of his command were involved in the destruction. The charge obtained countenance, at the time, in the notorious animosity of certain British regiments, those which had been many years in the Canadas, and of which General Sheaffe commanded one, General Proctor another, towards the abettors of the war in the United States. It was supposed, that they hardly regarded themselves as bound by the ordinary rules or customs of war in their contest with these states, and were prepared to commit any outrage or violence that subserved their purposes. But a fact so injurious to the character of a civilized nation, as this view of the case implies, not having been substantiated by indisputable evidence, has not been received into the histories of those times, written after many years had permitted impartiality to weigh all the circumstances of the case.*

General Pike was cut off in the bloom of manhood, at the early age of thirty-four. His remains were taken in the fleet to Sacket's Harbor, and there placed at the disposal of his relations and friends. His fall was much regretted throughout the nation. Probably no officer in the army, at that time, was held in higher estimation. This was not because he had seen much actual service, for he had hardly been in the presence of the enemy before the day on which he fell. It was on the promise, rather than the fulfilment, that the public mind rested his character for boldness and enterprise; and his fitness to direct and control men had been determined, to an extent that warranted much confidence, by his expeditions in the north-west

---

* General Armstrong, in his "History of the War of 1812," does not notice this charge against the British in his text. A note states that General Sheaffe said, the explosion was the result of accident, his own soldiers having been involved in its effects.

and the south-west. He had there given such proofs of these qualities, as established a reputation in advance. He had exhibited, moreover, an indefatigable activity in the drill of his regiment, requiring of all under his command an unwearied devotion to duty, and an exact and prompt obedience to orders.

His regiment became an example of zeal, discipline, and aptitude in movements; his men had an unbounded belief in his capacity, and his officers looked up to him with unusual respect and affection. He inspired that confidence in all under his orders, which is almost a certain evidence that it is merited.

At the opening of the war of 1812, we were almost without any fixed guides in tactics and discipline. The standard of the latter part of the revolution, and of subsequent times, "Old Steuben," which had been approved by Washington, and had led to some of the best triumphs of the closing years of that glorious period, had become obsolete, even before any substitute was provided. Hence, when new regiments came into service by scores in 1812, nothing was prescribed for regulation or for drill. The old regiments had their forms and customs, which preserved in them the aspect of regulars. But even these presented no uniform example. Some adopted the "nineteen manœuvres" of the English; others, the ninety and nine manœuvres of the French; while a few adhered to old Dundas; and fewer still to older Steuben.

Nothing was laid down by the proper authority; therefore all manner of things were taken up without any authority at all. Amid this confusion, or wide latitude of choice, General Pike, though brought up in the old school, was often tempted, by his ambitious desire for improvement, to run into novelties. With a prescribed rule, he would have been the most steady and uncompromising observer of it. But, in such a competition for beneficial change, he most naturally believed himself as capable as others of changing for the better.

In this spirit of innovation, the fifteenth regiment underwent many changes, and exhibited, even in those times when novelties and singularities were no rarities, perhaps the widest departure from common standards of any regiment in service. Adopting the French system of forming in three ranks, his third rank was armed in a manner peculiar to itself, having short guns, being the ordinary musket cut off some inches, and long pikes. It was said, by the wags of the day, that his own name suggested the manner, and the regiment was often called "Pike's regiment of pikes."

It may be well to state the issue of this experiment, which would have revived a portion of the long-exploded ancient armor, and in part dispensed with the advantages of powder. When exhibited in the drill, and especially in the "charge bayonet," these pikes presented a most bristling and formidable appearance; and could the files have preserved at all times their serried compactness, they might have contributed to the weight and success of a charge. With the extreme improbability of such a continual cohesion, this third rank was likely, under most circumstances, to deduct so much from the real strength of the line. At the landing at York, the regiment, being in the presence of its former Colonel, preserved their pikes; but, at the next battle in which this gallant and highly disciplined regiment was engaged, these cumbrous weapons, serviceable only in a charge,* were nearly all thrown away, with their accompanying short guns, and good English muskets, plentifully strewed around, were picked up in their stead. The regiment probably never paraded again with the pikes.

We have remarked, that the death of General Pike was much lamented by the public. But a far stronger feeling of regret pervaded the army.

---

* One of the rarest occurrences of an action. General Moreau is said to have remarked, that he never saw bayonets crossed but once.

Among the officers of the regiment, from which he had just been promoted, there was an unfeigned sorrow, as for a father and a friend. They had regarded him as a man, who was certain to lead them onward in the path of honor. His abilities and energy inspired them with reliance, and they were disposed to follow him, in any rank, with an assurance of success. This trust in a military character is seldom mistaken.

General Pike was married, in 1801, to Clarissa Brown, of Kentucky, by whom he had three daughters and one son. Only one of these children reached the maturity of life, a daughter, who married Symmes Harrison, the son of General Harrison, and became a widow, many years since, with several children.

Mrs. Pike withdrew to the seclusion of a family residence on the Ohio River, just below Cincinnati, soon after the fall of her gallant husband, where she has since lived. It is well recollected by most of the officers, who served on Lake Ontario in the early part of the campaign of 1813, that he regarded her with enthusiastic sentiments, believing her to share in all his ardent longings after distinction, and willing to make any sacrifice for their fulfilment. No doubt it was with a heart strengthened by such feelings, that she parted with him on the eve of the expedition in which he fell; though she may have felt, during her long widowhood, that the sacrifice, with all its honorable alleviations, has been at times as much as that heart could bear.

There was found an interesting memorandum on one of the blank pages of a copy of "Dodsley's Economy of Human Life," which General Pike habitually carried about with him. After affectionately alluding to his wife, and his son then living, he lays down two maxims, which he wishes may ever be present to the mind of his child, "as he rises from youth to manhood." "First; Preserve your honor free from blemish. Second; Be always ready to die for your country." This son was cut off too soon to exemplify the former in his life, or the latter in his death; but the father, in his life and his death, exemplified them both.

LIFE

OF

SAMUEL GORTON,

ONE OF THE FIRST SETTLERS OF WARWICK
IN RHODE ISLAND;

BY

JOHN M. MACKIE,
AUTHOR OF THE "LIFE OF LEIBNITZ."

SAMUEL GORTON.

CHAPTER I.

Introduction.

In the year 1636, there arrived in Boston a remarkable man, bearing the name of SAMUEL GORTON, an exile from England for conscience' sake and the love of liberty. He had left the land of his birth, at that unhappy period when the infatuated Charles, tired of proroguing and dissolving Parliaments, was endeavoring to rule without them; when the person and property of every patriot in the land were exposed to the arbitrary measures of the courts of Star Chamber and High Commission; when no person could exercise the sacred right of freedom of speech in the House of Commons, without running the risk of being sent to the Tower; when patents were granted for odious and oppressive monopolies; the royal forests extended in violation of the rights of private property; unconstitutional writs issued for raising ship money; levies of tonnage and poundage laid without the authority of Parliament; illegal proclamations made, restricting the freedom of industry; martial law declared without cause; soldiers billeted upon the citizens in time of peace; inquisitorial oaths tendered; and private papers searched on mere suspicion.

It was the time, also, when the bigoted Laud ruled with as high a hand in the church, as did his royal master in the state. Citizens, claiming the right of freely uttering what they honestly thought, on the subject of religion, were fined and imprisoned, or publicly whipped, and set in the pillory. Strict conformity was required to the established forms and ceremonies of public worship; Popish rites were introduced into the services of religion; and the pulpit was compelled to announce the royal permission for the practice of archery, May-games, and morris-dances on Sunday. Grave divines and learned civilians did not escape having their noses slit, their ears cropped, and their foreheads branded for heterodoxy. Church and state, in fact, were leagued together to keep the rising people of England from the acquisition of their liberties.

Excepting the enjoyment of civil and religious freedom, however, England had, at that period, everything to offer to the affections and the hopes of her children. Her monarch, though most unwise in his public policy, was not destitute of many excellences of private character; her institutions were more liberal than those of any other state in Europe; both the useful and the elegant arts had made no inconsiderable progress; and the blessings of peace and plenty were diffused throughout the country.

But Samuel Gorton was one of the noble spirits, then abounding in England, who, esteeming liberty more than life, and counting no sacrifices too great for the maintenance of principle, could not dwell at ease in a land where the inalienable rights of humanity were not acknowledged, or were mocked at. With all its industrial prosperity, its pleasing attractions to the eye of sense, its proud public annals, and its dear private memories, England could not restrain him from adventuring upon the then dread Atlantic, and seeking out a spot among the self-denying settlers of a barren coast and a savage wilderness, where, in thought, and word, and act, *he might be free.* He left his native country, he says, "to enjoy liberty of conscience, in respect to faith towards God, and for no other end."

And yet, even in this new world, was he not destined to find at once the ample liberty which he sought for. It was only after years of bitter contention, after having been cast out from the society of his brethren, and having had some experience of civil war, of fines, of fetters, if not of stripes even, that, in the evening of life, he was allowed to settle down, by the side, and almost under the protection, of his red brethren of the wilderness, in the unmolested enjoyment of those political principles and religious sentiments, to whose defence he had devoted the vigor of his days.

CHAPTER II.

Gorton's Birth. — Ancestors. — Early Education. — Arrival in Boston. — Removal to Plymouth. — Difficulties with Ralph Smith. — Banishment from Plymouth.

THE materials for furnishing a sketch of the life and character of this truly gifted, though somewhat singular person, are unfortunately scanty. Gorton seldom alluded, in his writings, to his personal history; his disciples and companions, though not all illiterate, published likewise but few memorials of themselves or their leader; and what few facts respecting him are known, were recorded for the most part by the prejudiced pens of those, who were themselves his persecutors; or who, at least, looked upon him with abhorrence, as a mystical fanatic, and "a most prodigious minter of exorbitant novelties." Of his life, previously to the period of his arrival in this country, neither history nor tradition has preserved scarcely any well-marked traces.

The precise time of Gorton's birth is not known. It was, however, early in the seventeenth century. The place was the town of Gorton, in England, where not only he was born and bred, but so also were the "fathers of his body for many generations." He came to New England from London, where he appears to have practised a mechanical trade; as in a certain conveyance he calls himself "a citizen of London, clothier." In another, however, he assumes the loftier title of "Professor of the Mysteries of Christ;" while in one of his printed works, he adds to his name the appellation of "Gentleman." He was of a good family; his ancestors, as he himself observes, were not unknown in the records of the heraldry of England; and speaking of his wife, in connection with his residence at Plymouth, he said that she had been "as tenderly brought up as any man's wife then in that town." *

---

* Manuscript Letter to Nathaniel Morton.

Notwithstanding the taste manifested by him for the study of languages, and the intellectual culture displayed in the productions of his pen, his early years were not spent, probably, at any of the celebrated academies of England; as it is certain that his youthful mind was not informed and disciplined at either of her venerable universities. "I was not bred up," says he, "in the schools of human learning; and I bless God that I never was."* But the lack of these costly advantages did not lead him to undervalue the humbler opportunities of acquiring mental discipline and useful learning, which every-day life graciously offers to every man. Indeed, a mind naturally so well endowed as his, could not well fail of being educated, even though, as was the case with him, it was compelled to be its own teacher.

His religious training was received in the established church; for in an address, written by him in 1679, to Charles the Second, disowning the Puritans, he says that he sucked in his peculiar tenets "from the breasts of his mother, the church of England." Hence it may also be inferred, perhaps, that the independent mind of Gorton, as it was self-taught in the acquisition of learning, so, the views of Christian

---

* Gorton's Letter to Nathaniel Morton, in Hutchinson's *History of Massachusetts*, Vol. I. p. 550.

doctrine entertained by him differing widely from those of the society in which he was educated, was it also self-directed in its search for religious truth.

The year in which Gorton arrived in Boston was signalized by the administration of Sir Henry Vane, the enlightened friend of religious freedom, and also by the commencement of the public teachings of Anne Hutchinson, the gifted advocate of liberal views of Christianity. A new religious spirit had appeared in the colony of Massachusetts Bay. The Antinomian controversy, which was then raging like a conflagration through society, had brought forward a number of active, inquiring minds, who set themselves in opposition to the spiritual despotism of the existing hierarchy.

Two parties, accordingly, had sprung up in the infant state, the one maintaining the established order of civil government and religious discipline, the other insisting upon the necessity of reforms, claiming the right of private judgment in opposition to the dictates of clerical authority, and asserting the dignity of the individual man, by teaching his unity with the Holy Ghost. But the former party prevailed; and Gorton, whose sympathies, it may be presumed, were with the advocates of free inquiry, (though it does not appear, that, immediately on arriving in Boston, he openly took sides with either party,) soon left Massachusetts Bay for the somewhat more liberal colony of the Pilgrims.

An early writer, however, mentions a reason for Gorton's removal to Plymouth, different from the one above suggested. "Gorton continued a while in Boston," says Hubbard, "till a reverend minister of London (Mr. Walker) sent over directions to some friends to demand an hundred pound debt of him, which he having borrowed of a citizen, the citizen bequeathed it to some good use, whereof Mr. Walker was called to some trust."*

But this statement, though repeated substantially from one before made by Cotton Mather,† we are not disposed to credit. The alleged fact is mentioned by no other historians, though notices of Gorton's career have been written by other enemies than Hubbard and Mather; and if it be not more true than many representations respecting this person's character, contained in the "General History of New England," and in the "Magnalia," it certainly can be deserving of but little credence. It is the only imputation which has ever been breathed against Gorton's

---

* Hubbard, in *Mass. Hist. Coll.* 2d Series, Vol. VI, p. 402
† Magnalia Christi Americana, Vol. II. p. 437.

integrity, even by those who, in an age when heresy passed for a sin unpardonable, looked upon him as a heretic. Nor does the reason assigned for Gorton's leaving Boston seem to be a very good one; for any inconveniences, which the non-payment of the debt might occasion him in this place, would naturally attend him in Plymouth also. This allegation, therefore, so contrary to the whole spirit of a long life of severely tried virtue, must be regarded as wanting confirmation.

In Plymouth, it is probable that Gorton took up, if he had not done so before, the calling of a preacher; which, in connection with his secular employments, he afterwards followed through life. Though never regularly ordained by the hand of man, he considered himself as well called to the work of the ministry as were his brethren. "For a human call," says he, "I think mine to be as good as the degrees in the schools, or to pass under the hands and ceremonies of a titular bishop, or under the natural hands of a titular eldership, or to have the call of a people, by the power of stipend or contribution, without one of which, no contract; all of which I account as human, at the best."[*]

---

[*] Gorton's Letter to Nathaniel Morton, in Hutchinson's *Hist. of Massachusetts*, Vol. I. p. 552.

Upon the Plymouth colonists Gorton made, at first, a favorable impression. His bearing was courteous; his feelings lively; his mind vigorous and well informed. "He gave hopes that he would prove an useful instrument." But it was not long before the language of the eloquent new-comer began to strike the itching ears of the Pilgrims, as differing somewhat from that peculiar form of words, which had received the sanction of the church. The sensitive organs of certain elders already scented a heresy in the sentiments of this free-spoken enthusiast; and presently it was openly asserted, by the brethren and sisters, that this self-called preacher was "a proud and pestilent seducer."

Gorton was not suffered to remain long unmolested. It happened, at this time, that his wife's servant, a widow of good report, committed the heinous offence of smiling in church; and, being thereupon suspected of being unsound in doctrine, and opposed to the established church order, she was threatened with banishment from the colony as a common vagabond. Believing the woman not to be deserving of the punishment proposed to be inflicted on her, Gorton interfered in her behalf, and defended her cause against her accusers. This increased his unpopularity, and attracted to him the special attention of the minister of the colony, Mr. Ralph Smith. This reverend gentleman, the first pastor of the church in Plymouth, though externally of the strictest sect of the Puritans, had the misfortune to possess more zeal than prudence, and, being also destitute of worldly wisdom, did not make up this deficiency by the experiences of religion in the soul; so that, when he resigned his pastoral charge, the occasion gave rise to the reflection, "that many times the total vacancy of an office is easier to be borne, than the under-performance of it." [*]

Another circumstance, which contributed not a little to render Gorton particularly obnoxious to the pastor of the colony, was, that the wife of the latter, together with other members of his family, attracted by the eloquence, and probably impressed by the reasonings, of the self-appointed preacher, was in the habit of frequenting his house at the time of morning and evening prayers. Mr. Smith, therefore, determined to get rid, if possible, of his free-thinking parishioner. But, unfortunately, he had let to the latter a part of his own house for the period of four years. There was then only one course to be pursued, which was, to accuse Gorton of

---

[*] Eccl. Hist. of Mass. in *Mass. Hist. Coll.* 1st Series, Vol. VII. p. 277.

heresy before the civil court, and procure his expulsion not only from his hired house, but also from the colony. This was done.

The complaint against Gorton was entered in court, according to Morton, on the 4th of December, 1630; but it must have been the year previous, as Gorton was received an inhabitant at Aquetneck on the 20th of June, 1638.* The same writer further observes, that, when brought into the presence of the court, Gorton carried himself "mutinously and seditiously toward both magistrates and ministers." This may very likely be true. The accused was a believer in religious liberty.

The sublime truth, that the civil authority has no right to bind the conscience, which Divine Providence had taught to many minds in that age, but most clearly and fully to the great soul of Roger Williams, had sunk deep also into the heart of Samuel Gorton. He held himself, therefore, not responsible to courts, civil or ecclesiastical, for his religious belief. He maintained the sacred, sovereign right of every man to inquire for himself what is truth; to hold to what seems to him to be true, with an undisturbed mind, asking of no human tribunal for leave or license; and also freely to declare his own set-

---

* New England's Memorial, Davis's Edition, p. 203.

tled convictions in the face of all men. It was
not to be expected, therefore, that this man,
when called into court to answer for his religious opinions, would submit to be catechized
with any great degree of gentleness and humility. No more was it to be expected, that,
in such a court, the accused would escape conviction and punishment. The matter was, indeed, first referred to arbitrament. But after the
referees had been appointed, and Gorton had
submitted to them his papers, the case was again
brought before the court, which thereupon, says
Gorton, "proceeded to fine and imprisonment,
together with sentence given, that my family
should depart out of my own hired house within
the space of fourteen days, upon the penalty of
another great sum of money, (besides my fine
paid,) and their further wrath and displeasure,
which time to depart fell to be in a mighty
storm of snow as I have seen in the country;
my wife being turned out of doors in the said
storm, with a young child sucking at her breast,
(the infant having at that time the disease called
the measles breaking out upon it, which the
cold forced in again, causing sickness near unto
death,) who had been as tenderly brought up as
any man's wife then in that town; and myself
to travel in the wilderness I knew not whither,

the people comforting my wife and children when I was gone with this, that it was impossible for me to come alive to any plantation." *

Although it is hardly to be supposed, that the conversation of Gorton while in Plymouth, or his persecution there, had any great effect in gaining proselytes to his opinions, or in diffusing more liberal sentiments on the subject of religious liberty, still we are told, that he sowed seed there from the fruits whereof "some were seduced." †

---

* Gorton's MS. Letter to Nathaniel Morton.
† Grahame, in his *History of the United States*, (Vol. I. p. 248,) says that Gorton's career in Plymouth "was cut short by a conviction of swindling;" and also remarks, immediately afterwards, that Gorton, on repairing to the plantation of Providence, "nearly involved the people of this settlement in a war with the Indians." These charges, though Grahame refers to Gorges' *America painted to the Life*, and to Neal's *History of New England*, as authority for them, have no foundation in truth. We mention them as specimens of the mistakes, not unfrequent, into which this historian, notwithstanding his general accuracy and his scrupulous fidelity to truth, has been led by his authorities respecting the early history of Rhode Island.

CHAPTER III.

Gorton goes to Aquetneck. — Hardships of his Journey. — The Settlement at Aquetneck. — Gorton's Difficulties with the Authorities. — His Punishment.

BANISHED by the Pilgrims, who did not acknowledge the principle of toleration in religion, but merely wished to find, in this country, a refuge where they might enjoy and establish the peculiar religious opinions for which they had suffered persecution in England, Gorton was forced to set his face toward the wilderness in the west. Aquetneck, or Rhode Island, as it was afterwards called, had then recently been settled by a small number of exiles, or emigrants, from Massachusetts Bay; and to this beautiful island, the exile for conscience' sake wended his way, attracted, doubtless, by flattering reports of the richness of its soil, the salubrity of its climate, and the beauty of its shores, as well as by the pleasing hope of finding there, several days' journey beyond the settlements of civilized intolerance, a spot where he might build a free and happy home.

Thither Gorton was soon followed by some of his disciples in Plymouth. Speaking of the hardships to which he and his friends were subjected on being driven out from Plymouth and Massachusetts Bay, he says they were compelled " to wander in the wilderness in extremity of winter, yea, when the snow was up to the knee, and rivers to wade through up to the middle, and not so much as one of the Indians to be found in that extremity of weather to afford us either fire or any harbor, such as themselves had, being removed into swamps and thickets where they were not to be found; in which condition, in the continuation of the weather, we lay divers nights together, having no victuals but what we took on our backs, and our drink as the snow afforded unto us." *

The Island of Aquetneck had been purchased of the Narragansett sachems, Canonicus and Miantonomo, by William Coddington, John Clarke, and their associates. These persons, the most of whom had been disarmed by the government of Massachusetts Bay for remonstrating to the General Court against the banishment of the Reverend Mr. Wheelwright, one of the followers of Anne Hutchinson, and some of whom had themselves been disfranchised and expelled from the commonwealth, on account of their reception of the religious sentiments of this persecuted

---

* Simplicitie's Defence against Seven-headed Policy, p. 3.

lady, had sought refuge from spiritual oppression about the pleasant waters of the Narragansett Bay They possessed not, however, that clear apprehension of the great democratic principles of civil and religious liberty, which so remarkably distinguished the venerable settler of the neighboring colony of Providence. On this account, most probably, Gorton did not establish himself permanently at Aquetneck. He was received as an inhabitant on the 20th of June, 1638; but he made no purchase of lands, and consequently was never admitted a freeman of the colony.

Some of the early historians assert, that Gorton became involved in some difficulties with the government at Aquetneck; and that, in consequence, he was imprisoned, whipped, and banished from the island.* "There," says Lechford, "lately they whipped one Mr. Gorton, a grave man, for denying their power, and abusing some of their magistrates with uncivil terms, the Governor, Mr. Coddington, saying in Court, 'You that are for the King, lay hold on Gorton;' and he again on the other side called forth, 'All you that are for the King, lay hold on Coddington;' whereupon Gorton was banished the island. So, with his wife and children, he went to Providence. They began about a small trespass of

---

* Winthrop's *History of New England*, Vol. II. p. 59, Savage's edition. Morton's *Memorial*, p. 203, Davis's edition.

swine; but it is thought some other matter was ingredient." *

The truth of the above statement has been questioned; and it is somewhat singular, that no mention is made of these transactions in the colonial records. But there is no room for doubt that Gorton came into collision with the authorities of the island, and that he was subjected to some disgraceful punishment; for he refers to their "dealing" with him; and makes an allusion, in connection with the subject, to "whipping-posts;" and says that "some of Plymouth then in place were instigators of the island." †

The colony at Aquetneck, though established on the same great principles of civil and religious liberty as that at Providence, was somewhat less liberal than the latter in sentiment, and less consistent in practice. Gorton's peculiar opinions undoubtedly gave offence. Moreover, he was a man who held firmly to his opinions on all occasions, and whose earnest, impulsive nature led him openly to express and stoutly to defend them against all gainsayers. Nor would "a small trespass of swine" have been regarded by him, as an occasion too trifling for maintaining the cause of right with unyielding pertinacity, and with a total disregard of all personal conse-

---

* Winthrop, Vol. II. p. 59, note.
† Gorton's MS. Letter to Nathaniel Morton.

quences. He was endowed, moreover, with no very great measure of respect for persons set in the high places of civil or ecclesiastical authority. His confidence in the conclusions of his own judgment was too complete, his will too inflexible, and his sense of personal independence too lively, to admit of his always maintaining all due deference to tribunals, whose decisions his observation had taught him were often lacking in wisdom, and whose punishments his personal experience had made him feel were sometimes sadly wanting in mercy. At Plymouth he had acknowledged the authorities to be entitled to some respect, because they were duly commissioned; but they were not so at Aquetneck, and he declared that he was competent to "manage his own affairs himself."

And even were Gorton publicly whipped at Aquetneck, the stripes surely dishonored the giver, not the receiver of them. For if corporal chastisement was really inflicted on him, it was for no crime or immorality. Such charges are nowhere brought against this man, even by his enemies and persecutors. It must have been for his opinions, and these alone, that he was scourged; and for virtue to be whipped of injustice in this world is no uncommon circumstance, nor one that leaves a stain upon the sufferer.

CHAPTER IV.

Removes to Providence, and settles in Pawtuxet. — Controversies then prevailing in this Settlement. — Part taken in them by Gorton. — Unlawful Interference of the Massachusetts Authorities. — Gorton refuses to submit to their Jurisdiction. — Removes from Pawtuxet.

From Aquetneck, Gorton removed with his family to Providence; at what time is not exactly known, though it must have been previously to the 17th of November, 1641. Roger Williams, the liberal and humane founder of the state of Rhode Island, though disapproving of the peculiar sentiments of Gorton, kindly received him into his "shelter for persons distressed for conscience." Gorton, however, was never enrolled as an inhabitant of the town of Providence; but, in January, 1642, he purchased lands at Pawtuxet, then within the territory of Providence, though now contained in the limits of the town of Cranston. Here he was soon joined by a number of persons, who had been expelled from Aquetneck on account of their attachment to his principles, and whose personal regard for their teacher appears to have been sufficiently strong to induce them again to seek for his society, and to follow his fortunes.

The colony of Providence, at the time when Gorton took up his abode there, had received no charter of government from the mother country. The inhabitants were associated together by a few brief articles of voluntary agreement. Those matters, which could not well be transacted by the whole people in town meeting, were referred to "five Disposers," who were required to make a report to their constituents once in three months; at which time, also, a new election of these officers was held.

So democratic was this form of organization, and so small the degree of power delegated to the Disposers, that it was said by the Massachusetts colonists, who lived under a stronger and more aristocratic government, that their neighbors of Providence "would have no magistrates." Every man, in consequence of the almost entire absence of the authority of government, was a law to himself; and the result was, that a conflict of laws not unfrequently took place. There were not wanting heady and discordant spirits in this asylum, as it was called by its enemies, "for men of all sorts of consciences;" nor were there lacking subjects fitted to call forth a diversity of opinions, or to give rise to acrimonious and protracted controversies.

The most prolific source of disputes was the uncertainty of the boundaries between the two settlements at Moshassuck and at Pawtuxet. And it was in the midst of dissensions growing out of this matter, that Gorton arrived in Providence. Unhappily, he was not, like Roger Williams, a peacemaker. His impatience of authority, his fiery disposition, his almost reckless devotion to the cause of right, made him a warm partisan, although the genuine goodness of his heart prevented him from being a rancorous one.

Gorton, therefore, entered readily into the controversy, which at the time absorbed the attention of the colony, and which long after his departure continued to disturb its tranquillity. What was the precise point in dispute, or whether the party espoused by Gorton was right or not, we have no means of knowing. This party, at least, proved to be the strongest; and, as was to be expected, Gorton, being the foremost man in the settlement, became its "instructer and captain." The minds of the colonists engaged in the quarrel at length became so heated, that "they came armed into the field, each against the other." But Roger Williams appeared in their midst, and "pacified them for the present."*

The mild counsels of the sage of Moshassuck, however, were not long heeded. The authority of reason had become so weakened by passion,

---

* Winthrop, Vol. II. p. 59.

that it was only by a resort to physical force, that the controversy could be terminated. But the government at Providence was one of public opinion merely; and public opinion was too equally divided respecting the merits of the question in dispute, to render any efficient interference by the authorities possible. In this emergency, the weaker party, not relying upon the goodness of their cause for its triumphant issue, applied to the government of Massachusetts Bay for assistance. This was done on the 17th of November, 1641, in the form of a petition to the authorities, written by Benedict Arnold, and signed by himself, with twelve others of the colony of Providence.*

It set forth that Samuel Gorton and his company, sojourners among them, having espoused the cause of two colonists who had long been opposed to the petitioners, and having also gained over to their side six or seven of their townsmen, who had previously lived on good terms with their fellow-colonists, were licentiously bent on resisting all "honest order or government;" and more particularly, that these persons had by force of arms, and not without the shedding of "some few drops of blood on either side," prevented the petitioners from distraining the cattle of one of

---

* R. I. Hist. Coll. Vol. II. Appendix, No. 1.

their townsmen, in satisfaction of a judgment of arbitration duly rendered for debt. The petitioners therefore prayed for assistance, that the offenders against public order and justice might be "brought to satisfaction," and be prevented from making further disturbances.

The prayer of the petition was not granted. "We answered them," says Winthrop, "that we could not levy any war without a General Court. For counsel, we told them, that, except they did submit themselves to some jurisdiction, either Plymouth or ours, we had no calling or warrant to interpose in their contentions; but if they were once subject to any, then they had a calling to protect them." *

The petition was not signed by Roger Williams. So deeply distressed, however, was this benevolent patriot by the feud which threatened to destroy the prosperity, if not the existence, of his colony, that he wrote a letter to the government of Massachusetts Bay respecting this matter, wherein he said that "Mr. Gorton, having foully abused high and low at Aquetneck, is now bewitching and bemadding poor Providence." †
But both the particular expressions contained in the letters of Williams, and his general charac-

---

* Winthrop's *New England*, Vol. II. p. 59.
† General Court's Vindication, May 30th, 1665.

ter and conduct, forbid the belief that he was willing to submit in any way to the jurisdiction of the government, which had banished him from its territories, and which was fanatically opposed to principles that were dearer to him than life. The most he could have asked for was counsel, or temporary aid for the purpose of quelling a dangerous tumult.

The course pursued by the party opposed to Gorton was a very wrong one. The territory of Providence lay without the chartered limits of Massachusetts Bay; and the government of the latter colony had no right to extend its jurisdiction beyond those limits. The petition, moreover, was not the act of the government of Providence colony; it was not the act of a majority of its citizens; it was signed merely by thirteen private individuals. And these individuals were bound, by the civil compact established by general consent in the colony, to submit their grievances to the voluntarily and formally established authorities; or, if aggrieved by the decision of such authorities, to apply to the mother country for relief. Most clearly, such a minority had no right to call in the physical force of a foreign state to enable them to execute any processes, even had they been strictly legal, against the persons or the estates of their fellow-citizens.

The manifest injustice of the means resorted

to by Gorton's enemies may well lead to the suspicion, that the ends proposed to be accomplished by them were not honest. They were, confessedly, the "weaker party;" and in the course of the year following, they were reduced even to a much smaller number. Still some of the petitioners continued to persist in their purposes; and in September, 1642, they submitted themselves to the authority, and solicited the protection, of the government of Massachuetts Bay. But though this act was an implied, if not an express violation of the civil compact established by the inhabitants of Providence; though these persons had just before been wrongfully and insultingly driven out from the territories of Massachusetts; though they had made great sacrifices in founding a refuge for "soul liberty," and were strongly opposed to this proceeding of a very small minority of their number; yet the government of the Bay colony did not regard the wrongfulness of the request preferred to it. It was desirous of breaking up the refuge of heresy by the "fresh rivers of Moshassuck and Wanasquatucket;" and also of opening to its own citizens a passage to the waters of the Narragansett Bay.

Under pretence, therefore, of upholding the cause of justice, the opportunity was gladly embraced by this government to extend the limits of its territories. Nor did the Massachusetts authorities confine themselves to taking under their gracious protection the persons and estates of the few petitioners merely. They extended their jurisdiction over the whole colony of Providence; and on the 28th of October, 1642, issued a notification to the same, stating that William Arnold and others had submitted themselves to their protection, and requiring the colonists to refrain from doing them any further injury.*

This conduct of the Massachusetts colony in extending its laws beyond its chartered limits, and into the midst of an independent community, was rightly regarded by Gorton and his friends as a flagrant act of usurpation. They denied that Massachusetts had any right whatsoever to assume jurisdiction over the free colony of Providence. They spurned the invitation to appear in the courts of a foreign power, for the purpose of asking for justice against their fellow-citizens; and they resolved to refuse submission to the mandates of their meddling and domineering neighbor. Accordingly, a reply was sent to the "men of Massachusetts," from whom the notification had proceeded, dated on the 20th of November, and signed by Gorton, together with

---

* Hutchinson's *History of Massachusetts*, Vol. I. p. 113.

eleven others, wherein they absolutely and indignantly refused to yield the required allegiance.*

This paper, after the fashion of those days, was of a most extravagant length; rambled off in various digressions; was clouded with dark sayings; indulged in severe strictures on the Massachusetts theology and piety; and both in letter and spirit was not, to say the least, more characterized by reverence for the powers that were in the Bay colony, than were the claims of these upon their "neighbors of Providence" by modesty and justice. Immediately on the reception of this reply, the magistrates, taking counsel with the leading elders, sat in judgment upon it, and discovered therein heresies and blasphemies to the number of "twenty-six, or thereabouts." Thereupon the pulpit took up the theme; warned the people against such damnable errors; and stirred them up to seek out diligently all persons who held to them for punishment.

At the same time that this reply was despatched to Massachusetts, Gorton and his friends thought it advisable, leaving the pleasant meadows of Pawtuxet, to remove further off from the dangerous power of their Christian neighbors, and nearer to the friendly hospitalities of the

---

* Gorton's *Simplicitie's Defence*, p. 9.

uncivilized red men. For the preservation of their peace, said they, as well as out of compassion for their wives and little ones, and willing, it would seem, to suffer some wrong rather than do more, they abandoned their houses and the rest of their labors lying near to the pretended subjects of Massachusetts. They had much to escape from. Their enemies "had learned this device, that whereas some of us had small parcels of land laid out to build houses upon and plant corn, and all the rest lay common and undivided, as the custom of the country for the most part is, they would not permit us any more land to build upon or to feed our cattle, unless we would keep upon that which they confess to be our proper right; and they would admit of no division but by the foot or by the inch, and then we could neither have room to set a house, but part of it would stand on their land, nor put a cow to grass, but immediately her bounds were broken; and then presently must the one be pulled down, and the other put into the pound to make satisfaction, or till satisfaction were made for both." *

Reports were also brought to Gorton and his associates, that their lives were threatened by some of the ministers and magistrates of Mas-

---

* Gorton's *Simplicitie's Defence*, p. 5.

sachusetts. Gorton was advised to escape to the Dutch or Swedish settlements; but he replied that he could not go to a foreign prince for protection, "knowing he had neither been false to his King nor country, nor to his conscience in point of religion, so far as God had informed him."

CHAPTER V.

Founds Shawomet. — His Disputes with the Indian Chiefs Pomham and Sochonocho. — Massachusetts takes Part with the latter. — Armed Commission sent by Massachusetts to Shawomet. — It is opposed by Force. — Truce between the Parties. — Gorton and his Company consent to go to Massachusetts. — Are treated as Prisoners of War. — Are Imprisoned in Boston.

THE place to which Gorton and his eleven friends fled for refuge was called Shawomet, now Old Warwick, and was situate on the west side of Narragansett Bay, about six miles south of Pawtuxet. The first settlement, according to tradition, was on the north side of what is now called Mill Cove. There Gorton purchased of Miantonomo, sachem of the Narragansetts, "with the free and joint consent of the inhabitants," a large tract of land, about five miles in width, and stretching westward from the shore twenty miles. This tract now comprises the town of Coventry, and nearly the whole of the town of Warwick. The date of the deed is January 12th, 1642-3, and its consideration one hundred and forty-four fathoms of wampum.*

In this new abode, far removed from the precincts of Massachusetts sovereignty, the little company of exiles, knit together by common views and common sufferings, hardy if impoverished, and free though alone, hoped at last to rest in peace. But their hopes were destined to be disappointed. If they had removed far into the wilderness, it was yet not so far as the ambition of Massachusetts desired to extend her jurisdiction; and if the heresy of Gorton was no longer infused, by his "very glossing, but yet very deceitful tongue," into the ears of dwellers within Christian borders, still it existed within his own breast, and made him a man " not fit to live upon the face of the earth."

The Massachusetts authorities soon found a pretext for following Gorton with their warrants even to Shawomet. Two Narragansett chiefs, Pomham and Sochonocho, instigated, no doubt,

---

* This sum, at 5s. 8d. per fathom, was £40 16s.

by the Arnolds of Pawtuxet, who were enemies to Gorton and *protégés* of Massachusetts, set up a claim to the territory of Shawomet, which had recently been sold by Miantonomo; and subjecting themselves, with their lands, to the jurisdiction of the General Court at Boston, in June, 1643, prayed for the assistance of their white brethren in the recovery of their rights.* Pomham had signed the deed to Gorton and others; but he afterwards pretended, that it was done through fear of Miantonomo, and refused to accept his part of the price. His right, however, to dispute the validity of the sale, and to place the territory in question under the control of Massachusetts, appears not to have had any good foundation. Pomham and Sochonocho were inferior chiefs, having between two and three hundred men under them; and Miantonomo, as principal sachem of the country, possessed, according to the laws and customs of the Indian tribes, rightful authority to dispose of its lands.

This view is confirmed by the best authorities. Roger Williams, in a letter written several years afterwards to the General Court of Massachusetts, speaking of this transaction, says, "What was done was according to the law and tenor of the natives, I take it, in all New England and

---

* Winthrop's *History of New England*, Vol. II. p. 125.

America, namely, that the inferior sachems and subjects shall plant and remove at the pleasure of the highest and supreme sachems; and I humbly conceive, that it pleaseth the Most High and Only Wise to make use of such a bond of authority over them, without which they could not long subsist in human societies, in this wild condition wherein they are."*

There is, indeed, no direct proof that Pomham and Sochonocho were subject to Miantonomo. The latter, it is said, appearing in the General Court of Massachusetts, could not prove the existence of such a relation, at least not to the satisfaction of those whose interests led them to disbelieve it. Evidence to the contrary, moreover, was brought forward in the same Court. Cutshamekin, a sachem residing within the territory of Massachusetts, affirmed that Miantonomo had no interest in Pomham and Sochonocho; and that these were "as free sachems as himself." But Cutshamekin was himself merely a petty chief, who acknowledged the supremacy of Massasoit.

Benedict Arnold, also, who was interested in establishing the absolute sovereignty of the two sachems, from the circumstance, that, in the April previous to their submission to Massachu-

---

* Massachusetts State Papers.

setts, he had purchased lands near Pawtuxet of Sochonocho, declared "partly upon his own knowledge, and partly upon the relation of divers Indians of those parts, that the Indians belonging to these sachems did usually pay their deer-skins (which are a tribute belonging to the chief sachem) always to them, and never to Miantonomo, or any other sachem of Narragansett, which Miantonomo could not contradict." *

But testimony so doubtful as this will not convince the unprejudiced mind, that the Narragansetts, after the extinction of the Pequods the most numerous, as they were before the most civilized, of all the New England tribes; who had owned in the north the meadows of the Moshassuck and the Wanasquatucket, previously to the sale of the same to Roger Williams, and whose territories in the south extended to the shores of the ocean; who had held all the broad and fair islands of the bay which bears their name; whose war-whoop had brought tributary tribes from along the eastern coast of the Atlantic, to accompany them to battle against the Pequods; that a nation so ambitious, so potent, so enlightened, would allow two sachems, with no more than two or three hundred men, to live independent and unsub-

---

* Winthrop, Vol. II. p. 120.

dued within the very heart of their empire. Even Massasoit, the illustrious sagamore of the Wampanoags, as he himself acknowledged to Roger Williams, had subjected himself and his lands to the Narragansetts. We feel authorized, therefore, to credit the express testimony of Gorton, who says that the chief sachem of the Narragansetts was the "lawful and natural Prince" of Pomham and Sochonocho; and may believe that the former, as such, had good right, according to Indian usage, to dispose of lands inhabited by the latter.

But Massachusetts, having resolved on extending her jurisdiction beyond her chartered limits, took that view of the question in dispute, which was most favorable to the accomplishment of her own purposes. Having some time before sent two deputies, to inquire of Gorton and his associates if they owned the letter, which purported to have been written by them in reply to the notification sent to the colony of Providence, and having received an answer in the affirmative, the government, on the 12th day of September, 1643, issued a warrant against the inhabitants of Shawomet, summoning them to appear at the General Court, then convened at Boston, to answer the complaints of Pomham and Sochonocho; and at the same time offering them a safe conduct during their passage through its territory.

To this summons, the persons sent for contented themselves with returning, verbally, by the messenger who brought it, a firm and peremptory refusal to do as they were bidden. "We told them," says Gorton, "that we, being so far out of their jurisdictions, could not, neither would we, acknowledge subjection unto any in the place where we were, but only the state and government of old England, who only had right unto us, and from whom we doubted not but in due season we should receive direction for the well ordering of us in all civil respects; and, in the mean time, we lived peaceably together, desiring and endeavoring to do wrong to no man, neither English nor Indian, ending all our differences in a neighborly and loving way of arbitrators, mutually chosen amongst us."*

On the receipt of this reply to its warrant, the government despatched a notice, on the 19th day of the same month, to Gorton and his companions, informing them that it intended to send a commission to Shawomet, to investigate the whole matter in dispute, and to "receive such satisfaction from them as should appear in justice to be due." But they were also plainly told, that a sufficient guard would attend the commission to protect it from violence; and finally they

---

* Simplicitie's Defence, p. 33.

were warned, that, in case justice was not done by them, the government would proceed to "right itself by force of arms."*

The notice was soon followed by the commission itself. This consisted of Captain George Cook, Lieutenant Atherton, and Edward Johnson, author of the "Wonder-working Providence of Sion's Savior, in New England," and was accompanied by forty soldiers. The approach of this force was heralded at Shawomet before its arrival there. It was reported that a large body of military, with numerous Indians, were on their march to the settlement, and that they were commissioned to carry off the inhabitants by force, or else to put them to the sword.

But this rumor, though not discredited, did not daunt the fearless souls of the borderers. A letter, written undoubtedly by Gorton, but much more brief and plain spoken than the one composed by him in answer to the first notification from Massachusetts, was immediately sent to the commissioners, wherein they were informed that, if they came as friends to settle the difficulties between the two parties in the way of peace, they should be welcome, but, at the same time, warning them not to set foot upon the lands of Shawomet, in any hostile way, but upon

---

* Simplicitie's Defence, p. 34.

their peril. In reply, the commissioners wrote that they wished to have an interview with their friends of Shawomet, to see if they could not convert them to be of their own mind; else, accounting them as men destined for slaughter, they should, with all convenient speed, address themselves to the work of their extermination.

The return of this answer frightened the women and children. Some of them fled to other settlements; some betook themselves to the woods and the Indians, suffering, in consequence, fatal privations; and some did not escape without experiencing pretty rough treatment at the hands of the soldiers. Gorton, soon seeing a band of English and Indians approach, cried out to them not to come within the reach of his musket, and called to his friends, who had assembled in one of their houses for defence, to stand to their arms. But, at this juncture of affairs, some persons, arriving from Providence, where these proceedings of Massachusetts excited no little interest, urged upon Captain Cook and his officers to hold a parley with the opposite party.

After some objections on the part of the former, this was agreed upon. At the interview, the men of Shawomet inquiring of the strangers the cause of their coming, the latter alleged that the former had intruded upon the lands of the Indians; that they had done wrong to certain subjects of Massachusetts; and also that they held blasphemous errors, which they must either repent of, or go to the Bay, to answer in court respecting them. To this the men of Shawomet replied, that, being without the jurisdiction of Massachusetts, they could not yield allegiance; but they offered to submit their mutual differences, for adjustment, to the authorities of the mother country; and this offer not being accepted, they further proposed to refer the matters in dispute to the arbitration of disinterested men mutually chosen. A proposition so reasonable did not fail to commend itself to the good sense of the invaders; and they consented to a truce, until they could procure further instructions from Boston.*

Meanwhile the soldiers took such liberties, in the territory of their heretical enemies, as soldiers under similar circumstances are apt to take. They broke open and searched the houses; they killed the cattle, to procure provisions for themselves and their Indians; they gave a rough reception to those, who came to sympathize with the invaded; and fired their muskets, without being particularly cautious as to the direction of the muzzles. Witnessing these transactions, four of the colonists from Providence, at the head

---

* Simplicitie's Defence, &c. p. 41.

of whom was the excellent and venerable Chad Brown, privily wrote to the Governor of Massachusetts, giving him a particular account of the parley at which they had been present, and praying him to accept of the fair and reasonable proposals sent to him by the party of Gorton. But Governor Winthrop, in his reply, declined acceding to the proposition made to him, reiterating the charge against the settlers of Shawomet of being "blasphemers against God and all magistrates;" and expressing his distrust of any arbitration that might be made by persons of Providence, or Rhode Island, "divers of whom he knew too well to refer any matters unto." *

The truce was terminated by the return of the messenger of the commissioners, bringing an unfavorable answer to the proposal for an arbitration. This event was announced, on the part of the invaders, by the firing of guns, and the immediate seizure of all the cattle of the settlement; while, at the same time, a messenger was sent to Gorton and his party, informing them that their propositions could in no case be accepted by Massachusetts. Refusing the request of the settlers for another parley, the invading force straightway proceeded to intrench themselves, and opened their fire upon the enemy's

---

* Simplicitie's Defence, pp. 44, 45.

quarters. Thereupon the besieged hung out the colors of old England; but seeing that their "words were shot good enough to keep aloof" their adversaries, they refrained from using their muskets. The assault continued for several days. The trenches were gradually brought up; an ineffectual attempt was made to fire the house in which the settlers had taken refuge; bullets were freely discharged by one party, and scoffs as freely returned by the other; but, though invited on by insults, neither the captain nor his soldiers showed any eagerness to risk their lives too near to men, who had muskets in their hands, and who perchance might use them.

At length, the invaders sent to Massachusetts for aid; and the besieged, seeing that in the end they would have to yield, and not wishing that English blood should be spilled by Englishmen, sought once more for a parley, and finally consented to accompany the commissioners to Massachusetts, provided they might go as "free men and neighbors." These conditions having been allowed, the merry roll of the drum summoned the troops to return home. But, previously to departing, having been admitted into the castle of the besieged, they immediately, in violation of the articles of capitulation, seized upon the arms of the settlers. The cattle of the latter were also driven off,* their goods left exposed to the pillage of the Indians, and they were themselves marched away as inglorious captives of war.

On the route, the prisoners, being eleven in number, were guarded very strictly. Orders were given to the soldiers to knock them down, if they should utter a word of insolence; and to run any one through, who might step aside from the line of advance. When, on arriving within the territory of Massachusetts, the troops came to a town, their chaplain, who accompanied the expedition for the purpose of administering counsel, both temporal and spiritual, "went to prayers in the open streets, that the people might take notice that what they had done was done in a holy manner, and in the name of the Lord."

At Dorchester, where a large concourse of people had assembled, together with several ministers, to witness the passage of the troops through the town, the prisoners were stationed apart, and volleys of musketry fired over their heads in token of victory; and finally, at Boston, the soldiers were formally received by the Governor, who, passing through their ranks, gave them

---

* Gorton says that he and his friends had eighty head of cattle taken from them and sold.

his benediction, saying, "God bless and prosper you; God bless and prosper you." Gorton and his party, on complaining to his Excellency that they had not been treated according to the terms of the capitulation, were told that they were no more nor less than captives, and that they must go to the common jail, "without either bail or mainprize."

CHAPTER VI.

Gorton and his Fellow-Prisoners accused of Heresy in Court. — The Trial. — The accused found guilty. — Their Sentence. — Gorton confined in Charlestown. — Prisoners released.

Gorton and his fellow-captives were thrown into prison, to await the meeting of the General Court. When the Court was convened, the prisoners were brought forth and publicly accused; not of having fraudulently possessed themselves of the lands of Pomham and Sochonocho; not of having done any wrong to any of the inhabitants of Pawtuxet; for no man appeared to enter a civil complaint against them.

The charge preferred against them was, that they were *heretics;* and upon this charge they were to be tried for their lives. "It was alleged against us by the authorities," says Gorton, "that we denied the human nature of Christ, which they gathered from this, that we professed his death to be effectual to the fathers, before the time of his incarnation in the womb of the Virgin; also, that we denied all the churches of Jesus Christ, because we could not join with them in that way of church order, which they had established amongst them; again, that we denied all the holy ordinances of Christ, because we could not join with them in their way of administration; as also, that we denied all civil magistracy, because we could not yield to their authority, to be exercised in those parts where we lived, (that place being about four-and-twenty miles out of their bounds,) which we should not once have questioned, if we had been within the compass of their jurisdiction."

These charges were directly denied by the accused, who called for the public reading of the letter of Gorton in answer to the first notification from Massachusetts, from which paper the charges had been drawn. But this was refused; and when, moreover, the accused continued orally to disavow the construction put upon the sentiments of this letter, they were ordered to be silent.

The Court, having failed, at the first trial, of convicting Gorton or his friends of the crime with which they were charged, afterwards held several private sessions, at which they were assisted by many of the clergy, and at which the accused were examined apart, but without success. In the intervals between the sitting of the Court, also, the prisoners were visited and questioned by the elders and church members; and on Sunday, on which day the prisoners were sometimes brought into the meeting-house, that they might have the privilege of listening to godly preaching, Mr. Wilson, the first minister of the church in Boston, urged the magistrates and people not to let the heretics go, as the King of Israel did Benhadad, but to take their lives. Mr. John Cotton also justified their capture, and the treatment to which they had been subjected, on the ground that it was the duty of the saints of the Most High to subdue unto themselves the kingdoms of the unbelievers.*

At length, after many long days of inquiry and deliberation, the ministers and magistrates proposed to Gorton four questions, which were

---

* Simplicitie's Defence, pp. 53, 54.

to be answered in writing by him, at the peril of his life, and that, too, within the space of fifteen minutes. These were as follows.

1. "Whether the Fathers, who died before Christ was born of the Virgin Mary, were justified and saved only by the blood which he shed, and the death which he suffered after his incarnation!

2. "Whether the only price of our redemption were not the death of Christ upon the cross, with the rest of his sufferings and obediences in the time of his life here, after he was born of the Virgin Mary!

3. "Who is that God whom he thinks we serve?

4. "What he means when he saith, We worship the star of our God Remphan, Chion, Molech?"*

The time granted for replying to these questions was afterwards extended to half an hour; and finally permission was given to Gorton to bring in his answers on the morning of the next Court day. With these answers, when read in Court, the magistrates could find no fault. They were said, however, to be contrary to the sentiments expressed in the letter of Gorton replying to the notification from Massachusetts; and he

---

* Simplicitie's Defence, p. 56.

was therefore required to retract those sentiments. This he refused to do; and finally he was again remanded to prison, after having been asked by the Governor *what faith was*, and having made answer, that it was "the substance of things hoped for, and the evidence of things not seen."

Not long afterwards, Gorton was again brought forth to listen to the formal charge of the Court. This was as follows.

"Upon much examination and serious consideration of your writings, with your answers about them, we do charge you to be a blasphemous enemy of the true religion of our Lord Jesus Christ, and his holy ordinances, and also of all civil authority among the people of God, and particularly in this jurisdiction." *

When asked whether he would acknowledge this charge to be just, Gorton denied that it was so, and did not demean himself so civilly as his accusers thought would have been becoming in him.

The sentence of Gorton soon followed. The elders, being consulted as to what punishment was due, by the word of God, to the offence of blasphemy and heresy, replied that the punishment was death. Of the magistrates, all but three thought that Gorton ought to die; but the

---

* Winthrop, Vol. II. p. 146.

greater part of the deputies dissenting, the opinion of the elders and magistrates did not prevail. According to Gorton's account, the majority against this opinion consisted of but two votes. The order finally agreed upon, and adopted unanimously, was the following.

"It is ordered, that Samuel Gorton shall be confined to Charlestown, there to be set on work, and to wear such bolts or irons, as may hinder his escape, and to continue during the pleasure of the Court; provided, that, if he shall break his said confinement, or shall in the mean time either by speech or writing publish, declare, or maintain any of the blasphemous or abominable heresies, wherewith he hath been charged by the General Court, contained in either of the two books sent unto us by him or Randall Houlden, or shall reproach or reprove the churches of our Lord Jesus Christ in these United Colonies, or the civil government, or the public ordinances of God therein, (unless it be by answer to some question propounded to him, or conference with any elder, or with any other licensed to speak with him privately under the hand of one of the assistants,) that, immediately upon accusation of any such writing or speech, he shall, by such assistant to whom such accusation shall be brought, be committed to prison till the next Court of Assistants, then and there to be tried by a jury, whether he hath so spoken or written ; and upon his conviction thereof shall be condemned to death and executed. Dated the 3d of the 9th month, 1643.*"

John Hicks, Randall Houlden, Robert Potter, Richard Carder, Francis Weston, and John Warner, were sentenced to be confined on the same conditions. William Waddell, Richard Waterman, and Nicholas Power, were treated more leniently.

The prisoners, after having been brought in irons to the meeting-house, that they might be exposed to the public gaze, and also might avail themselves of one more opportunity of listening to a discourse from Mr. Cotton, were sent abroad to the different towns where they were to pass the winter. Gorton was confined in Charlestown. Respecting the occupations or reflections with which he relieved the long hours of his imprisonment, nothing is known, except that he wrote a long letter to the ruling elder of the church in Charlestown, requesting permission to preach a sermon on a particular text of Scripture, and stating, at the same time, the general views he designed to deduce from it. The request was not granted; although, in Boston, Gorton had sometimes been allowed to address the peo-

---

* Winthrop, Vol. II. p. 147.

ple immediately after the conclusion of public religious service on Sunday. The prisoners, however, did not fail, though in bonds, to find opportunities to disseminate their peculiar doctrines, boldly declaring them to all comers.

But public sentiment would not permit Gorton and his companions to be long retained in custody. Accordingly, notwithstanding the efforts made by some of the ministers to prevent any favors being shown them, the Court ordered them to be released in January, 1644; though with the provision, that in case they should be found, after fourteen days from the period of their liberation, within the territory of Massachusetts, or in or near Providence, or any of the lands of Pomham or Sochonocho, they should suffer death.* But when this order of the Court was presented to Gorton by the constable, accompanied by a smith to file off his fetters, he refused to part with them on the conditions prescribed, and declared that he would wait for "fairer terms of release." When, however, the constable, returning with the chief men of the town, ordered the irons to be removed by force, Gorton relaxing his resolution left the prison.

---

* Winthrop, Vol. II. p. 156. Simplicitie's Defence, p. 74.

CHAPTER VII.

Gorton and his Friends kindly treated in Boston. — Expelled by the Governor. — They go to Aquetneck. — Are kindly received by the Narragansett Indians. — Subjection of the latter to the English Crown. — Gorton, with two of his Friends, goes to England. — They complain to the English Commissioners of the Massachusetts Government. — Their Complaint favorably received, and an Order issued to Massachusetts. — Gorton Preaches in England with great Success. — Is accused before a Committee of Parliament of preaching without License. — Is acquitted.

GORTON and his friends, after having been released from confinement, were so kindly received into various houses in Boston, that the jealousy of the magistrates was aroused; and the Governor took upon himself the responsibility of issuing a warrant commanding them to leave town within the space of two hours. With little provision, accordingly, for a long journey through a wilderness exhibiting few marks of civilization, though with limbs lightened from the weight of chains, and with free consciences, they set out for Rhode Island. The hospitalities of savage wigwams were not denied them on their way; and they reached Shawomet in safety. There, previously to proceeding to 'Rhode Island, observing that Shawomet was not expressly named in the order of the Court, banishing them from the jurisdiction of Massachusetts, they wrote to Governor Winthrop, inquiring whether the terms of the act of expulsion were to be understood as excluding them from that place. To this letter, purporting to have been written "by order of the government of Shawomet," and expressed in terms not particularly submissive, but rather well supplied with the old leaven of contumacy, the Governor sharply replied, that, being excluded from the lands of Pomham and Sochonocho, they were excluded from Shawomet; and that, if they settled there, they would do so upon peril of their lives.[*]

On the receipt of this reply, the outcasts continued their journey to Aquetneck. The Indians of Narragansett, hearing of their return, expressed their surprise that they had escaped with their lives, and welcomed them back with joy. Messengers from the sachems conducted them to the seat of the aged and venerable Canonicus, where they were "courteously entertained;" and thence to the residence of Pessicus, successor to the noble-hearted Miantonomo, at which place they

---

[*] Simplicitie's Defence, p. 78.

were received by several sachems, with their chief counsellors. At the same time, also, was held a general council of the sachems and princes of the Narragansetts, who, taking counsel of their white friends of Shawomet, and being influenced by their dislike of Massachusetts, resolved to place themselves under the protection of that great and mighty Prince, Charles, King of England, and executed a formal deed of subjection.

At Rhode Island, Gorton and his followers, hiring houses and grounds, proceeded to plant the latter for the maintenance of themselves and their families. But even here their enemies did not cease to attempt to molest, though they had not the power actually to disturb them. The Governor of Massachusetts wrote to a person at Aquetneck, on whom he supposed he could rely, expressing a desire that the inhabitants of the island might be persuaded to surrender up the Gortonites, or a part of them, to the authorities of the Bay. But this request the islanders indignantly refused to comply with; and the exiles continued to find a hospitable shelter in their hired homes, until the granting of a charter to the inhabitants of the Narragansett Bay by Charles the First.

Some time in the year 1644, probably in the summer, Gorton went to England, embarking at the Dutch plantation of New York. He was accompanied by two of his friends and fellow-sufferers, Randall Houlden and John Greene. The object of their journey was, besides conveying to the English government the act of the Narragansett Indians submitting themselves to its jurisdiction, to lay before the Commissioners of Foreign Plantations a complaint against the government of Massachusetts for its treatment of the inhabitants of Shawomet, together with a petition for such action on the part of the Commissioners as might be necessary for restoring to the petitioners and their associates their just and lawful rights.

The petitioners met with a favorable hearing; and, in consequence of their representations, an order was passed by the Commissioners, expostulating with the authorities of Massachusetts for "their want of charity," requiring them to allow the inhabitants of Shawomet "to pass peaceably through their government," and forbidding them to molest again the latter on account of their religion or lands. On the reception of this order in Massachusetts, however, an agent, Mr. Edward Winslow of Plymouth, was sent out to England to present the answer of the government of the colony to the memorial of Gorton. He was authorized to assume the bold position, at a later period still more firmly maintained, "that the doings of the Massachusetts colony were not subject to any reëxamination in England." But his arguments and statements failed to change materially the minds of the Commissioners. They took the ground that the territory of Shawomet was without the bounds of the patent granted to the colony of Massachusetts; and that, consequently, the inhabitants of the former could not rightfully be subjected in any way to the government of the latter.

Besides the above-mentioned memorial to the Commissioners, Gorton published, in 1646, a "more particular and full relation" of the matters with reference to which he had come to England, in a book entitled "*Simplicitie's Defence against Seven-Headed Policy.*"*

During his residence in England, Mr. Gorton, at the solicitation of his friends, spent considerable time at London, and elsewhere, in publicly preaching the gospel. In this vocation he labored with a good degree of success, and very general satisfaction. His extraordinary powers of speech not only drew around him crowds of the common people, but also attracted the attention of persons of intelligence and cultivation. In some places, even the clergy conde-

---

* This work, in the course of a year, passed through a second edition; and was answered by Winslow in his "*Hypocrisy Unmasked.*"

scended to be hearers of the word spoken by this man sent from God, though not from the schools; and the minds of men high in rank and station were moved by the eloquence, which was simply a rude gift of nature, not an elegant accomplishment of art.

"I preached," says Gorton, "the word of God publicly, in divers as eminent places as any were then in London, as also about London, and places more remote; many times the ministers of the places being hearers, and sometimes many together, at appointed lectures in the country. I have spoken in the audience of all sorts of people and personages under the title of a bishop or a king, and was invited to speak in the presence of such as had the title of Excellency, and was lovingly embraced wherever I came, in the word uttered, with the most eminent Christians in the place; and for leave-taking at our departure, not unlike the ancient custom of the saints on record in the Holy Scripture; and I dare say, as evident testimony of God's power going forth with his word spoken, manifested, as ever any in New England had; publicly and immediately after the word delivered, the people giving thanks to God that ever such a word came to be uttered among them, with entreaty for stay and further manifestation, in as eminent places as are in England, where myself did know that doctors of note had formerly preached, and at that time such as had more honor put upon them than ordinarily preachers have, who gave me the call thither, in way of loving and Christian fellowship, the like abounding in the hearers."*

The notice taken of Gorton, however, did not fail to give offence to the friends of the regular ministry; and at the instigation of some of these, he was summoned before a committee of Parliament to give an account of himself. He was accused of preaching "without a call," not being a "university man." But he faced his accusers boldly; and, after having been examined by the committee respecting his procedure and doctrine, he was honorably dismissed "as a preacher of the gospel.†"

---

* Gorton's *Defence against Morton's Memorial*, in Hutchinson's *History of Massachusetts*, Vol. L p. 251.
† Ibid. Vol. I. p. 252.

CHAPTER VIII.

Returns to America, and disembarks at Boston. — Warrant issued against him by the Governor of Massachusetts. — He proceeds to Shawomet, then called Warwick. — Massachusetts relinquishes her Claims to Warwick. — Gorton's public Services after his Return from England. — His Mode of Life. — Death. — Family.

In the spring of 1648, after a residence of nearly four years in England, Gorton returned to this country. He disembarked at Boston; but it was no sooner known that he had arrived there, than a warrant was issued for his apprehension. He had not, however, ventured among his old enemies unprotected. A letter which he exhibited from the Earl of Warwick, requesting the authorities of Massachusetts to allow him free passage through their territories, secured to him his liberty. Yet the order for arresting him was recalled only by the casting vote of the Governor; and the period allowed for his departure was limited to a single week.*

Arriving at Shawomet, then named Warwick in grateful acknowledgment of the important

---

* Winthrop's *History of New England*, Vol. II. p. 322.

services rendered to its inhabitants by the noble Earl who bore that name, Gorton had the satisfaction of finding his old friends and followers already reëstablished there. Massachusetts had not, indeed, relinquished her claims to the Warwick territory; but no further attempts were made to disturb the peace, or invade the liberties of the settlers. At length, in 1651, upon the petition of the inhabitants of Pawtuxet to be dismissed from the jurisdiction of Massachusetts, that colony entirely gave up her ill-grounded pretensions to the soil of her neighbors; and, finally, at the order of Charles the Second, in 1678, she also repealed the act of banishment against Gorton and his associates.* Thus at last Warwick had peace.

This little settlement, situate in the heart of a savage wilderness, and exposed during its infancy to so many perils from civilized fanaticism, continued henceforth gradually to increase in numbers and general prosperity. In 1647, it was admitted a member of the union formed by the colonies of Providence, Newport, and Portsmouth, under the charter obtained by Roger Williams, in 1644, from the English commissioners of the American colonies. Warwick, indeed, was not mentioned in this charter; but the settlement had

---

* Massachusetts Records.

been recognized and protected by the Earl of Warwick and the other English commissioners; and in the charter afterwards granted by Charles the Second, it was endowed with the same rights and privileges as its sister colonies. The fertility of its lands, and its conveniences for trade with the Indians, early gave to the settlement ample means for pecuniary support; while the intelligent character of its inhabitants, and the extraordinary freedom of its institutions, made Warwick from the first a distinguished member of that little confederacy of colonies, which in a fanatical age adopted, and, with a consistency hardly equalled in any other states, carried out into practice, the great doctrines of toleration in religion, and of equal civil liberty regulated by law.

Of Gorton's life after his return to Warwick, there is not much known. He appears to have retained to the close of his days the affectionate esteem of his followers and fellow-citizens. Much of his time was given to public business; and the records, both of the town and the colony in which he resided, show that his old age was constantly honored by the gift of the most important civil offices. He was repeatedly elected a member of the town council of Warwick, and still oftener a commissioner to the General Assembly of the Rhode Island colonies; and was, also, frequently chosen by his fellow-citizens to draw up state papers of importance, now unfortunately no longer extant.

On Sundays, Gorton discharged the duties of a teacher of the gospel, instructing, with few forms or ceremonies of worship, but with such wisdom as a life of manifold experiences had taught, and such learning as the diligent perusal of the Holy Scriptures in their original tongues had furnished, the simple minds of the settlers, and the benighted souls of the Indians, in the words of eternal life. He went in and out, to the end of what we may believe was a good and green old age, a patriarch among the people. Nor, late in life, did the fires of mystic enthusiasm grow dim in the eyes of this teacher of so called strange doctrines. No longer driven out from among men by religious persecution, no longer harassed by the warrants and the weapons of ambitious fanaticism, the great calamities of life overpast and its tasks well nigh finished, he was able to give his leisure hours to the undisturbed contemplation of the great, saving truths of his day and generation. The ancient, solitary woods often allured him out, at morning and evening, to meditate in their solemn shades; and even the silent night was wont to witness the fervor of his aspirations, or the tranquil joy of his self communings.

The precise time of Gorton's death, like that

of his birth, is not known. It occurred, however, between the 27th of November and the 10th of December, 1677, at which period he had attained, according to the testimony of contemporary writers, a "great age."*

Gorton is known to have had three sons, Samuel, John, and Benjamin; and six daughters; Maher, who married Daniel Coles; Mary, who married Peter Greene, and afterwards John Sanford; Sarah, who married William Mace; Anna, who married John Warner; Elizabeth, who married John Crandall; and Susannah, who married Benjamin Barton. His son, Samuel Gorton, lived to be ninety-four years old; and most of the children survived to a great age.

The place of Gorton's residence, during the last few years of his life, is about two miles distant from the spot where he is supposed to have been living at the time he was taken captive by the commission from Massachusetts. It lies at the head of a small cove, which winds its way, through pleasant meadows, a little distance inland from what was formerly called Cowesett, now Greenwich Bay. The house faced the water, and had a south-western exposure, whereby it was fanned in summer by refreshing breezes from the sea, and was visited in winter by the

---

* Eliot's *Biographical Dictionary*, Article, *Gorton.*

warm airs, fabled to blow from the Indian's Heaven. In other directions, gently sloping hills sheltered it from the inclemencies of a northern climate; a prattling brook, still skirted with the remains of ancient elms, ran, hard by, down the gradual declivity into the cove; and on both sides were spread out ample fields, the fertility of whose soil must have annually clothed them with variegated beauty and the golden rewards of labor. No fairer spot can be found upon the Narragansett shores; none, within whose quiet, sunny solitude the founder of Shawomet could better have spent the tranquil evening of his eventful and much harassed life. Also, upon the rising grounds in the vicinity, his aged eyes were often gladdened with the sight of the pleasant shores and placid waters of the bay, of its numerous islands, of Mount Hope in the distance, of the heights of Providence in the north, and of the line of ocean, glittering in sunlight, on the southern horizon.

Tradition says, that parts of the timber and stone of Gorton's house are still preserved in the dwelling, which stands near the site of the ancient homestead, and which is now inhabited by some of his descendants. It also points to the family burying-ground, shaded by the sole remaining branch of an aged apple-tree, and lying a short distance in the rear of the house, as the place where the hoary patriarch was interred. But the exact spot, where his ashes' repose, is marked by no pious stone or monumental marble. Yet, if without other honors, may it at least ever be their privilege to sleep beneath the greensward of a free state!

As a testimony of the last of Gorton's disciples to the excellence of his life and character, the following extract from the manuscript diary of Dr. Ezra Stiles, afterwards President of Yale College, may be read with interest.

"At Providence, November 18th, 1771, I visited Mr. John Angell, aged eighty years, born October 18th, 1691, a plain, blunt-spoken man; right old English frankness. He is not a Quaker, nor Baptist, nor Presbyterian, but a Gortonist, and the only one I have seen. Gorton lives now only in him; his only disciple left. He says that he knows of no other, and that he is alone. He gave me an account of Gorton's disciples, first and last, and showed me some of Gorton's printed books, and some of his manuscripts. He said Gorton wrote in Heaven, and no one can understand his writings, but those who live in Heaven, while on earth. He said Gorton had beat down all outward ordinances of baptism and the Lord's supper, with unanswerable demonstration; that Gorton preached in London, in Oliver's time, and had a church and living of five hundred pounds a year offered him; but he believed no sum would have tempted him to take a farthing for preaching. He told me that his grandfather, Thomas Angell, came from Salem to Providence with Roger Williams; that Gorton did not agree with Roger Williams, who was for outward ordinances to be set up again by new apostles.

"I asked him if Gorton was a Quaker, as he seemed to agree with them in rejecting outward ordinances. He said, no; and that, when George Fox, (I think,) or one of the first Friends, came over, he went to Warwick to see Gorton, but was a mere babe to Gorton. The Friends had come out of the world in some ways, but still were in darkness or twilight; but that Gorton was far beyond them, he said, high way up to the dispensation of light. The Quakers were in no wise to be compared with him; nor any man else can be, since the primitive times of the church, especially since they came out of Popish darkness. He said, Gorton was a holy man; wept day and night for the sins and blindness of the world; his eyes were a fountain of tears, and always full of tears; a man full of thought and study; had a long walk out through the trees, or woods by his house, where he constantly walked morning and evening, and even in the depth of the night, alone by himself, for contemplation and the enjoyment of the dispensation of light. He was universally beloved by all his neighbors, and the Indians, who esteemed him not only as a friend, but one high in communion with God in Heaven; and indeed he lived in Heaven."

CHAPTER IX.

Gorton's Character. — His Relations with the Indians. — His Opinions.

THE character of Gorton has so fully appeared in connection with the events narrated in this memoir, that few words will suffice for the subject in conclusion.

By those who looked on Gorton as a heretic, he was characterized as self-sufficient, supercilious, insolent, intractable, a "subtle deceiver," one "soon moved to passion," a disturber of the peace of society, and of the quiet of men's consciences. These persons acknowledged, however, that he was both learned and eloquent; that, if his tongue was deceitful, it was also a "very glossing one;" that, though it were to secure his own ends, he was unto all "courteous in his carriage;" and that, if he was plausible and ingenious, yet, by his ingenuity, he generally succeeded in "satisfying the candid." That Gorton could not have been a bad man; that, on the contrary, he must have possessed great and shining virtues; is sufficiently evident from the fidelity with which many of his early adherents followed through life his changing fortunes, and by their never-failing confidence in his worthiness to fill public offices of the highest trust and of the greatest importance to the general weal.

The community, in the midst of which he lived, trusted and honored him to the last; and few testimonials to integrity of character are better than this. To the charge made against him, by Morton, of being a "sordid man," he could truly, as well as indignantly, reply, "Whose ox or whose ass have I taken; or when or where have I lived upon other men's labors, and not wrought with my own hands, for things honest in the sight of men, to eat my own bread?"* And if the other accusation made against Gorton, by the same writer, of his being a "passionate person," have more truth in it, still it cannot be denied, that his passion was without bitterness, that it was rarely aroused, save in the defence of principle or for the sake of truth; and that, in strict

---

* Gorton's *Defence against Morton's Memorial*, in Hutchinson's *History of Massachusetts*, Vol. I. Appendix, No. 20.

conformity with verity, he could affirm, "The thirty-third year is upon expiration since I arrived first in New England, in which tract of time I have washed my face with tears day and night *in the ordinances of Jesus Christ.*" *

Gorton, undoubtedly, was not destitute of striking faults of character. He was strongly opinionative; and, firmly persuaded that he himself was right, he also was very apt to think that other people were in the wrong. He therefore dealt a good deal in contemptuous denunciation of men and men's opinions, which were not after his own fashion. Nevertheless, he was far from being so foul-mouthed as most of his contemporaries.

In advancing and carrying out his own views, Gorton was unyielding and uncompromising, even to obstinacy. Whoever gainsaid them, he was at swords' points with; whoever did not receive them in their entire length and breadth, he likewise could hold no fellowship with. He made the mistake, common with enthusiastic minds, of believing that the wide universe was constructed exactly on his narrow system of principles, and that upon their unqualified reception depended the welfare of society and the salvation of men's souls. His principles were, in-

---

* Gorton's MS. Letter to Nathaniel Morton.

deed, most liberal; but the vehemence, the rigor, with which he maintained them, approached almost to illiberality.

That, however, which constituted one of Gorton's greatest failings, in the estimation of the age in which he lived, but which at the present day will be viewed rather in the light of a great virtue, was his devoted love of liberty. In the earlier part of his life, he may have been too impatient of restraint; he was wanting, certainly, in reverence for regularly constituted authority in church or state; and his strong sense of personal independence made him rather disinclined to submit, in any degree, to the control of other minds. Until finally established in Warwick, Gorton was always in the party of opposition, in the minority. He could not bring his mind to conform to law, however highly sanctioned, when it seemed to him to be unjust; as he would yield no manner of allegiance to doctrines, which appeared to his reason to be untrue.

He was never satisfied, until after having established himself in the position where he could indulge unblamed in free thought and free speech; where he could feel, that there was over him no civil authority at variance with the perfect law of liberty, and no ecclesiastical rule, which conflicted with the dictates of conscience or the teachings of Scripture. Gorton may have been not a little self-willed, not a little heady; but it is not in the attainment of any personal, petty ends, that we see him manifest these traits of character; it is rather for the defence of what he believed to be the right, for the furtherance of the truth, for the establishment of human freedom.

Gorton's treatment of the Quakers may here be briefly referred to, as an illustration of his practical love of freedom. He differed widely from them in many points of doctrine, and he strenuously opposed what he conceived to be their errors. But, notwithstanding this difference of opinion, he gladly gave shelter to these outcasts; and when some of their number were thrown into prison by the civil authorities at Boston, he wrote to them letters of sympathy, and offered them all the aid in his power.*

Among other charges, which have been brought against Gorton, is that of having instigated the Narragansett chief, Miantonomo, to make war upon Uncas, sachem of the Mohegans.† In proof of this, it is said that Gorton gave a coat of mail to Miantonomo; ‡ and that, when the latter

---

* See APPENDIX.

† Stone, in his *Memoir of Uncas and Miantonomo*, p. 100, says, that the Narragansett chief was urged to make war upon his rival by "the noted schismatic, Samuel Gorton."

‡ Hubbard's *General History of New England*, in *Mass. Hist. Coll.* 2d Series, Vol. VI. p. 450.

was taken captive by Uncas, he wrote two letters to the Mohegan chief, demanding the release of the Narragansett, and threatening him with the vengeance of the English, in case of refusal.* This is slender evidence. That Gorton may have presented Miantonomo with a suit of armor, is not improbable; the Indian was his friend; and also that he solicited the life of the illustrious captive will certainly not be denied; for even the savage soul of Uncas is said to have revolted against taking the life of his unfortunate but magnanimous rival; and it was only the selfish prudence of the commissioners of the United Colonies, together with the hatred conceived by them against all who favored the Rhode Island exiles, which murdered, in cold blood, the great chieftain of the Narragansetts.

Gorton and the other settlers of Rhode Island lived on friendly terms with their red neighbors, by whom they had been most hospitably received, and towards whom they, in turn, always acted in good faith; so that Roger Williams could say with truth, "Through all the Indian towns and countries, how frequently do many, and ofttimes our Englishmen, travel alone with safety and loving kindness!"† Surrounded by

---

* Winthrop, Vol. II. pp. 165, 166.
† Roger Williams's MS. Letter to the Governor of Massachusetts.

Christian foes, Gorton had good reasons for cultivating the friendship of the rude, yet not altogether heartless children of nature, in whose territories he had taken refuge. He also instructed them in the truths of the Holy Scripture, and sometimes sat, not unhonored, around their council fires, and smoked with their braves the pipe of peace. That his red brethren thus revered and confided in him, is greatly to his credit.

The principal reason, however, of the unfavorable accounts given of Gorton by the early Plymouth and Massachusetts writers, is, that he was a religious enthusiast, the founder of a new sect, or, in their phrase, a "damnable heretic." Morton says that he was " deeply leavened with blasphemous and familistical opinions;" * and the Puritan writers, generally, considered him a teacher of strange doctrines, similar to those imputed to the Familists.

The Family of Love, so called, was a sect established in the sixteenth century in Holland, by Henry Nicholas, who maintained that he was commissioned by Heaven to teach that the essence of religion consists not in the belief of any particular religious creed, or the observance of any peculiar form of public worship, but

---

* Morton's *Memorial*, Davis's edition, p. 202.

simply in the feeling of divine love. The Service of Love was declared to be the dispensation of the Holy Ghost, surpassing that of Christ, which was the dispensation of belief, and that also of Moses, which was the dispensation of law. The Familists believed in the indwelling of the Holy Spirit, allegorized the doctrines of revelation; and viewed the facts of Scripture as not having any historical, but only a spiritual importance. In England, where the sect made, for a time, no little progress, they held private assemblies for devotion, "for which they tasted of the severities of the government," and were charged with unbecoming laxity of morals, at the same time that they were making extraordinary pretences to spiritual perfection. As the Seraphic Family danced, sang, and made merry, they were denounced by George Fox as a "motley tribe of fanatics." *

As to what really were the religious doctrines held and taught by Gorton, there has been considerable diversity of opinion. It is, indeed, no easy, perhaps quite an impossible matter, to obtain from his writings any clear and adequate

---

* Mosheim's *Eccl. Hist.* Vol. III. pp. 351, 352. Henry More's *Grand Explanation of the Mystery of Godliness*, Book 6, Ch. 12 – 18. Neal's *History of the Puritans*, Vol. I. p. 297. Sewel's *History of the Quakers*, Book 3, pp. 88, 89, 344.

view of his peculiar tenets. It is more than probable that he himself had no distinct apprehension of them. His thoughts are very obscurely expressed in his writings; his style is exceedingly involved; his leading ideas are unfolded but incidentally and partially. Gorton's intellectual capacity was, indeed, great; but his sentiment prevailed over his reason. His mind was rather brilliant than sound; too impulsive to be clear. Accordingly, one does not find in his works any detailed system of faith set forth, much less any peculiar system; and the conclusion to which the reader comes, at last, is, that Gorton's heterodoxy consisted more in the original, mystic cast of his thoughts, in the use of peculiar forms of expression, and especially in the censorious, condemnatory spirit of his allusions to opinions on religion at variance with his own, than in any essential departure from the great doctrines of the gospel, as held by the church of the Puritans. After Gorton had replied to the questions put to him on his trial for heresy, in the General Court of Massachusetts, the Governor said to him, that "they were one with him in those answers; for they held as he did."*

In general, however, it may be said that Gor-

---

* Simplicitie's Defence, p. 62.

ton made little account of any forms of religious worship, and laid not much stress upon most of the dogmas of Christian theology. A right temper of heart was, in his view, the one thing needful, and the union of the believer with Christ in love the great saving doctrine of revelation. The reliance of the Puritans on creeds and forms was a subject of frequent animadversion with Gorton. "The world," said he, "hath still some fast to keep, some Sabbath to sanctify, some sermon to preach or heare, some Battel to fight, some church to constitute, some officers to raise up, or orders to reform, and reëdify, before it can take God upon his word, *that we are complete in Christ.*" *

By the union of believers with Christ, and the consequent indwelling in them of divine power, Gorton held that they became partakers of the perfection of God. Thus he asserts that "We are blessed in him, (Christ,) by becoming one with that righteousness that is perfection in the height thereof, which knows nor can admit of any gradual distinction at all, being the righteousness of him who is God over all, blessed from eternity to eternity; and such righteousness and perfection can only give the spirit of man content; for if he can comprehend

---

* Gorton's *Incorruptible Key,* p. 73.

it, and go beyond, either in looking forward or backward, he makes an end of his happiness, and is at a loss in himself." *

Respecting the nature of Christ, Gorton taught that it was both human and divine; the two parts whereof were neither united, nor will they ever be separated in time; and both together constitute *one eternal being*. Christ's death and humiliation, he considered also to be of infinite duration; for with him "are all things ever present, being himself the fulness thereof." This death and humiliation he regarded, though not in the sense of those who receive the doctrine of universal salvation, as the propitiation for "the sins of the whole world."

Viewed in connection, these two doctrines of the divinity of Christ, and of the life of the believing soul in him, will appear at the present day to have somewhat of a pantheistic character. Indeed, one of the early writers, in speaking of Gorton, went so far as to say that he "magnified his own glorious light, that could see himself to be personally Christ, God-man." † The concentrating tendency, so to speak, of Gorton's mind, was certainly very strong. The

---

* Ibid. *Introduction*, p. 6.
† Johnson's *History of New England*, Book 2, Ch. 23, p. 186.

scope and range of his thoughts were wide, but it was his habit to reduce all particular truths to general ones. To behold all things in Christ; to see them revolving in him in harmonious relations; to trace all the channels of life, the impulses of goodness up to him, as to the one, infinite, universal Fountain, "needing nothing out of itself to send forth its streams, but only its own fulness;" this was the aspiration of his mind, and its chief delight.

In illustration of a general tendency of this sort in Gorton's mind, it may be mentioned, also, that he differed from his brethren of Plymouth and Massachusetts, in his views of the relation between the present life and the future. While they, undervaluing this state of existence, concentrated all their hopes of happiness, if not of improvement, on that which is to succeed it, he, on the contrary, affirmed that the soul now exists in eternity; and was reported to have taught, that there is no heaven or hell, save in the mind.* The soul seemed to him to be independent of place, as the future and the past were but the eternal *now*. "Such doctrine," he says, "as sets forth a time to come, of more worth and glory than either is, or hath been,

---

* John Eliot, in *Mass. Hist. Coll.* 3d Series, Vol. IV. p. 135.

keeps the manna till to-morrow, to the breeding of worms in it." *

Gorton, it may be further adduced on this subject, was of the belief that all the gifts of the Divine Spirit are offered to all souls alike. Each, becoming a partaker of the divine nature, may be filled with all the fulness of God. Each is placed in similar relations to the infinite, and must be always viewed in its connection with the great whole; "as it is, in the art of philosophy," says Gorton, "that in the full and accurate discussing of any particular creature, in its nature, operation, and office, relations and respects, we must bring in the whole creation, to set it forth to perfection." † Gorton, accordingly, was very far from believing that the favors of the Deity are confined to any particular sect, or lavished with peculiar partiality upon any chosen saints. Men have but their own narrow views and perverse wills to blame, not the all-embracing goodness of Him who made and loveth all, if they fail of being gathered together by one and the same shepherd into the fold of grace. "The ground of these particular and nominal Religions, (as Independent, Presbyterian,

---

* Gorton's *Saltmarsh returned from the Dead*, Dedicatory Epistle.
† *Incorruptible Key*, p. 2.

Anabaptist, Papist, Generallist, for they all stand on one root,) is, because they limit and infringe the grace of the Gospel." *

In the same spirit, the external ordinances of religion were little esteemed by Gorton. He did not recognize the rites of the Lord's supper, and of baptism, in the mode in which they were observed in his day by Christian churches, as being either obligatory in conscience or beneficial in practice. Of the latter sacrament he said, "If we will profess and practise the perfect Baptism, unto which our Apostle leads us, when he saith, *Let us go on unto perfection*, then we must unite and contract them all into one; and so shall we find the ordinance of Baptism to be found faulty in all churches under Heaven, unless they have learned to centre them all in one; and if they do so, it will not be found in any, but only in the Son of God, whose dipping or washing comprehends them all, and so hath in it all spiritual and holy dippings and washings whatsoever." †

Gorton was also strongly opposed to the clergy, as an established order and separate class of society. Cotton Mather says of the inhabit-

---

* Gorton's *Saltmarsh*, Introduction.
† Incorruptible Key, 2d Part, p. 14.

ants of Warwick, and of the Rhode Island settlers generally, that "they have an extreme aversion to a regular ministry, and would never, till of late, allow any such to preach among them, though the Massachusetts Ministers offered to do it without putting them to any expense;"* a most generous offer, surely, on the part of the loving ministers of Massachusetts;† to propose to preach the gospel (as they understood it, of course) to the banished heretics of Rhode Island; "a generation," as Mather pleasantly calls them, "of Libertines, Familists, Antinomians, and Quakers, inhabiting the fag end of creation."

Gorton probably would have thought such preaching, as he did the "sermons of Occido and Occidio," which he was indulged with the privilege of hearing during his bonds in Boston, "meat not to be digested, but only by the heart or stomach of an ostrich;" and would have considered it as, at most, not exceeding in value the modest price that was set upon it. By some it was said of Gorton in particular, that " he would have all men to be preachers." But this is only so far true, as that Gorton thought any

---

* Neal's *History of New England*, p. 179.
† Gorton's *Saltmarsh returned from the Dead*, p. 172.

person qualified to preach, who had been anointed for the office of public teaching by the Spirit of God; and, in his estimation, no other person could be duly prepared, "not if all the hands in the world were laid on him in his ordination, or a thousand rivers of oil brought in for his unction." An established church, or one having any connection with the state, was no less offensive to Gorton than a regularly constituted and paid ministry. He railed sturdily against both; but he was not opposed to well-educated teachers of religion, for he himself was uncommonly learned in the original languages of Scripture; and he approved of regular meetings for public worship and religious instruction. Callender says, "I am informed that Gorton and his followers maintained a religious meeting, on the first day of the week, for above sixty years; and that their worship consisted of prayers to God, of preaching, or expounding the Scriptures, and singing of psalms." *

It is easier to make out what were Gorton's political, than what were his religious opinions. He was often accused of being opposed to civil magistracy; but it is clear, both from his writ-

---

* Callender's *Historical Discourse*, in *R. I. Hist. Coll.* Vol. IV. p. 92.

ings and his life, that he was not. "Observe diligently in this treatise," says he, in the Introduction to his Incorruptible Key, "that it gives all power and dominion unto the Son of God, both in Heaven and in earth; so it also gives, notwithstanding, due authority to all civil magistrates; without which, their right cannot be given unto them, if their place and office be not bounded within the compass and lists of civil things. For Christ's power and authority is spiritual; so that if once the magistrate be engaged, by virtue of that his office, to deal in the things of God, and to intermeddle between God and the consciences of men, he is then also bound over, in conscience, to subdue, to the uttermost of his power, all other civil States unto himself; and to engage them to serve and worship the same God he serves, whatever idol he hath set up unto himself, or his Levitical priests have framed and fashioned for him; and so must, of necessity, greed and endeavor after the subjecting of all civil States unto himself; else doth he not deal faithfully with his God. But keep the office of the magistracy, according to sobriety, within the compass of civil things; that is, to have relation to whatever concerns the relation between creature and creature, simply as they stand in reference one unto another in that respect; and then in that way only, it is the preservation and honor of all States, in their several ways of rule and government."

Like Roger Williams, Gorton was a decided and consistent advocate of religious toleration, of unqualified freedom of conscience. He did not, in fact, approve much human government, either civil or ecclesiastical; but he acknowledged with awe the government of God in the soul, and believed it was only through the pious recognition of his supremacy, that man, becoming a law to himself, could be fitted for the enjoyment of perfect liberty. No preference, moreover, was given by him to the "first born after the flesh;" but he held to the equality of all men before the law. After the venerable founder of Providence, no man was more instrumental in establishing the foundations of equal civil rights, and of "soul-liberty," in Rhode Island, than Samuel Gorton.

By his bold example, by his written and his spoken word, he did much that should make his name ever freshly remembered by the friends of civil and religious liberty throughout the wide country which is now rejoicing in the inheritance of principles planted, in part, by his hand; for he did much towards introducing into this land the great experiment of self-government, the issue of which is to decide; for a succession of ages, whether Humanity, at the present stage of her progress, is capable of reducing to reality the vision of perfect liberty, which she doth ever, though slowly, pursue; or whether, exhausted by her accelerated pace, she is destined once more to sink down for a time into the arms of a despotic state, and a strongly organized hierarchy.

APPENDIX

Account of Samuel Gorton's Writings

THE writings of Gorton, which have been preserved to the present day, are generally of a theological character, and for the most part consist of commentaries on portions of Scripture. His "Simplicitie's Defence," however, is an historical narrative; and there are a few letters of his extant. The style of these writings has no lack of the faults, which are seen in the works of most of the early New England authors. It is often obscure, prolix, rambling, and allegorical; it also abounds with scriptural allusions, which sometimes are not without beauty and expressiveness. As the works of Gorton are now extremely rare, I shall give their titles at length.[*]

1. "SIMPLICITIE'S DEFENCE *against Seven-Headed Policy.* Or, Innocency Vindicated, being injustly

---

[*] A volume containing all the published writings of Gorton, except his letter to Nathaniel Morton, is in the possession of the learned antiquarian, Mr. William R. Staples, of Providence, Rhode Island. There is a copy of "Simplicitie's Defence," the "Incorruptible Key," and "Saltmarsh," in the library of Harvard University. Some of his works are also in possession of the Rhode Island Historical Society, and of Mr. John C. Brown, of Providence.

accused and sorely censured by that Seven-headed church government united in New England; or, That servant so impious in his master's Absence, revived, and now thus re-acting in New-England. Or, The Combate of the United Colonies, not onely against some of the Natives and Subjects, but against the authority also of the Kingdome of *England*, with their execution of Laws, in the Name and Authority of the Servant, (or of themselves,) and not in the Name and Authority of the Lord, or fountain of the Government. Wherein is declared an Act of a Great People and Country of the *Indians* in those Parts, both Princes and People (unanimously) in their voluntary Submission and Subjection unto the Protection and Government of Old England, (from the Fame they hear thereof,) together with the true Manner and Forme of it, as it appears under their own Hands and Seals; being stirred up, and provoked thereto, by the Combate and Courses abovesaid. Throughout which Treatise is secretly intermingled that great Opposition, which is in the goings-forth of those two grand Spirits, that are and ever have been extant in the World, (through the Sons of Men,) from the Beginning and Foundation thereof. *Imprimatur, Aug. 3d,* 1646. Diligently perused, approved, and licensed to the Presse, according to Order, by publike Authority.—London; Printed by John Macock, and are to be sold by Luke Fawne, at his shop in *Paul's Church-yard,* at the sign of the *Parrot.* 1646."

In 1647, this work was republished, under a title somewhat different from the preceding one, as follows;—

"SIMPLICITIE'S DEFENCE *against Seven-Headed Policy.* Or, a true Complaint of a peaceable People, being Part of the English in New-England, made unto the State of Old England, against cruell Persecutors, united in Church Government in those Parts. Wherein is made manifest the manifold Outrages, Cruelties, Oppressions, and Taxations, by cruell and close Imprisonments, Fire and Sword, Deprivation of Goods, Lands, and Livelyhood; and such like barbarous Inhumanities, exercised upon the People of Providence Plantations in the Narryganset Bay, by those of the Massachusetts, with the Rest of the United Colonies, stretching themselves beyond the Bounds of all their own Jurisdictions, perpetrated and acted in such an unreasonable and barbarous Manner, as many thereby have lost their Lives. As it hath been faithfully declared to the Honorable Committee of Lords and Commons for Forrain Plantations; whereupon they gave present Orders for Redress. The light and Consideration whereof hath moved a great country of the Indians and Natives in those Parts, Princes and People, to submit unto the Crown of England, and earnestly to sue to the State thereof for safeguard and shelter from like cruelties. Imprimatur, Aug. 3d, 1646. Diligently perused, approved, and licensed to the Presse, according to order, by publike Authority. — London; Printed by John Macock, and are to be sold by George Whittington, at the Blue Anchor, near the Royal Exchange, in Cornhil. 1647."

The work, published under the above titles, contains one hundred and eleven pages small quarto, and is an historical narrative of the difficulties between the first settlers of Warwick, and the colony of Massachusetts Bay, growing out of the attempt of the government of the latter to extend its jurisdiction over the persons and lands of the former. The account it gives of the controversy in its origin, progress, and issue, is believed to be full and impartial. It also contains copies of many valuable letters, that passed between the two parties, as well as several long and rambling theological disquisitions, of little interest at the present day, though doubtless esteemed of some value at the time when they were written. The narrative is dedicated to the Earl of Warwick, who extended his protection to the infant colony of Shawomet; and is also introduced by an "Epistle to the Reader," together with some anonymous doggerel verses addressed to the author, and his reply in verse of the same character.

The "Defence" has been republished by the Rhode Island Historical Society, in the second volume of their "Collections," accompanied with numerous learned notes, explanatory of the text, and appendixes containing valuable original documents, by William R. Staples, Associate Justice of the Supreme Judicial Court in the State of Rhode Island. The editor has also prefixed to this work a brief sketch of the life of Gorton, to which the author of this memoir is happy to acknowledge himself indebted for many facts and important suggestions.

2. "AN INCORRUPTIBLE KEY, composed of the CX PSALME, wherewith you may open the Rest of the Holy Scriptures; Turning itself only according to the

Composure and Art of that Lock, of the Closure and
Secresie of that great Mystery of God manifest in the
Flesh, but justified only by the Spirit, which it evi-
dently openeth and revealeth, out of Fall and Resur-
rection, Sin and Righteousness, Ascension and De-
scension, Heighth and Depth, First and Last, Begin-
ning and Ending, Flesh and Spirit, Wisdome and
Foolishnesse, Strength and Weakness, Mortality and
Immortality, Jew and Gentile, Light and Darknesse,
Unity and Multiplication, Fruitfulness and Barrenness,
Curse and Blessing, Man and Woman, Kingdom
and Priesthood, Heaven and Earth, Allsufficiency and
Deficiency, God and Man. And out of every Unity
made up of twaine, it openeth that great two-leafed
Gate, which is the sole Entrie into the City of God, of
New Jerusalem, *into which none but the King of
glory can enter;* and as that Porter openeth the Doore
of the Sheepfold, *by which whosoever entreth is the
Shepheard of the Sheep;* See Isa. 45. 1. Psal. 24. 7,
8, 9, 10. John 10. 1, 2, 3; Or, (according to the
Signification of the Word translated *Psalme,*) it is
a Pruning-knife, to lop off from the Church of Christ
all superfluous Twigs *of earthly and carnal Com-
mandments,* Leviticall Services or Ministery, and fad-
ing and vanishing Priests, or Ministers, who are
taken away and cease, and are not established and
confirmed by Death, as holding no Correspondency
with the princely Dignity, Office and Ministry of our
Melchisedek, who is the only Minister and Ministry
of the Sanctuary, and of that true Tabernacle which
the Lord pitcht, and not Man. For it supplants the
Old Man, and implants the New; abrogates the Old

Testament or Covenant, and confirms the New, unto a thousand Generations, or in Generations forever. By Samuel Gorton, *Gent.*, and at the time of penning hereof, in the Place of Judicature (upon Aquethneck, alias Road Island) of Providence Plantations in the Nanhyganset Bay, New England. Printed in the Yeere 1647."

The character of this treatise may be inferred, in a measure, from its title. It is a practical, exegetical, though more or less mystical commentary on the one hundred and tenth Psalm. It is divided into two parts; the first comprising one hundred and twenty, and the second one hundred and nineteen small quarto pages. The work is introduced by an affectionate and apostolical epistle "To the Worthies and much honored in the Gospel, those who occasioned the penning of this Treatise, by Letters out of the Massachusets, together with all our endeered and longed-after Society, that love and have learned the Truth as it is in Jesus, in Providence Plantations, in the Nanhyganset Bay, New England." Following this epistle is an address to the "Courteous Reader," wherein the penning of the treatise is stated to have been in compliance with the wishes expressed in several letters from "some of the most eminent and approved Church-members among them of the Massachusets." These were persons, who had been dissatisfied with Mr. John Cotton's interpretation of the psalm in question, and who therefore applied to Gorton for his interpretation of it.

3. "SALTMARSH Returned from the Dead, in *Amicus Philalethes;* or, The Resurrection of JAMES

the Apostle, out of the Grave of Carnall Glosses, for the Correction of the universall Apostacy, which cruelly buried him who yet liveth. Appearing in the comely Ornaments of his Fifth Chapter, in an Exercise, June 4, 1654. Having laid by his grave Clothes, in a despised Village remote from England, but wishing well, and heartily desiring the true Prosperity thereof. John 11. 25, *I am the Resurrection and the Life; he that believeth in me, though he were dead, yet shall he live.* — London, Printed for *Giles Calvert*, and are to be sold at the Black Spred-Eagle, at the West-end of Pauls, 1655."

This commentary is signed by Samuel Gorton, Professor of Christ; and contains one hundred and ninety-eight pages small quarto. It is prefaced by two epistles dedicatory, one addressed "To my honored and beloved friends in London who, in a solitary season in that populous Citie, were so great refreshment unto me, by their undeserved society;" and the other, "To my much respected and honored friends in and about Lynne, in Norfolke, in whom I have perceived grave and joyfull Acclamations at the publication of the Gospel." The occasion of Gorton's composing this treatise was the wish, several times repeated in letters from his friends in London, that he would write to them "concerning the opening of a portion of the word of God." Therefore he "made bold to set upon the writing of it, yea when others slept, because of his daily occasions."

4. "AN ANTIDOTE Against the Common Plague of the World; Or, An Answer to a small Treatise, (as in water, face, answereth to face,) intitled *Salt-*

marsh returned from the dead; And by transplacing the letters of his name, this is *Smartlash* ascended into the Throne of Equity, for the Arraignment of false Interpretours of the Word of God. Summoned out of all Ages to appear, under the Penalty of Death, challenging the Consent, or forbidding to gainsay the common approved Priesthood of this Age.. *What hast thou done? the voice of thy brother's blood cries unto me from the ground.* Gen. 4. 10. — London; Printed by F. M. for A. C. 1657."

The "Antidote" is dedicated, in a modest but manly epistle, "To His Highness, Oliver, Lord Protector of England, Scotland, and Ireland, with the Dominions thereto belonging." Gorton viewed Cromwell, on account of his piety, as well as other qualities of character, "as the mirror of this age, as also exemplary for that to come." " For," said he, addressing the Protector, .."I could never learn that you have pursued the honor of the world, but only have been constrained thro the agency of a mighty hand of God pursuing yourself, to yield yourself over thereunto, when necessitie hath clothed you upon, and adorned you therewith." The letter dedicatory is succeeded by an Epistle to the Reader, being a Paraphrase of the Ninth Chapter of the First Epistle of the apostle Paul to the Corinthians. The " Antidote" itself is a Commentary on the portion of the Twenty-third chapter of Matthew's Gospel, which pronounces woe upon the scribes and Pharisees. Like the " Saltmarsh," this treatise is practical in its character; contains much verbal criticism, and many references to other parts of Scripture; and is not so full, as are the "Incorruptible Key" and some other of Gorton's writings, of obscure theological speculations. It is signed Samuel Gorton, and is dated from "Warwick, in the Nanhyganset Bay, this present October the 20th, 1656, New England."

Gorton also prepared for publication a running commentary on a portion of the Gospel of Matthew; chapter 6, verses 9—13. This manuscript, preserved until recently by the Gorton family, is now in the possession of the Rhode Island Historical Society, and well deserves a place among their published "Collections." It consists of one hundred and thirty folio pages, written in an extremely small, but legible and very beautiful character. The delicate penmanship of this tract shows, that the hand which wrote it was not one that had been stiffened by toil. It is the hand-writing of a scholar, rather than of a day-laborer. In style and character, this composition resembles the more practical of the author's commentaries on the Scriptures.

Among the literary works of Gorton may also be enumerated two letters, written by him to certain persons of the sect of the Quakers, and published in 1657, as an appendix to his "Antidote." The religious sentiments of the Quakers being, in many particulars, greatly at variance with his own, these letters show, that the writer's charity was not confined to those of his own communion, but that his fervent, active sympathies extended to the oppressed of every creed and name. The letters bear date from Warwick, one, September 10th, 1656, and the other, October 6th, 1656. They were published under the following title.

5. "*Certain Copies of Letters, which passed betwixt the Penman of this Treatise and certain men newly come out of Old England into New;* Who, when they were arrived at Boston in the Massachusets Bay, the Governour being informed they were such as are called Quakers, he sent Officers to fetch them ashoar, and being forthwith brought into Examination what their Business was in these Parts, they answered, To spread the Gospel, and to do the Worke of the Lord; whereupon they were all committed to Prison, both Men and Women, there to remaine till the Return of the Ship, and then to be carried back into England, the Master being bound in £500, with others for security with him, to set them ashoar in England againe, and that upon his own Cost and Charge, lest the Purity of the Religion professed in the Churches of New-England should be defiled with Errour."

The Letter written by Gorton, in reply to Nathaniel Morton's Memorial, was published by Hutchinson, in the Appendix to the first volume of his "History of Massachusets Bay," in a garbled and very imperfect form. A manuscript copy of the original letter, which has never been published entire, is now in the possession of Mr. Edward A. Crowningshield, of Boston, to whose politeness in allowing me to make several extracts from it, introduced into the early part of the preceding memoir, I am happy to acknowledge myself under great obligations. This manuscript, signed by Samuel Gorton, and bearing date at Warwick, June 30th, 1669, is entitled "A Copie of an Answer sent to Nathaniel Morton, of

New Plimouth, concerning some part of his Booke intituled New England's Memorial." There can hardly be a doubt, that this copy was made by Gorton himself, as the hand-writing of it is the same as that of the manuscript commentary in the possession of the Rhode Island Historical Society, and closely resembles that of an ancient paper, preserved in the records of the town of Warwick, and attributed to Gorton. The style of this Letter to Morton is somewhat remarkable, as being more plain, pointed, and concise, than that of Gorton's other published writings.

Allen, in his Biographical Dictionary, (article on Gorton,) attributes to him the authorship of a work entitled "A Glass for the People of New England," printed in 1676. But this is probably an error, as Bishop, in his "New England judged," says this work was written by Samuel Grove, or Grover.

www.ingramcontent.com/pod-product-compliance
Lightning Source LLC
Chambersburg PA
CBHW051741300426
44115CB00007B/654